T0354711

The Bright Survivor
Let Me Tell You Your Story

Sharon Shih

THE BRIGHT SURVIVOR
LET ME TELL YOU YOUR STORY

iUniverse books may be ordered through booksellers or by contacting:

iUniverse
1663 Liberty Drive
Bloomington, IN 47403
www.iuniverse.com
844-349-9409

ISBN: 978-1-6632-5880-9 (sc)
ISBN: 978-1-6632-5881-6 (e)

Library of Congress Control Number: 2023923861

Print information available on the last page.

iUniverse rev. date: 12/28/2023

To my mother, a Chinese housewife, who devoted herself to her husband and took care of her own and others' children.

Contents

BOOK 2: PRETEEN, TEENAGER, COLLEGE AND BEYOND

BOOK 3: FAMILY TRIPS

Introduction

Shortly after the birth of her son, she applied to immigrate to Canada. A few months later, she and her husband were called to the Consulate General of Canada in New York City for the immigration interview. At the end of their interview, the immigration officer said, "You have a son who is Canadian. Make sure that he gets all that a Canadian deserves." The family of three settled in Canada.

The Bright Survivor is about the parents and their Canadian-born son. Its narrator is the mother who accompanied him for nearly twenty years. The boy was born in Toronto, grew up in Ottawa, graduated from Waterloo, and started his career in Toronto. His parents, who were new to Canada, spent two decades building their careers and bringing up their Canadian-born child. The book contains every aspect of life related to their son as he grew from infancy to a young professional.

Six chapters of the book present the life of the boy in a sequence: infant, toddler, preschooler, preteen, teenager, and college student. When he was an infant, he stayed with home care while his mother worked two part-time jobs in different countries. As a toddler, he stayed with the live-in nanny when his mother went on business trips. During his elementary school years, his parents tried their best to find him an environment where he could focus on his schoolwork. As a teenager, he traveled across town to attend a year of private school and four years of high school. The International Baccalaureate program at his high school turned out to be the best fit for him. He then moved on to the co-op program for his university education. Each chapter contains the boy's behavior, family life, his friends, and (whenever applicable) his caretakers.

Three chapters are on specific topics: Chinese nannies, gifted identification, and hobbies. Stories about different Chinese nannies provide a glimpse of the families of the Chinese immigrants in Ottawa. Identifying the boy as gifted details a case that was known to the respective school board and the Ontario Special Education Tribunal. Stories on nurturing hobbies reflect the effort, both physical and financial, that a family made over the years.

The last three chapters are about family trips that his mother remembered the most. They traveled to China to meet relatives, pay respects to ancestors, and tour historical landmarks. In North America, the family flew or drove long distances to visit relatives and friends, and to explore nature and the people of the land they call home. The family also took a few pre-arranged vacations to see the world outside their old and new home countries. Although away from home, these were the precious time periods when the family stayed mostly in the same room or car tightly together.

The chapters are augmented by a Prologue and an Epilogue in the setting before the child was born and after the young man left home. In the Prologue, his mother moved from Madison, Wisconsin, to Toronto to be close to her husband, who was in Buffalo, New York. Her pregnancy started as a surprise and was followed by months of uncertainty. In the Epilogue, to be close to their son in downtown Toronto, his parents sold their house in Ottawa and moved into a condo in Scarborough for their retirement.

The book is a case study of the new generation of Chinese immigrants in Canada. Instead of making a life in Chinatown, they left China for North America to complete their education. Instead of going back to China like the Chinese scholars a century ago, they opted for a peaceful life in Canada. They worked among immigrants from other countries. Many of them eventually became middle class and technology oriented. With both parents working full time and lacking relatives, their children grew up in home care, daycare, after-school programs, and camps. To be integrated and excel, they sent their children to extracurricular classes and programs. Feeling homebound or obligated, the families travel to China to maintain the connection. Being first-generation immigrants, they traveled to see the world, especially North America, their new home.

The book reflects the learning curves and the mindset to learn (all the time) of the parents. New to the country, they did not have the basic background of Canada nor help from families in China. The parents learned to raise their Canadian-born child along the way and sometimes wondered if it could have been handled differently. There is ample literature in various media about immigrants, family conflicts, and growing pains. However, the intent of the book is to cover every timeline of a small family when raising a child. The book contains a lot of facts and occasional afterthoughts on specific matters. However, the pros and cons are left for the readers to discover when they find similarities in the content of a specific age or environment.

In the years of the latest pandemic, young Asian or Chinese descendants have become more conscientious about their ethnicity. They feel a kind of belonging to a specific branch in our multiculturalism. They are college students and young professionals who have excelled because of their diligence, endurance, and tolerance learned while growing up with their parents. The author hopes to reconnect them to the pieces of happy, sad, and annoying moments they remembered when they were toddlers, preteens, teenagers, or youths. Some stories, hopefully, will fill the gap between them and their parents, who raised them as Canadians, but were often thought to be very Chinese.

Sharon Shih, Fall of 2023

"You have a son who is Canadian. Make sure that he gets all that a Canadian deserves."

— Immigration officer at the Consulate General of Canada in New York

Prologue

In the winter of 1991, I moved from Madison, Wisconsin, USA, to Toronto, Canada. Leaving the country where I had all of my academic accomplishments, I became a postdoctoral researcher in the department of physics at the University of Toronto (U of T). Ying, my husband, was working on his doctoral degree at the State University of New York - Buffalo. Ying and I had been married for over four years and had no children. We were in our forties. I said once, "We can have a grandchild, skipping a level." We just laughed. Being almost 700 miles apart, we tried to avoid the action.

My decision to move put a temporary stop on my job hunting. Instead of a potential position with an oil company in Houston, Texas, the research position at U of T was closer to Buffalo, although it is in a different country. Before leaving Madison, I was informed that my proposal to the National Science Foundation (NSF) went through. It was good news but came too late. I told my professor that I would join the research after the grant arrived. Ying and I left Madison, the beautiful state capital with government offices, the university, and the lakes.

Our journey to Toronto was a two-day drive with a pair of walkie-talkies between my car and Ying's U-Haul. After Chicago and Detroit, we had our first lesson in driving separate vehicles in a snowstorm. On the long stretch of Highway 401, we passed Windsor and London towards Toronto downtown. Luckily, there was not a lot of traffic. I could see the lanes by alternating low and high beams, and Ying just followed the taillight of my car. My comment for the major Canadian highway afterwards was that there should be some real lights besides reflectors.

Toronto was full of lights. With me in Toronto, Ying and I were finally less than 100 miles apart. In a few days, I fell in love with the big city, although I had to move from a room downtown to a cleaner apartment in Scarborough. Toronto was peaceful compared to other metropolises like Chicago or New York. The beef short ribs from the European Meat Market and the Vancouver crabs flown in on the same day were very welcoming. The daily commute between U-of-T downtown campus and Scarborough was a bit of a pain, but I was just one among thousands of commuters. Navigating downtown, I soon learned a few hand gestures to either notify my intention or show my appreciation.

One night in early spring of 1992, I noticed a hard lump in my lower abdomen when I was in bed. It was not painful but was not going away. Being in good health most of my life without a family physician, I became concerned. After monitoring it for a few days, I thought that a tumor in my abdomen would merit a visit to any hospital. I walked into the Toronto General Hospital during my lunch break. I told the receptionist that I had a lump and needed to see a doctor. Although not really an emergency, my case was handled promptly, including a basic checkup, blood test, and even an ultrasound (after liters of water!). By late afternoon, I was met by the doctor, who had assessed me when I checked in. She congratulated me because I was pregnant. "Really?" That was all I said. She then continued her explanation of my case. The ultrasound showed that the fetus ("tiny-you") was growing with fibroids in my uterus. Because of my age and the complications, I was immediately referred to an obstetrician, Dr. Morris.

In the months that followed, I got to know Dr. Heather Morris of the Women's College Hospital through my monthly ultrasound and many bi-weekly visits. In the second trimester, she told me that the fibroids would grow and get softened because of the changing hormones. I could take as much Tylenol as I needed, but not any other painkillers. Indeed, I had to take plenty of. Besides the pain, I did not have serious morning sickness. I happily worked as usual. Ying came over from Buffalo on the weekends so that we could cook or go for big meals to satisfy my growing appetite.

Soon the amino synthesis showed that the fetus was normal and that "tiny-you" was an XY boy. However, the fibroids were also growing. The diameter of the two large ones was several centimeters. Going to any prenatal class never crossed my mind. Instead, my focus was on being ready for something bad to happen. It was more like, "how far can I go with the baby and the fibroids?" My peers at work always had the ear to listen during our many walks along St. George Street or Spadina Avenue. For Dr. Morris, I was an older female with complications. She showed me and my fibroids to her students during some of my visits. She was attentive to any symptoms I reported and explained and treated them patiently. On the walls in her office, there were many baby pictures. I was never bored while waiting for her.

In early May, six months into my pregnancy, Dr. Morris happily updated the status of "tiny-you": the baby had become a complete human; he would live if he wanted to come out earlier than expected. It was the second milestone in your life while the first, my inception, went unnoticed and likely happened in the country on the other side of the border. Ying announced my pregnancy to his family in China. His mother wanted to help. She applied to come over. She went shopping for baby clothes and sewed several baby-sized blankets and comforters. Ying passed the news to his peers in Buffalo, too. Some of them immediately promised to provide different baby furniture. We started preparing the baby room.

Dr. Morris scheduled the date of birth to be a week before the expected date. I secured a month of maternity leave with my boss. In the weeks before my operation, Dr. Morris asked me to inform the ambulance, if it was needed, that the baby did not go down. Luckily, the ambulance was never called. "Tiny-you" by then was diagonally between two 6- and 8-cm fibroids in my womb. My bulging belly was visibly higher than any woman in the late stage of pregnancy. The top of the bulge contained one fibroid on the left side and your feet and legs on the right. Under the tight skin, the left side was hard solid while the right side was active, especially when I was steady, trying to rest at night. The poking and kicking sent wonderful messages that you were alive. It must have been hard for "tiny-you" to get around from time to time.

This is the beginning of the story about you before you were born. You came and grew while I had to feed both you and the fibroids while working full time on my research projects. In the end, you survived and won. Like Dr. Morris said, "The human body is a mystery."

BOOK ONE

Baby, toddler, preschooler

The Baby

We watched the Disney movie *Dumbo* many times after you started watching TV. In the movie, Mrs. Jumbo, the veteran elephant of a circus, waited anxiously. A flock of storks was delivering babies. A little bundle strung to a parachute was flying to each expecting mother. At last, a stork flew over her railway cart and delivered her bundle. Mrs. Jumbo opened the bundle and loved her baby, big ears and all, with her whole heart. Here is how you came to the world and started your real life.

Your Birth

Your birthday was to be August 24, 1992. In the afternoon of the 23rd (Sunday), I did the finishing touch on the poster for a conference. When leaving the office, I met a professor in the elevator. He smiled at my condition and knowingly said, "Still working because of her?" I proudly replied, "Baby boy and his birthday is tomorrow."

Before 8 o'clock on the 24th, Ying and I arrived at the hospital. I checked in, and it was a room with four beds in the maternity section. The nurse came with the gown. She asked a few questions and took my temperature and blood pressure. As instructed, I was soon changed and got wheeled into the operating room, which was as spacious as I had seen in the TV shows. Dr. Morris came by with her usual smile. For six months, I was a patient at the

Women's College Hospital. Dr. Morris was on top of my case after I was diagnosed as an older pregnant woman with multiple fibroids. A few of her students, whom I had met on my previous visits, were also in the room. They were there to do the chores because my surgery was just one of the few on Dr. Morris' list for the day. As she explained a few times already, the operation was a C-section, and anesthesia was epidural. In simple terms, the baby would come out through an incision in my lower abdomen, and I should remain awake during the surgery. According to the form I had signed, my uterus (with the fibroids) would be removed if serious hemorrhaging occurred during the operation.

The operation bed was very flat and hard. A divider was installed to block my view of the area beyond my chest. People were arriving and bustling around on the other side of the divider. Ying stood next to me on this side. I looked at the ceiling, wishing it had some pictures, like those in a dental office. The air conditioning was strong. A few minutes later, the intravenous was connected, and I was told to roll over onto my side. An injection was administered to my lower back. It was to numb the local area on my back enough for the larger needle of the epidural. The big needle, the real anesthesia to last for my entire operation, came as a big push, and I was told to curl up a bit and relax. The needle then went in and found the right location between the two vertebrae in my spine. That was the end of the preparation. I should be awake during the operation. Strangely, I felt my response, especially in English, was fading when I tried to refresh my memory of the procedure that was underway. People were moving around, and Ying was eager to get a view of the operation on the other side of the divider.

The operation started. I felt a few dull cuts. As I later learned, it was a horizontal incision across my lower abdomen. Because of the baby's position, the cut was a little higher than normal, above the bikini line. The doctors cut through layers of skin and muscles to expose the uterus. The incision then opened the uterus. In my case, Dr. Morris's expertise was to reach up to find the baby among all the blobs and water without breaking or bruising anything. I was quite alert at the time because my uterus was on the line. The serious hemorrhaging did not happen, and my uterus remained. The doctors hoped the hormone changes after the birth would do magic to shrink the fibroids so that I would be back to normal. It did not take long before Dr. Morris pulled out the baby. She patted the baby twice, and the latter cries came out. You were out and alive! A baby in Chinese culture is a year old when he is born. In that way, your age would include "tiny-you" doing all the struggles inside me. Here you were out at age zero and started counting… Figuratively, your age only started when you cried to announce your arrival.

I overheard that everything about you was normal. Ying and I had worried about whether your arms, legs, neck, or even fingers might not have enough space to grow among the fibroids. Everything was fine. I was hugely relieved and fell asleep before any pain kicked in.

First Day

I woke up and found that the other beds in the room were occupied. Ying was around. I was still connected with the needles and catheter. There was dull pain, and I could feel the flatness of my abdomen. However, the muscles that had been working together did not cooperate when I tried to raise my head. Finally, "tiny-you" and its world were gone; maybe I would miss the time when I could feel your heart beating and see your foot poking.

In a tray on the cart next to my bed, you were wrapped tightly in a light blue sheet. After being soaked in the liquid inside my womb for months, your face was reddish and puffy, and the skin of your hands was wrinkled. Although not pretty, you had plenty of hair on your head, and it was very black. You weighed less than seven pounds and were approximately seventeen inches long. There was a band on your left wrist, saying "Shih, no name," an implication of how unprepared your parents were. Ying and I worked on your name. He gave you a Chinese name, Jiyun, meaning the clouds on the horizon. He wanted you to be free. Your English name is James, following the pronunciation of your Chinese name. Before the end of the day, we filled out the application for your birth certificate.

A nurse brought a small, half-filled bottle of infant formula, an imitation of human milk. She also asked me to put you on my nipples so you could be familiar with them. You suckled at my nipple! However, my milk would not come soon. The C-section, instead of natural birth, did not provide the mother with the required stimulation for the next step of feeding the offspring.

According to her, a newborn won't be hungry in the first 24 hours, and you would likely lose some weight to get rid of the puffiness. The nurse then showed us how to feed you. An important training for us was to help you burp. The reason was that a newborn does not have enough muscle or proper coordination to expel the air out for the milk to go down. Evolution from tube feeding inside the womb to a normal human digestive process required a bit of help at the beginning, I thought. Help in burping included standing you straight against the adult and patting your back lightly until the air (and sometimes milk) came out of you. Ying soon became an expert in burping. He also learned to put a piece of soft towel between your chin and his shirt as a cushion and a sputum collector.

Since we did not attend any prenatal class, the nurse gave us the first lesson on how to change diapers. The naked you in front of me showed more hair on your head, neck, and back. Ying seemed calmer than me on these things because he has a younger sister and a nephew. He was familiar with the scene and the smell. The diaper was disposable. It could be cloth, as we learned later. However, our first lesson was with the disposable diaper and baby wipe. The smallest diaper fitted you well, and the tape at its two ends made the operation safe and easy. You were quite comfortable after being wiped clean. We learned soon that you would certainly let us know if the diaper was soiled.

Throughout the day when you were available, we tried feeding and changing diapers. Once or twice, I felt your skull under the thick hairs. As said in the book, I could identify the pieces of bones and sutures, the most fragile part of an infant. It would take a long time for the shell of human intelligence to close tight. My busy work and advanced age did not create a big baby, but the good food and a lot of walking to get the good food made every part of you fully functional. Your abnormally large amount of hair, Ying believed, had something to do with the many beef short ribs from the European meat market, one of my favorite meats. I fully agreed. Other than the pain and complications of my pregnancy, I really enjoyed the months of my life in Toronto.

For the night, you were sent back to the nursery because I could not yet get out of bed without a lot of pain. By then, the catheter and related tubes were pulled out, but I still needed to spend the night with the intravenous pain killer and antibiotics. Obviously, my focus was to make safe rounds with the rack to any place, such as the washroom. My appetite was back. I could finish everything on the tray at mealtimes. Ying went to the hospital cafeteria to have a bite and eventually went home when he was asked to leave. I was tired and slept through the night. Still, I remembered that my attempts to turn were held back by the rack and wires and that people were in and out often, but as quiet as possible.

Suture

Dr. Morris came by the next morning during her daily rounds. She was happy that I had no fever and, hence, no implications for infection. In contrast to the mothers who went through the normal birth, I had to stay at the hospital for a week to wait for the wound to heal. Dr. Morris or other doctors making the daily rounds checked my chart and the suture of the C-section every time.

The nurse on duty changed the gauze from time to time. She came by, removed the soiled one, and went to her next patient. Instead of applying the fresh gauze immediately, she seemed to believe in healing in fresh air. The wound stayed open longer and longer each day. She also asked me to take showers to "wash, wash, and wash it clean." She helped me to the shower room for the first time and showed me the trick of showering with the least pain. So, I took a shower every day. Since I don't swim, those were almost all the cold or lukewarm showers I had in my whole life. After the shower, I would lie in the bed and leave the wound open until she came around to put the clean gauze on.

I had ample opportunities to examine the suture while waiting for a new gauze. It was an approximately five-inch horizontal cut. It was closed tight, and, as far as I could see, stapled together, zigzagging whenever necessary. I was told that there were two layers of closure. The inner one to close the uterus was by surgical thread, and the thread would be absorbed and eventually disappear. The outer one for my tummy was stapled, and the staples would be removed when no longer needed. On the day you were born, the doctors doing the chores for Dr. Morris had to work on the layers of skin, fat, and muscles covering a big void after you were out. Therefore, the closure was not a piece of fine work. The compilation was likely done by one person squeezing the layers tightly together and the other pressing the stabler along. Some staples were holding three layers together, while the others were holding two or four. The new skin or muscle would grow and replace the old ones, I thought. I wondered whether the final product would be a smooth line when it was completely healed. At least, the length of the visible scar should be shorter.

I had doubts about leaving the wound open. The air was not germ free, although the ward was cleaned diligently. I also had doubts about the shower policy. In the back of my mind, the old Chinese tradition told me that a mom with a newborn should not touch cold water or go out for the first thirty days. However, there was nothing in my mind about what would be done if the mother had a C-section. An applicable old Chinese saying is that it takes one hundred days to heal bone or muscle injuries. Amazingly, my body (probably with the magic hormone) put up with everything without a lot of complaint.

The hospital food was healthy, but not anything like fish or chicken broth to bring the milk. I was weak, and the healing was slow. My co-worker at U of T, a researcher from the Chinese Academy of Science, believed in black-bone chicken. It is a type of chicken with high carnosine that is good for the muscle and nervous system. She searched through the grocery stores in Chinatown and spent a fortune on one. She then cooked it and brought me the entire pot of chicken soup. I had a bowl of soup, and it tasted very good. I asked her to take the rest back and told her that the soup would be good for her, too. It turned out that I made the right decision. The grease in the soup did not get along with my weak stomach.

Since I was still healing, my time with you was limited. The milk eventually came, and you were fed by both me and the infant formula. Ying tried to come every day and leave after you were sent back to the nursery. The new moms in the room came and left, mostly staying less than three days. I envied them, most of whom were ten to fifteen years younger than me. In addition, healing without a C-section cut quickly gets the hormone back on track in a mother. These young moms would be as good as new in a few weeks, and ready for another child, and another child...

Your First Medical Treatment

Dr. Edward dropped by on the third day. He was a pediatrician visiting the newborns in several hospitals. By default, he became your doctor. You were the first one among the three of us to have a family doctor. He asked about you and left his business card. It did not take long for him to come back. By then, he had examined you in the nursery. He said that your jaundice was higher-than-normal. It is the excessive yellow pigment in a newborn, and the problem is relatively common for babies from oriental mothers. The key was that the yellowish color was advancing after your birth. His advice was to treat the jaundice in order to prevent any damage.

The light therapy was arranged immediately. In the afternoon, a technician pushed in a different cart mounted with equipment. Your wrappings were removed. With only a diaper and a protective eye patch, you were placed under a special lamp that emitted blue-green light. I was told that the light would change the shape and structure of the yellow pigment in such a way that it would come out in your urine and stool. Almost naked under the light, you twisted and kicked in the tray. Instead of crying, you were howling desperately. Out of the womb and then out of the tight bundle, you felt very unprotected. It made me very sad. I lightly squeezed your hands and feet, hoping to connect with you or at least to divert your attention. As instructed, I put your legs and arms back under the light from time to time. I was so relieved at the end of the treatment. Once you were wrapped in the blanket and back in your own cart. You fell asleep quietly. You were so tired. Gladly, I was told that you only needed the treatment once.

Having handled the lamb and cubs in my previous life as a herdsman, I understood with my heart the weak and helpless state of the human offspring. The animal cubs come out with the placenta and can stand up themselves. They just shake off the gunk and immediately look for their mother's nipples. The mother is usually back on her feet, watching, and sometimes licking, the baby. Soon, the cub will walk lingeringly next to the mother. In the springtime on a pasture, the howling from either the mother or lamb is often heard, especially in the morning or in the evening after a long day of grazing. If only a short distance from each other, the mom and baby could identify each other, run, and quickly reunite. It is also the time for the herdsmen to ensure the entirety of his sheep flock. With a bit of help from the herder, the animals will all be paired up, and the flock is quiet with barely auditable noise, like a family at a well-behaved dinner table. The human offspring belongs to a home. You, my baby, could only cry to send out your message when feeling the loss of protection. You will be immobile, bundled tightly most of the time for months, and attended to by your loved ones, always at home.

On the fourth day, I was off the intravenous and could sit

up and walk a bit. Therefore, you were to stay at my bedside overnight. You were used to the pattern of being fed by me and then from the formula bottle. As a new mother, I checked the state of your diaper often. Together, we were quite peaceful, never bothering the neighbors much. So, you stayed. I did my duty as a mom for the first night.

Going Home

The staples in the C-section suture were taken out on the fourth day. They left small holes along the ugly wound. While checking along afterwards, I noticed a hole that was bigger than any stable marks at the spot where the layers were seriously mismatched. There was a bit of itchiness, and the nearby area was pinkish and warm. It could be a sign of infection. I blamed it on my slow healing. When Dr. Morris came by on the Friday morning (beginning of the fifth day in your life), she said that I could go home the next day or wait for her next round on the Monday next. I was eager to go home.

The students of Dr. Morris discharged us in the morning of the next day. They made sure that I knew how to follow up if anything needed medical attention. I was surprised when I looked at the bill when checking out of the hospital. For my surgery, medical treatments afterwards, and the five-and-half days of hospital stay, I only needed to pay the cost of the rental phone. When the wound was treated for the last time, the situation was borderline. The soiled gauze had sizable yellow spots, and the worst area along the wound was a bit swollen. However, the threatening wound was of less importance than my desire to go home.

Ying came to pick us up. We changed you into our own cotton blanket. It wasn't really fall yet and was warm outside. Ying got our car baby-ready days before. The oversized car seat, which was given to him by his friends at school, was in the middle of the back seat. For the first time, you were strapped into the car seat. I got into the back as well. There was a dull pain when I had to extend the range of my movement to get into the car. Ying drove out of the hospital compound, then on Bloor Street, and then on Don Valley Parkway. You were fast asleep because of the motion of the car. I felt light and happy, like a soldier going home.

However, you woke up and started crying by the stop-and-go on Eglinton Avenue after we were off the highway. Eglinton has so many traffic lights. I wondered if you inherited my car sickness. First time with a crying baby on board, Ying eventually ran the traffic light when we were only two intersections away from home. Almost immediately, the patrol car was behind us. An officer came over and talked to Ying. Ying was then asked to step out. I could only hear him saying repeatedly that the baby was crying and that his wife was just out of the hospital. It turned out that he did not have his driver's license with him and did not know where I kept the car insurance paper, either. The result was three traffic tickets, two of which could be removed, provided he went in with valid information the next day. We arrived home in no time after the patrol let us go.

It took longer than two months to get your birth certificate. For a while, I wondered if it got lost because of the "Shih, no name" or my non-resident status. It finally came after a few calls to track the progress. You became the only one in the family with a birth certificate.

Welcoming "tiny-you" into the world was the first step in our relationship. It was a whole new experience for all three of us. I am forever grateful to Dr. Heather Morris at the Women's College Hospital. With her medical judgment and expertise, she was always positive about my rocky road to having my first and only child. I had my first experience in a Canadian hospital to observe and communicate with professionals outside my expertise. It was also my first encounter with the health insurance in Canada, which was envied by many of my friends in other countries.

The First Sixteen Months

"**T**hey explore the world of things and begin to figure out the fundamentals of cause and effect…. Children need an environment that allows for the next developmental achievement but doesn't push them into it." — Dr. Benjamin Spock[1]

Your First Home

Our home then was a two-bedroom apartment. It was near the intersection of Eglinton Avenue and Kennedy Road in Scarborough. The parking lots of the apartment building were next to the strip mall with a No Frills. The Eglington subway (now with GO train) station was on the other side of Eglinton. To reach U of T downtown campus, I tried taking the subway at first, but soon found myself not immune to the germs in the public facilities, especially in winter. Parking around U of T was tricky. The parking ticket I got once was expensive. However, I found driving in downtown Toronto wasn't bad at all. With my condition, I finally settled on carpooling with a coworker, and we shared a parking spot for faculties on the King's College Circle. As I was getting heavier, driving to work became necessary. My

---

[1] The text is from "The First Year, Four to Twelve Months" of *Dr. Spock's Baby and Child Care* by Dr. Benjamin Spock, M.D.. It is from the 9th edition of the book (revised and updated by Robert Needlman, M.D.) The first edition of his book on the content was published in 1946.

Chevy Celebrity, with a mileage already exceeding 150,000 miles, served me well.

The help in China did not come. We tried to get Ying's mother over to help. Her application was rejected because of "Immigration Tendency", which was the phrase used to turn away hundreds of applicants in those years. His mother sent the baby clothes and several baby-size blankets in the mail. The package arrived before your birth. The lack of help required at home led to our decision that Ying would take a three-month leave of absence from his thesis work. It was good for both of us. The consequence of the delay and subsequent additional family duties was that he had to make many trips between the USA and Canada over the next three years.

We arranged one of the two bedrooms to be a baby's room. It contained the baby bed Ying got from his friend in Buffalo. The bed was made of solid wood. One of its sides could be removed, and its base could be moved up and down. In addition, we bought a crib with wheels. It would be large enough for you in the first three months. In fact, you were in our room at night most of the time. Your room functioned as a storage for your gears such as diapers, boxes of infant formula, and even some toys for later use. A part of the kitchen counter became the baby's space for bottles, nipples, formula cans, and related utensils.

Our apartment had a large living-dining area. The smaller section next to the kitchen was used for dining or as an extension of the kitchen. It had a foldable table and four foldable chairs. The large living room was relatively empty, with a desk and a couple of chairs, which Ying and I used for work or study. We filled it with a new three-seat couch with a pull-out bed from La-Z-Boy. It was the first piece of new furniture we bought after many years of our student life in North America. The couch, which is as old as you are, served the family well. Many visitors, including our relatives and your friends from school, slept in it. It was moved to Ottawa and now moved back to Toronto with Ying and me. We kept the living room clean so that you could be left anywhere while I might be away, and Ying might be busy with other things. Additional pieces were added to the living room once you started crawling and walking. Still, you always had space to "roam".

We bought a humidifier for the night when the heating in the building was turned on. In a few months, we made our home childproof.

Second Round to the Hospital

Life was busy but on track for a few days until the infection around my C-section suture went out of control. Less than a week after I returned home, a part of the wound became glaring red and started oozing yellow fluid. One night, Ying had to load you and me into the car for a trip to the hospital because of my rising fever. This time we drove to the entrance of the Emergency. The doctor on duty had a look at my infection and reckoned that the situation was bad, possibly because the suture was not closed properly. I was to stay, and Ying left with you.

A different doctor was called down to the emergency room, and my wound was cleaned up. The infection had created a deep hole that was originally formed by the prong of a staple holding the zigzagging layers together. To avoid further rotting, a strip of gauze was partly inserted into the hole to drain any new fluid. On the top of the "drainage," the doctor applied a fresh gauze pad. I was connected intravenously. This time, I was rolled into the ward for surgery recovery. It was clean and quiet. The nurse came by at least three times that night to check my temperature and the wound. My fever was down when the doctor making the morning rounds came by. The prognosis was that the infection was serious, and therefore, I had to stay for a few days.

This led to Ying's daily trips to take you to the hospital so that I could feed you once or twice. I could imagine that you were hot, probably crying in the oversized car seat in the back of the car on the way. Ying was tired, but he never showed frustration. Sending you home was also hard. I was sad, feeling that the age factor had been really overlooked before all this happened. I wondered how you two would manage at home. The sequence of chores until the next daylight included feeding, bathing, and then getting up and down for a bottle or a diaper throughout the night. Luckily, with the intravenous and good cleanup, my situation improved quickly. I was home after a five-day stay at the hospital.

The follow-ups were done by the daily call of a home-visiting nurse. She would replace the strip in the hole and the gauze pad covering the wound on each visit. By then, my one-month maternity leave was ending, and I had to return to my full-time job. Because I could not be at home during her shift, the nurse taught Ying to redress the wound and asked him to do it daily. There was still a hole, waiting for new flesh to be filled. Every evening, Ying used the tweezers to pull out the soiled strip, cleaned the wound, and then inserted a clean one tightly so that the hole would stay dry. We had such an operation daily for two or three weeks until the new flash filled the hole. I was just glad that my work only required sitting in front of a computer most of the time. Driving daily along the Don Valley was actually the most peaceful moment of the day.

It was an amazing first month of your life. We went through pain and chaos and came out safely. As a result, my C-section suture is forever an ugly scar. It was hard, thick, and itchy for many years, and it hurt whenever I laughed, coughed, or sneezed. Under the depression along the now brownish line defining the original suture, the layers never grew back to normal.

Dr. Spock and Your First 100 Days

The first one-hundred days of your life were for Ying and me to overcome the steep learning curve in a new culture of bringing up a baby in Canada. My friend in the States sent me her congratulations with (one edition of) Dr. Benjamin Spock's *Baby and Child Care*. Ying and I started reading it even before you were born. We followed his checklist in the "Right from Start" section to get ready for your homecoming. We agreed wholeheartedly with his views on baby basics since we could not yet afford any luxuries. It was the go-to book for answers and explanations on various topics, such as behavior, digestion, and common illnesses.

We learned to warm up the formula bottle using warm water instead of the microwave oven. We learned to sanitize the nipples at the right temperature after overheating a few sets. I even learned to collect my milk, although I never had a lot. We bought a baby bathtub and a series of baby wash and wipe materials. Ying gave you the first few baths because I could hardly bend. You were not colicky, but I did open Dr. Spock many times to check and compare your crying, feeding, and sleeping patterns. The answer I got was usually that it happens and that it is not a problem until something worse happens. Things were often back to normal before the "something worse." A thought that often came to my mind was "can't wait for when you are in" the next growth spur or age stage. In fact, juggling between work and you, I was often surprised when your next accomplishment came into view.

Ying is always very proud of the three months during which he was on duty taking care of you. Most of all, you were well around 50 percent of the growth curve, and we heard no complaints during the few visits to Dr. Edward's office. The remaining two months of his stay at home after my maternity leave were busy but peaceful. Ying started tabulating your daily activities, which included sleep, formula, water, stool, and urine. The record was written on the back of scrap paper from his research on nuclear physics or mine in seismic data analysis. I still have two stacks of records on you in the filing cabinet. You had a good eating and sleep pattern if all the gears were properly prepared.

I fed you in the morning before leaving for work. For a short while, I could pump some milk in the early afternoon and bring it home after work. Then my milk was gone, probably because of my work and the infection. In the years that followed, watching my co-workers enjoy the twelve or even eighteen months of maternity leave, I envied them. A year of close mother-and-baby contact will not only bring many months of breastfeeding but also a much more relaxing process for a family to take in a new member.

We did not buy any fancy baby toys or monitors. Ying was there with you all the time. He made a human swing by laying you in a folded baby blanket. He said that you could stay asleep, or at least silent, for half an hour when he swung you back and forth for five minutes. His invention was probably inspired by your prolonged crying.

On sunny days, Ying would unwrap you and lay you on a piece of cotton cloth. In this way, you would get some vitamin D in the sunshine. Indeed, you always had great black hair. Following the instructions from Drs. Edward and Spock, we let you sleep on your side. Your head got the shape of a "foreigner" as later commented by our relatives.

Bottle feeding brought a few problems. You turned away from the bottle a few times until we figured out that the nipples were overcooked. I had to run out to get a new pack. The size of the hole in a nipple mattered, too. After you were completely on formula, you got constipation — no stool. We called Dr. Edward and were told to add a teaspoon of corn syrup to the formula bottle. That solved your problem. You have had a sweet tooth from the beginning.

Otherwise, you were healthy for the first three months. As the book says, the newborn has the mother's antibodies for the first few months. At the end of his three-month leave of absence, Ying left for school. He started his weekly or bi-weekly trips between Toronto and Buffalo. Before he left home, we moved your bed into my bedroom and set up a brand-new playpen in the living room. In this way, I could synchronize my activities with yours and easily check on you in the evening and at night.

Home Care

Setting you up with home care turned out to be tough. Ying and I found a home care for you before he returned to school. The sitter and I agreed on the starting date and the time duration you would stay at her home care. The family was taking care of two babies, one toddler, and one after-school child. Its setup was within the quota of a home care service. On the first day, I delivered you with three bottles of formula. When I picked you up, I was told that you had not finished a single bottle. The lady reassured me, "He will be used to my house and will drink when he is hungry." When I brought you home, you finished a bottle and a half! I was sad. Regardless of your first rocky day, we had fun in the evening, and you slept well at night.

On the second day, you had finished half of the bottle when I picked you up. You again had a "big drink" once you got home. On the third day, I brought you back home with three full bottles. I was desperate, although the lady did not think that there was a problem. Looking at you, I really wished you could tell me what had happened. I discussed the situation with Ying, and we agreed on looking for a new home care.

In the evening of the same day, I saw a note offering home-care service on the bulletin board at the nearby No Frills, and the note was written in Chinese. A lady answered the phone when I called. I explained my urgent situation, and she told me to come over. I put you in the car and drove to her house, which was not far along Kennedy Road from our home.

This was how I met Jiang Taitai. Later, I called her your lifesaver. I never asked about her full name. "Jiang" was her last name, and "Taitai" in Chinese was equivalent to "Mrs." in English. She was from Taiwan. She lived with her two-year-old son, Kevin. Her husband was in Taiwan doing business to support the family. She was hoping to earn some grocery money while bringing up her son in Canada. She wasn't sure if she could handle a baby that went on a hunger strike at other people's house, but she liked you and thought that you could be Kevin's playmate.

The next morning, I packed three bottles of formula for you and drove to her house. She asked me to take you in with your car seat so that you could rest comfortably in something you were familiar with. When I went to pick you up in the evening, she said something I remembered for the rest of my life: "Your baby isn't easy to feed. I tried many, many times, but only finished one and a half bottles." I was hugely relieved. She then told me you had a nap when Kevin took his and that Kevin came around to check on you and cheer you up many times. She said that things would be better, and therefore, her decision was to take you in.

You were under her care for almost an entire year. You and Kevin were a good pair. After a few months, you were out of the car seat at her place. You learned to hold the bottle and then to hold a spoon. You mostly imitated Kevin in learning new skills, while Jiang was leading me through your progress. She set the rules for the two of you. For example, each of you had a highchair, and a meal was served at the table. Everyone should sit in the highchair to finish their meal. You took your nap next to Kevin every day and played along with Kevin all the time. You loved their company so much that I had to sit there watching sometimes when I got there to pick you up.

The routine was that I packed you up with bottles of formula (and later with baby food) in the morning and left you with Jiang Taitai. I then carpooled (either drove or waited at home) with a coworker near Midland and Eglinton. The working day was from 9 to 4:30 because my friend had two girls in elementary school to take care of. Once or twice a week, I walked to Chinatown to buy a lunch plate that included a portion of rice and three portions of meat and veggies of my choice. I usually had leftovers to bring home for my dinner. Life with you in the evening would be relaxing and fun.

If all the documents for border crossing were up to date, Ying always came back on the weekends. We often went to picnics in the park and then did a bit of shopping. He tried to help and be the father. I had a picture of him reading with you on his lap in front of his paper; the father and son were very well aligned and focused. I sent the pictures around, and the feedback was that you were predestined to be a scholar.

The Little Canadian

Life with my work and baby was well underway. Ying and I discussed and made our decision to immigrate to Canada, although he already had a green card to stay in the States. Like many Chinese of my generation, our intention for immigration was to make it easier to get a job and settle down. I hired an agent and started the process. A few years later, when I became a Canadian citizen, my coworker asked about my feelings. I said, "I am more important now. I am one in the millions of Canadians, while I was one in the billions of Chinese before." It was a plain truth that this is a vast country with a lot fewer people. Going through the first half of our life in China, studying abroad, and then settling down abroad were just a few chapters of our life.

A few months after filing for immigration, Ying and I were called to an interview at the Consulate General of Canada in New York City. During the interview, most of the questions were expected, except for the one about my education. The immigration clerk pointed out that I had a deficiency in education. The reason was that I did not have the compulsory twelve-year primary and secondary education, which is a standard in Canada. We briefly explained the interruption of my education in China, and my postgraduate degrees received in the States. At the end of the interview, the clerk said, "You have a son who is Canadian. Make sure that he gets all that a Canadian deserves." Ying and I discussed the meaning of his comment on our way back. Do we need to make any special effort? The answer was probably yes; the clerk was concerned about us coming from a very different cultural background. However, we were just at the first step of immigration, and you were only a few months old. It was too early to research the topic.

No matter what, you, the little Canadian, were growing bigger and became much superior to the lamb and cubs I had handled before. Pretty soon, I needed to put the pillows around you if I left you in my bed. I flipped you over a few times when you rolled and buried your head somewhere. I noticed you popping up your head in the dark when I woke up during the night. It might be diaper time. You often tried to cling to the side of the playpen once you learned to sit up. As soon as you learned to stand up, you were often up in your bed or the playpen, shaking anything that could make a noise. You tried so hard with each little progress and claimed it.

It was a character-building process. In the playpen, you insisted on standing up yourself. You would fall back to start all over if I had helped. Standing steady was probably a huge milestone that separates humans from most other mammals. You graduated from the playpen and started wobbling in the walker. You extended your interest beyond your age-appropriate clean toys. When I was in the kitchen, you often shook and propelled yourself towards me with a big smile on your face and no fear. You navigated along the shelves and cupboards under the counter, playing with anything in your path. Watching you master every skill with the greatest effort, I wondered what a person could accomplish if they were never tired and worked at 100 percent all the time.

To plant a bit of caution into your little mind, I put you on the counter next to the oven. I turned on one burner. I told you the word "hot" and pulled one of your fingers close to the heat. Unfortunately, your finger somehow got too close to the hot surface. You cried, and I had to hold you close to the sink and let the cold water run through your little fingers. It was your first encounter with pain and fear. You stopped going to the kitchen for a while afterward. Another incident happened in the garage downstairs. On a regular afternoon, the garage door suddenly started rolling up when we passed by on our way to my car. The rolling sound really shocked you. You screamed. I had to bury your head in my chest to shield the noise and get into my car as fast as possible. I soon found out that you have a sensitive ear. You would curl up or jitter in response to thunder or even a loud bang on the door. You never had ear infections, which was a common sickness for children. Your sensitive ear was mentioned by others from time to time in the later years.

We had a proper stroller and a cloth carrier for you. If the weather permitted, we often had outings on the weekends when Ying was around. The outings were usually very pleasant. We found that the parks along the Don Valley were very green and augmented with different colors year-round. Families came to the park to picnic. Parents and children from one or multiple families played frisbee or water guns. For a small group of three, we sat you on the green next to your stroller. There were enough activities for you to look around. Ying's brother, who was on a business trip from China, came with us one time. He held you and ran back and forth to fly you into the sky. Besides the parks, we went shopping sometimes. The malls along Eglinton were usually packed on weekends. In a store like Kmart or Zellers, you only busily watched instead of reaching out to grab or pull if you already had something in your hand. Ying and I were impressed that you understood the simple concept of ownership. I still have a picture of you holding a plastic spoon among the clothing racks.

Gradually, you were introduced to our social activities. Summer in Toronto is for gatherings. My boss and coworkers had BBQs or dinner parties. I was usually not the host because I was still new, and Ying came back home only on weekends. My boss left China when he was a teenager. He did his postgraduate work at the University of California, Berkeley, and became a professor at U of T. He organized team buildings as far as Barrie. You would be fine if you were not cranky because of an unfinished nap in the car. Most of the time, the children of my coworkers took care of you.

We celebrated your first birthday with Jiang Taitai and Kevin. The layered cake with fruit from one of the Chinese bakeries was fluffy and not very sweet. With everybody's help, you learned to blow a single candle on the big cake. Our relatives in China and the States were happy to see a boy with a big smile and both hands and feet on top of his highchair. For the Christmas after your one-year birthday, we were invited to the party at one of my distant cousins. He was in his sixties and well respected. His house was large enough for over fifty people. I learned for the first time that we were all related. They came to settle in Toronto years or generations ago, from Asia, Europe, Australia, and South America. You behaved well because the food was delicious, and several of your cousins or nieces took turns entertaining you. Being almost the youngest at the party, you got a big Christmas present at the end.

My Two Part-Time Jobs

A few months after your birth, the fund of my NSF proposal at the University of Wisconsin materialized. My professor and

I communicated about options for the project. I could either withdraw from the project, i.e., give up the grant, or do my part of the research in Wisconsin. I chose the latter, and my professor was glad to have me back as the principal researcher on a similar subject I did my doctorate work on. My choice was a difficult one, but I deemed it necessary because I was still on track to settle down with my career. Financially, the salary of a non-tenure track associate professor in the States was higher than that of a post-doc researcher at U of T.

I got two part-time jobs and a baby. The agreement was that I would go to Madison to work for two weeks every other month. Your whereabouts during my two-week business trip were also arranged. You would spend the night at Jiang Taitai's house from Monday to Thursday. On the weekend I was away, Ying would come back on Friday evening to pick you up. He would stay for the extended weekend with you and go to Buffalo on Monday morning after delivering you to Jiang's house. The distance between Toronto and Madison, Wisconsin, is 670 miles. During the long days of late spring, summer, and early fall, my typical business trip would start at Jiang's house after leaving you with her. My journey for the day included driving past London, Detroit, and Chicago and arriving in Madison in the evening. At the end of my business trip, I would drive the same route in reverse and pick you up on my way home in the evening.

My professor knew the hardship I was in and let me stay in his house. His wife, who was a professor of biochemistry at the same university, did all the chores to help me settle in. She was as senior as her husband in academic ranking. Optimistic and believing in

34

an individual's effort, she said that the dream would come true for a few lucky ones. She won my respect immediately. She was certainly the major contributor in raising their four children. "They are all grown up now," she told me. For a few years, they were teenagers, and all lived in the house. "We often waited in the evening, wondering if everybody would come home without trouble," she said. The professors juggled between their career and kids for quite a while on the way.

My professor did the chores outside the house, such as re-landscaping the garden and fixing the house and cars. These were the right hobbies for a physicist. I still remember what he told me on my first day in his office. Besides presentations and research papers, his doctoral student must be successful in field operations. To get the degree, the student must have at least one successful NSF proposal. It took me five years to complete. I was involved in a few field projects with him. He lost his youngest son in a project across the East African Rift. The sad news came when I was alone with a school van and my tent in eastern California for geothermal study. I had to collect the instruments and drive back to Wisconsin by myself at the end of the deployment. We never talked about this.

Being able to stay with them was really an honor for me. Their house on the top of a hill certainly had the owners with the highest possible education in the area. It was the place people took their children to get a professor-made rice crispy ball on a Halloween night. The house was filled with everything that might be necessary for the children and adults all the time. In the evenings, it was filled with the fragrance of the food and sometimes, the laundry. I often saw the wife with one of her visiting children busy in and out on family projects. I probably helped after dinner. However, I worked hard on my research as I remember.

Other than my feeling of a bit more progress in my career, the extra money earned was mostly used for gas and babysitting. Jiang Taitai charged $40 a night, which I did not argue. For her, taking care of you without a parent nearby meant an enormous responsibility. Ying had to plan extra time to go through customs so that he could pick you up at a reasonable time on Friday. He handled you as well as whatever he needed to do in his thesis work on those extended weekends.

After four trips to Madison, you got sick for the first time. Returning from my Wisconsin duties, I noticed rashes on your chin and neck. My further checking at home showed that you got rashes all over. Ying said that you had a little when he left you the previous Monday. I took you to Dr. Edward. His diagnosis was that the rash was likely related to sweat and a lack of cleaning. The weather was indeed getting warmer. I bought baby powder. On each of the subsequent evenings, I gave you a lukewarm bath and applied a bit of baby powder over the rashes. You were quite happy back in my queen-size bed at home. The rashes were gone after a few days.

I felt guilty because I wasn't doing well as a mother. I was supposed to know the best and should not expect the same from anybody else. Gradually, my two part-time jobs were becoming harder to handle. The situation often was that I would face a pile of work at each location, Madison or Toronto, waiting for me to clean up after every long drive. I felt guilty of being unable to fulfill the expectations of my counterpart. The result of the two part-time jobs was a few more research publications. However, the academic track was getting dimmer after a few interviews for a faculty position. I doubted my belated ambition of becoming a female professor in geophysics.

Right after the new year of 1994, we moved. I put you in the car and started the four-hour journey on Highway 401 East and then on Highway 7. Ying drove his own car, following the moving truck. We moved from Toronto to Ottawa. I gave up the academic route and switched to a full-time industry position with a Kanata company that makes seismic systems. You were not yet a year and a half old. Our hectic life in Toronto was over.

Ying started traveling between Ottawa and Buffalo. It takes three times as long because the distance is almost three hundred and forty miles.

Preschool Years

People said that Ottawa is a winter postcard. It has white snowscapes, enormous ice sculptures, and frosty trees illuminated by twinkling lights. We arrived in Ottawa after the New Year of 1994. Environment Canada had extreme weather warnings on those days. It was close to -20°C with bright sunlight, and we learned what the windchill factor meant immediately. In the twenty-five years we were there, Ying and I worked full time almost all the time, and you grew from a toddler into a young man.

1800 Baseline Road

Before we moved, I checked the rentals in Ottawa and made a day trip to compare and sign up. I could not afford to rent a house yet, and Kanata at the time did not have many apartment buildings. At the end of my day trip, I settled on renting a unit in the apartment building on the Nepean side of Baseline Road.

1800 Baseline Road is a large compound with townhouses in a cluster and a long apartment building next to the sidewalk of Baseline. I rented a sublet unit in the apartment building. It was the first time I had been in a building with two floors that share the same hallway. With all the units facing south, the hallway between the two floors certainly shields a lot of cold air in winter. It is a smart design. The unit I rented had a few steps leading down to its door, which led to the hallway. The apartment was clean. Like the one we had in Toronto, it had a large living-dining area, two bedrooms, and a nice kitchen area close to the door. I had an assigned outdoor parking area inside the compound. The company I worked for was in Kanata. It took around twenty minutes each way for me to travel between home and work on a normal day. It was before the telecommunication boom. My traveling was against the major traffic flow of people living in Kanata, a suburb, and working in the government offices in Ottawa. The city of Ottawa was considerably smaller than Toronto, and it was unamalgamated then.

The Ottawa side is located across the Baseline Road. I could see at least one rundown apartment building with cracked windows and peeling paint. A little pond with reeds was a block away from 1800 Baseline on the same side of the street. There was only a MacDonald's at the current big box store-filled shopping center at the corner of Woodroffe Avenue and Baseline Road. We could walk on a trail on the grass-covered land, passing the pond, before reaching MacDonald's. There were several low-rise office buildings on the north side of Baseline. I transferred my State Farm car insurance to an agent on the second floor in one building. In a few days, I found our family physician, Dr. Douglas, close to the intersection of Hunt Club and Greenbank Roads. She was nice and patient, as calm as Dr. Edward we had in Toronto. She provided medical care to you, me, and my parents-in-law over the years. I got to know how hard it was to find a female family doctor after she retired.

Using the remaining days before I reported to my work, I

found Qin Nainai, our first Chinese live-in nanny. I asked her to work six days a week. My reason was that you were too young. With her around on Saturdays, it would give Qin and me some overlap time to shop for the weekly supplies in case you needed to stay at home. Besides, anybody in her family could visit any time since their house was on Clyde Avenue, which was about a five-minute drive. She and her family agreed. In those years, the phone line was safe without spam. I would call from work around lunchtime every day to check and discuss if anything was needed.

A few days after we settled in the apartment at 1800 Baseline Road, I was notified that my immigration papers had gone through. The next step was to "land," which means reentering Canada at a Canadian customs office to receive the new status of a permanent resident of the country. Ying and I left you, the Canadian, at Qin Nainai's home one day. We drove south and made a circle to exit and re-enter at the Canadian customs office in Lansdowne near Kingston. The landing was straightforward.

Ying went back to school after our move and "landing." It was his first long trip, driving from Ottawa to Buffalo.

Nanny and Toddler

With me working and coming home every day to find you in reliable hands, life was peaceful most of the time. Other than the few words in Chinese you had before we moved to Ottawa, your Chinese was expanding with a certain flavor of a Chinese dialect. Qin Nainai took you out in the stroller to walk around the compound whenever the weather allowed. Her daughter came to visit at least once every week. With their influence, you were sometimes running around in girlish clothes, having a lot of fun. When I came home from work, you were eager to show and tell me what you had learned. You gave orders to yourself to put on the shoes and wear a hat, and asked Nainai to get the stroller and bag. Qin was proud that you remembered quickly what she had told you. I was confused sometimes with your words from Qin's dialect. You never forgot the few stairs on the way to the door. You climbed the stairs on all fours. When going out, you promptly stopped a meter away from the first step, turned around, and climbed down backwards. I wondered if you had a nasty fall before you figured out the routine.

My daily phone calls eventually led to your attention on the phone at home. Statistically, it should take a long time before a combination of an off-hook phone and dialing the numbers 9, 1, and 1. On a normal evening after work, I was on my last stretch, driving along Baseline to get home. I followed a police car into the courtyard of the compound. After parking my car, I followed the officer into the building and then took the elevator to our floor. I asked the officer where he was going, and he said my unit number. I was almost in a panic. Once I opened the door and peeked inside, I immediately realized what might have happened. I explained to the officer that there was a one-year-old toddler with his sitter. He insisted on checking. He came in and checked. Neither of you remembered anything. I apologized and sent the unhappy officer away. I asked Qin to keep you away from the phone. Like letting you know the oven is hot, I had a serious conversation with you about the phone and the possibility of having big strangers over. Nainai should be the only one using the phone while I was away. It never happened again.

Our first year in Ottawa was full of discoveries. We observed the bright and cold winter, and then the beautiful spring filled with tulips and lilies. On weekends, we spent a lot of time outdoors in the parks and at a few local fairs. We then learned that the summer in the Ottawa Valley could be unexpectedly hot. It was the heatwave of 1994. By the time I realized that the un-air-conditioned apartment was too hot, most of the fans were sold out at the nearby stores. One day after work, we had a quick dinner at MacDonald's. I then left you and Qin there with a cold drink and a dish of ice cream and went hunting for a fan. Eventually, I found a high-grade turbo fan at Sears. It was expensive. However, it functioned very well. I set it near the window of the living room. It did not have a stand, but it was powerful. The result of the turbo was that the room cooled down relatively quietly. I had to make the setup childproof before I left for work the next morning. Luckily, the heatwave was gone in a few days.

Because of the heat, good-hearted Qin looked for baby powder to keep you cool after the bath. However, she found Ajax and used it instead until I noticed the smell in the bathroom. Later, the pallets of deodorant for the garbage bin were mistaken for candies. After these incidents, I set the space under the kitchen sink to store all the cleaners. I put the snacks in the kitchen cupboard above the counter and kept enough skin care products on the bathroom counter. In addition, I would be the only person doing the housecleaning chores, and I would only clean on Sundays. It was a part of my learning curve. No damage was done.

Family of Three

After your first trip to China, the research part of Ying's thesis work was completed. Therefore, he could stay longer at home. Occasionally, he traveled to school to discuss his progress with his professor. You were two years old and should be potty trained. A vivid picture in my mind then was that you were naked with an oversized disposable diaper when we were in China. You were running around in the courtyard of the apartment buildings when you stayed with Ying's parents in Beijing. You were a scene, if not a fashion show, in the few days you were there. Babies in China mostly wore cloth diapers and were rid of them around one-year-old. After they found out that you came with a diaper, your aunt did some research to get you disposable ones while I was attending a conference. The baby pants there had a large opening in the rear, which was convenient for a child to leak when needed.

It wasn't difficult to train you since you were probably aware of the issue after your trip to China. We got you the potty and explained the steps. Ying took care of you during the day when you were at home. You were still with a diaper when going to any home care. At night, I woke you up once or twice to lead you to the washroom, hoping you would pee. Obviously, the daytime training was the first one to complete. It took a lot longer at night for the need to pee to become important enough to wake you up, especially when you were tired or in a dream. I had many nights to get up to put the sleepy you on the toilet. Also, there were many times to ask you to stay on the toilet and try to finish your business (stool) for the day. Your parents, two scientists, focused on diaper training for a while because it was about time. Other than a few accidents, you were off the diaper in a few weeks for outings, home care, and at home. You were already at a stage of talking into senses.

It was also a process to introduce you to your own bed and own room. To get your potty trained, you were moved into a standard single bed with bedding that was relatively water resistant. After the bedtime story, you could sleep by yourself for several hours. However, the hours after you were back from the midnight pee could be chaotic. I put you back in bed and waited for a few minutes to make sure that you went back to sleep. However, you often ended up between Ying and me in the early morning hours. For you, it was fun to run barefoot on the floor as soon as you saw the daylight. It was usually a pleasant surprise to notice you, and either Ying or I would pull you up and put you between us to keep you warm.

There was a Chinese buffet restaurant in the Emerald Plaza on Maitland Avenue. It changed hands over the years. One of its names was Yangtze Buffet. It became our favorite because it was spacious, with plenty of selections. The ordering and subsequent waiting of a formal dining would wear out the limited patience of the little one. With me working full time, it was nice and probably necessary to eat out occasionally to get the well-cooked varieties. We started going to Yangtze when you still needed a highchair. Once you were out of the highchair, you couldn't wait to have your own plate and follow me around. You never dropped your plate or bumped into anybody. However, your selections, which included fried rice, fries, a sausage, corn, and carrots, maybe a bun, were only a few among probably more than one hundred items.

That was how we met the "lollipop lady", who was a server at the restaurant. The acquaintance started when I took you there for dinner. She liked you and asked about you and me while setting up the highchair and serving us tea. You behaved when I went to get food for both of us. She came around a few times to check on you and soon brought you a lollipop. It was a pleasant surprise! I really appreciated it because you spent a long time on your first lollipop while I worked on the food on my plate. We went back there many times over the years. You got a lollipop every time she was there. After many years, we went back there from Kanata when you were in town. We found her still working there. It was at least fifteen years since her first lollipop. She was happy to see you as a college student. She said that she changed places, and then retired but still came back whenever needed.

In the few months of our family of three, you got your first pneumonia. On a chilly day in late September, Ying took you out fishing in the afternoon. The late fall at Britannia Park was beautiful. Ying told me that the fishing pole was a cleaned-up branch he had picked up on the shore and that the string was one of his shoelaces. It was quiet around the lakes. You two had fun flying the string and watching the rings of water spread and disappear until he realized you were cold. You were in a sweatshirt and wrapped in a double-layered coat. Still, the wind on the lake near sunset took no time to chill you to the core. Ying said that he grabbed you and felt that you were shivering. You two came back as soon as possible. You developed a fever the same night and the following day and night.

I took you to Dr. Yang, a pediatrician, at the Centrepoint Clinic. The doctor asked about your history and listened to your chest. She said that she could hear a heart murmur, which might be just an infection. You were given a tiny amount of fruit-flavored antibiotics at the beginning stage of pneumonia. In addition, you needed to be checked at the Children's Hospital once the antibiotic was done. It got me worried since there was a family history of weak respiratory systems on Ying's side. The word "infection" for a child combined with the very limited dose of antibiotic a child can take implies the possibility of a lifelong impact. I could only hope that the antibiotic and your own immune system would defeat the infection. Ying took you to the Children's Hospital for a follow-up in the afternoon after two weeks. It was your first X-ray. Everything was fine in the picture, and no murmur was heard. This was the only experience we had with a pediatrician in Ottawa.

Home Cares

After your first trip to China, we used home care because Ying was often at home. The first one was at the corner of Baseline and Clyde. It was in a townhouse, and the lady took care of two children of your age and several after-school ones. She was experienced. You played well along with the group. You were well fed there because you did not need any snacks after we brought you home. The downside was that you were always in front of the

TV every time I picked you up. The couple was also watching TV, waiting for me. Their dinner was ready and would start right after we left. It implied that the agreed pickup time was too late. Another thing I noticed soon was that the cigarette smell in your hair every day, although I did not find it in their house. We quit after a month.

The second caregiver was in Centrepoint. She was an older lady, and her house was decorated with pieces of her knitting and crochet. The colors of her works were mostly light pink or green, reminding me of paintings by Monet. Her products were laid on top of the hardwood furniture and even on the pieces in her washroom. It was tidy and clean everywhere. She took care of a little girl of your age and several after-school children. During the day, several cupboards and baskets of books and toys were out in a large room for children to play with. She was polite but with little interaction with the children other than serving lunch and snacks. I don't remember if I ever got any feedback. You and the girl got along well. The little girl arrived early, often waiting for you in the mornings. When I picked you up in the evenings, you were always the last one in the room that was already tidied up.

For a few days, you took a few candies with you and probably always shared them with the little girl. One day, I noticed scratch marks on your forehead and arms. I showed them to the lady but did not receive any answer. You later told me in the car that you forgot to bring candies that day. It was really the consequence of our own actions. I stopped the candy supply and let you take one or two little toys instead. The candy dealing was soon forgotten.

You stayed with the lady for the months of spring and summer until we moved to Kanata before school started in the fall.

There were other helping hands. You probably remember Dajiejie ("Big sister" in Chinese). She was the wife of a visiting doctor from China. They were introduced to us by my previous coworker at U of T, who asked if we could be friends with the young couple. The couple left their own baby in China so that they could settle down in Canada. It turned out that the wife became the one to be called whenever I had an urgent babysitting request. The man did medical research at Ottawa University. He studied in his spare time to complete various programs in order to find a position that was close enough to his expertise. His wife, who was an electrical engineer in China, worked from time to time for high-tech companies in Ottawa. She sponsored her parents to come to Canada. The family grew to five, including her parents and her daughter, when reunited in Ottawa. The man later found a job with a pharmaceutical company in the States. By the time they moved to the States, you were quite familiar with their two girls, one of whom was Canadian born.

Ying graduated and returned to stay in the spring of 1995. He needed to build his career in North America. He worked odd jobs while searching and waiting for a position in nuclear physics. The opportunity eventually came, but the company next to AECL (Atomic Energy Canada Limited) was in Chalk River. It is about one hundred and fifty kilometers from Ottawa. People working there usually live in the town of Deep River, a few kilometers down Highway 17. To be closer to my work and his work, we moved to Kanata. We rented a townhouse on Clarkson Crescent in Kanata, and you started your life in daycare.

Daycare

There was a daycare at the end of Glen Cairn in Kanata in those days. It was in the same compound as a senior center. The daycare and senior center shared the kitchen facilities. All the food and snacks were of high quality for older people and, therefore, included a lot of freshly cooked food and freshly cut fruit. Once a week, the children of the daycare were brought over to the senior center to have a party with the people there. I liked the setup when I visited. You were accepted because you were three years old and potty trained. You were in the group of older children at the daycare.

The daycare started taking in children at 7:30 in the morning. The children, who got there around 7:30, were served breakfast. A snack was served in the mid-morning, and then lunch was served. A nap was mandatory before the afternoon activities. Another snack would be served if the child was not picked up at 3:30. The daycare was open until 5:30 pm. I liked the long and flexible time you could stay at the daycare.

We usually had breakfast at home, and I dropped you off at the daycare around 8 on my way to work. Occasionally, we went for a treat at McDonald's at the corner of Hazeldean Road and Terry Fox Drive. For the treat, we were at its drive through at 7:30. With the food in hand, I parked the car anywhere in the large parking lots of the strip mall. In the car with the window rolled down, I worked on my muffin while you had hash browns and juice. After the meal, I took you to the daycare at the usual time and then drove to my work. However, my full-time job in the industry was product or sales driven. There were days when I left you at the daycare at 7:30, and you had breakfast there.

It took a few days for you to get used to napping after lunch. As usual, you were happy to explore the blocks and letters yourself. You didn't mind sharing toys or waiting for your turn when there were other children around. When the weather permitted, the children were outside in both the morning and afternoon. You soon learned some new skills, such as getting into your shoes (with Velcro) and getting in your winter coat by putting your arms in the sleeves and making a flip. I noticed the size and shape of the plasticware used at the daycare and bought similar sets for home use. The teachers at the daycare said that you were a bright little boy. For a while, when parents started coming in to pick up their children in the afternoon, you would stand or sit close to the door and say hi to every parent. I felt guilty when I heard about this. I tried not to make you the last child to be picked up. There are plenty of discussions online about the impact on the last kid to be picked up and what to tell the child.

You probably remember Trish, the daycare teacher, who took you in when I went on my first trip to Colombia. Ying could not help because he was sharing an apartment in Deep River with two other men. The best he could do was to come back every weekend. For my ten-day business trip, Trish volunteered because she knew you and she certainly had the qualification. I hesitated for a moment, but I did not have any alternatives. I dropped by to check her home in Carp one night. She and her husband, a music teacher, were both at home. Aside from cooking a bit more food that was suitable for your appetite, she was certain that your stay would not be a hassle for her at all. You just follow her to daycare in the morning and back home in the evening. She did not want me to pay for her babysitting. I brought back a small flower vase from the local artisan when I returned from Colombia, and she happily accepted it. It worked out very well. I felt like you even missed her home environment from time to time, the home of a much younger couple.

Junior Kindergarten

After a year of daycare, you turned four years old, and the options then were to continue with the daycare or start junior kindergarten. In early spring, a private junior kindergarten had an open house on a weekend, and we went. It was only a three-minute drive away from home, and the teachers at the school were excellent. Being with peers of the same age and in a small group setting should be a step forward compared to daycare. I signed you up. We said goodbye to Trish and the other teachers at the daycare.

The junior kindergarten was inside the Presbyterian church around the corner of McCurdy Drive and Maple Grove Road. There were two experienced teachers and less than twenty children. It was a big step for you, as you were called a student for the first time in your life. The same applied to your peers, who were from families that opted for junior kindergarten instead of staying at home or daycare. The students were required to pack lunch and were served one snack in the morning. No nap after lunch was required. The school had extended hours after 3:30 for working parents. My routine in the afternoon was to leave my work around 4 o'clock and to pick you up on my way home.

September went by, and you liked the school. It was a transition from playing to a learning environment. There was still a lot of playing time to explore the basic virtue, the proper behavior of which had already been emphasized at the daycare level. In addition, the group setting was introduced mainly for art and crafts. You learned to use glue, tape, and scissors, which later became a part of school supplies in your pencil box throughout your elementary years. For Halloween, the class had a costume party where your old sweatshirt was fully decorated. Christmas cards were made before the end of the fall term, and the gift exchange was done between the teacher and the students. It was the first time I helped you to prepare a gift for others. It then came Valentine when the children in the class made cards for each of his/her classmates. I was surprised when you brought a bag of cards home, and we had fun looking through the cards. Mother's Day and Father's Day followed. The class made cards each time, and the teacher wrote some common phrases for students to copy when they made the cards. I was also learning about these newly added expressions of love and family. It provided new content when we looked through children's books in bookstores and libraries.

The emphasis at the school was on expanding the vocabulary. In the large classroom, there were boxes of miniature people, animals, and furniture from all aspects of the world. Thanks to the Webster's book I read to you often, the teachers were impressed by the big words such as "paleontology" you used when dinosaurs were shown to the class. Otherwise, children made letters and numbers, but were never forced to write them correctly. Other than the maze and puzzles, you had never been interested in writing or drawing since your toddler age. It took at least another year for you to figure out the direction of letters "p", "q", "b", and "d" and even longer to write a proper "6" or "9".

You were awarded once with a yellow heart of caring for your good behavior. Here is what happened. When the class was dismissed on a normal day, the children were leaving the room and probably running to meet their parents. In a hurry, somebody bumped into the coat rack, and the rack fell on a child, Eva. She was under the coat rack when others were going out, running or screaming. You were the one to turn around to Eva and get her out from under the rack. The teachers noticed and awarded you promptly. You were one of the younger ones in your class because you were born at the end of August. You were among the ones of smaller size in your class picture.

Family of Two

On the way home from daycare, we sometimes had dinner at the KFC at the corner of Castlefrank and Hazeldean Roads. We often sat next to a window, watching the construction across the street. In a few years, the site became the host of Pizza Hut and Arby's. At KFC, you had your kid's meal of chicken nuggets, and

I had crispy drumsticks with coleslaw. The operations across the street usually had your full attention. Therefore, it was safe to leave you at the table for a minute in case I needed to get extra napkins or straws. If we started our meal when the construction was still ongoing, you would insist on staying until the last big yellow machine left the site. Soon, we started collecting construction machines from Zellers and Kmart. For a while, you had a set of five or six, including a backhoe, bulldozer, and forklift. I called the set "yellow fever," and we made some stories with the help of some picture books. Another construction site at the time was the current Centrum Shopping Centre. The large piece of land there was all flattened with piles of rocks and gravel and one or two trucks or construction machines. By the time we got there, the daily operation was done. Still, we had the tall and dusty tires of a truck to admire and new shapes of the building material to check.

Pretty soon, you started showing up at my work in the evenings because I needed to complete my bit of the work for the day. Mitch, my coworker who originally came from Yugoslavia, also worked hard. He often took you to his office and gave you markers to doodle on his board. Both of his children were already attending Canterbury High School. There were cornfields next to my office building. After I completed my work, I took you there a few times to search for empty bird nests. In the fall, you chased after the geese when hundreds of them were constantly flying up and down, getting ready for their long journey south.

Time after supper or after we finally came home in the evening was not long before I cleaned you up and sent you to bed. It was the first time we lived in a townhouse. I let you go by yourself between the first and second floors. You worked your way, still on all fours, meandering on the carpet-covered stairs. The door leading to the basement was closed, and the stairs behind the door were uncarpeted. We had a children's-grade five-game-in-one setup in the basement. On weekends, with Ying around, one of us would hold you up so that we could play a formal game with the ping-pong table of a much-reduced size. On weekdays, I took you downstairs some evenings and just let you poke or smack the ball in the pool or on the ping-pong table. After running around a bit, I let you pick some fruit and put it in the orange Halloween lantern. You were on my back and holding the lantern in your hand on our way upstairs. The last course of the day was fruit. Shortly after I cleaned up the kitchen, we raced upstairs to have a bath and a bit of tooth brushing. With one or two stories from the picture books at your bedside, you were fast asleep.

Living in the clusters of townhouses in the Kanata residential area, I took you out to walk and play in the nearby sandpit on weekends. We sometimes walked past garage sales at the end of a family driveway. Unlike my previous experiences, the items directly from a single-family house were mostly clean and well kept. This prompted me to hunt for books I could read to you. Our favorite book, which had been picked up from other people's driveway, was the 1978 edition of *Webster's Beginning Book of Facts* (Webster's). The book has no index, but its "Contents" section at the beginning is alphabetical. It was at your bedside for several years. Besides the books of rhymes and fantasies from different countries, I read every section of Webster's at bedtime for hundreds of nights. Facts on mining, animals, and plants were your favorite. I probably read the section on "Venus's flytrap" more than a hundred times. I still have the book.

Compared to a live-in nanny, the downside of a home care or daycare for a working parent is that the parent must pick up a sick child. Another rule is that the sick child must be kept at home until the fever went down or the antibiotic cycle was complete. They were very justified requests if I had any backup at home. It happened at least twice in your year at the daycare. I took you to the family doctor or a nearby walk-in clinic first and then brought you home. Both times, you got the common cold likely from other children with siblings, and the fever would be gone in two or three days. It only required countertop children's medicine, which was a must for a family with a young child. The small company I worked for was familiar with parents rushing out after these calls. I could do a bit of work from home while taking care of you. The occasions provided me with time to build your playground in the large living room of the townhouse. I never had many toys when I was your age. It gave me the opportunity to learn about the age-appropriate toys at Toys R Us or Mrs. Twiggy Winkles. Life was busy but peaceful, even with these occasional downtimes. The daycare provided a good and ordered environment and healthy food for your day. In the year you were in daycare, I could deal with my full-time job and take care of you in the morning and evening.

In early fall, after you started junior kindergarten, you got cold after you went to Bryce's home for his birthday party. Your cough worsened and became pneumonia. While you were kept home on antibiotics, I got infected by you and got bronchitis instead. I never had such nasty coughs that seemed to last forever. It was early October when we were finally rid of the antibiotics. To catch up with my work as well as have some help at home, I hired Luo Nainai, who was introduced to me by Qin Nainai. Subsequently, Sun Nainai came in place of Luo for a few days before Ying came back for the holidays at the end of the year. It was nice to be back in the routine for the family of three, and we had a peaceful Christmas and New Year. Wang Nainai came after Ying went back to work. Her stay brought back a stable life to support my full-time work and your flexible schedules in kindergartens.

Transition to a New Phase

With Ying having a full-time job and renting a place in Deep River, we started looking for a house to buy. As we were told, paying the mortgage to own a house eventually is better than paying rent to others all the time, especially paying for two rentals. In house hunting, I met Joan Smith after I picked two or three houses to visit on my own. Joan Smith became my agent because she immediately understood my needs after I did not like my picks and visited a house she was selling. She found several houses, and I indeed picked two of them as candidates. Ying came back over the weekend, and he liked the larger one better because it had potential. For the first time in my life, I was in the actual process of bargaining. The deal was struck after the two sides passed the contract back and forth a few times, with updated prices and conditions. It was a tense week with Ying, either at home or remotely reachable all the time. Shortly after the New Year of 1997, we bought a single house on Sicard Way, which is a bubble off McCurdy Drive. I hired an inspector and a lawyer when needed. Getting the deed and the keys on the closing day was uneventful. With a lot of help from Wang Nainai and our friends, we moved into the house in the spring of 1997.

Financially, it was hard at the beginning because of the down payment on the house. To gather the money for the size of the down payment that did not require an insurance on the mortgage, I borrowed from Qin Nainai and others. In Chinese culture, it was unthinkable that I would ask my nanny to lend me money. She did not hesitate to help me, and in the end, I paid her back with a normal interest. The mortgage was backed by the salary for my full-time job. My boss told me it was a part of everybody's life here. Signing papers with my bank had no trouble, but it mentally introduced the fact that I was formally in debt for the first time in my life. Ying and I went through paperwork for the house, lawyer, and insurance — all things for the first time in our lives. The second fact was that I became the owner of a property. In contrast, I only had cash transactions for second-hand cars, furniture, and rental up to that point.

A new phase of our life began in 1997. We became property owners in debt.

Cuckoo and Santa

You and I came across a cuckoo clock while house hunting. In one house in Kanata North, we went past a cuckoo clock in the living room. The little bird suddenly came out and cuckoo. It shocked you, and I explained to you that the bird came out to alert people every hour or every thirty minutes. You stayed in front of the cuckoo clock while I followed the owner of the house to check around. I had a relatively long conversation with the owner because you insisted on waiting for the next cuckoo. In the end, I pulled you away and said that maybe Santa would send you one if you were a good boy.

To keep my promise, I looked for a real cuckoo clock for months. It was only sold at the specialty shops of clocks, and there were very few in Ottawa. Eventually, I went to the one on Bank Street. The shop was full of fancy clocks from around the world. Most cuckoo clocks were from Germany. I bought the most classic one, which was also less expensive. I thought it would be a delightful piece of decoration in the kitchen.

You found it under the tree on Christmas morning. Although it was no longer the most sensational one among your gifts, you remembered what I had said about the good boy. It took some work for Ying to put a nail in the right spot on the kitchen wall and set it up. Its complete mechanical operation required almost perfect balance of the clock on the wall. We had fun carefully pulling the strings daily for a long time. The dials were heavy. You were excited but careful in studying every piece of the clock. We let it cuckoo throughout the Christmas break.

Wang Nainai came back after the New Year. You took her around to show all the additions of yours, which included the cuckoo clock in the kitchen. Santa brought it to you because you were a good boy. Her comment was straightforward: "What a wonderful piece! Your mother spent a fortune on it. It is very nice in the kitchen!" This was the first time you heard that Santa or Santa's gift was paid. Her words were forgotten soon. We kept the tradition of a real Christmas tree and gifts under the tree for many years.

As for the cuckoo clock, we soon learned to turn off the cuckoo at night, although we liked cuckoo around during the day. I had to take it back to the shop to get it serviced after a few years. The shop moved to St Laurent Shopping Center. We visited the German Pavilion in Epcot to check on the clock display when we were at Disney World in Florida. I still have it wrapped somewhere after moving to Toronto. Maybe a shop will take it back to use its parts.

A Distant Father

Aside from his three-month leave-of-absence from school when you were born, Ying's role as a father was mostly remote in the first few years of your life. He was a student in Buffalo when you were a baby and then was away working in Chalk River when you were a toddler. On the weekends when he was at home, he tried very hard to do what he regarded as a father's duty. He also filled in to take care of you when I was on business trips. However, the contrast between a father being away and the mother (or a nanny) being around all the time was obvious in your early memories. It led to a distant relationship between you two. On his side, his role for you in our family of three was a backup in taking care of you, even in the years after he moved back to Ottawa. On your side, you did not include him as a part of the family at first and never sought him as a person to consult with as you grew up.

With increased interaction outside the home, you developed a sense of ownership. When we were at 1800 Baseline, Ying was an infrequent visitor because of the distance between Ottawa and Buffalo. In addition, his research required a lot of computing time on the mainframe system at school. Near the end of his research for his thesis, he stayed at school for weeks and then came home to stay for an extended weekend. People you were familiar with were Qin Nainai and her daughter. On his visit, Ying was a stranger to you for the first day and then became your friend after playing with you and feeding you. But you never let him put you to bed. When he was packing his car and leaving, he gathered his luggage and piled it near the few stairs in front of the door. Sometimes, you went to the pile and pulled the pieces one by one back to the living room area. We thought you wanted him to stay until you started pulling the bag he was carrying. Qin Nainai held you back and explained to you that Ying is your father and that he needed his stuff for his trip. We had to divert your attention to something else to let Ying go. It was probably sad for Ying, thinking that you had totally forgotten about the first three months when he spent almost 100 percent of his time taking care of you.

After Ying completed his degree, we had a few months as a family of three. The virtue of sharing was still vague in your mind. One time in the hot summer, the family traveled to my office because of my work. We walked around in the field and stopped inside to cool down. We had a bottle of cold drink to share. After you and I had our turns, Ying started drinking. You watched, reached out for the bottle, and murmured, "The drink tasted awful." Ying did not understand and gave you the bottle, anyway. What a complicated mind! I thought. You must have learned this from either me or the nanny. However, what we told you meant that something was not good for you. You picked it up, but your application to the occasion was awful. Was the concept of good in your mind already twisted between you and the grown-up world?

When working in Chalk River, Ying usually started driving home after work on Friday. After catching up with his dinner, he would come to your bedside while I was reading to you. Sometimes, he would fall asleep next to your bed since he had a long day and a long drive home. However, he made sure that he would continue his story on the Monkey King the next night when you were in bed. He would be on his way back to Deep River on Sunday afternoon.

Mind and Temper of a Toddler

The progress and changes in the life of a toddler are probably faster than those of an adult life compressed together. Changes from bottle to bowl, from swallow to chew, from diaper to potty, from walker to tricycle, and from car seat to booster just took place. Transitions seemed to happen naturally but not necessarily smoothly, in sequence or in parallel. For me, there were a lot of readings. For you, you sometimes picked up the wrong words, feeling embarrassed or frustrated in the first few tries. At the end of each action, common sense prevails.

For all the drives I needed in dealing with the nannies and

my full-time job, you were in the car a lot. Keeping you in your car seat was a headache that lingered for months. We never had a rear-facing car seat, which was not common during your time. From the beginning (age 0) to the end (age 4), you were in the normal-size car seat given by Ying's friend in Buffalo. It was too big at the beginning and probably tight with snow pants after you were three years old. Once you slipped out and found comfort in the back of the car, it became hard to keep you in your car seat. You started escaping from the car seat when you were way below thirty lbs. If you were alone and not tired, you often started your operation soon after I started my car. I had to reach back to put one hand on your legs while I was driving. I had to feel your feet from time to time if your boots were already on the floor and we still had a long way to go before getting off the highway. It was a battle every time but soon forgotten because we had other things to do. Somehow, I never thought of buying a new car seat or switching to a booster in a timely manner. With a nanny in the back, she entertained you during the drive. By the time we drove to Disney World in Florida, you were totally against a booster seat, although you were still under forty lbs. Thinking back, Ying and I must have been very civilized drivers, so that you were not "damaged" by the missing proper support in the car.

Occasionally, you were in a bad mood or even had one or two tantrums. Weaning you off the occasional bad habits such as biting, spitting, and tearing things was an additional short-term task. Without siblings, you were excited to have the company of someone of a similar age inside or outside the home. Good or bad (just-learned) skills were a part of the show-and-tell during the gathering. The curiosity after my intervention was usually short-lived, in a sequence of discovery, testing, and giving up. I was disgusted at first but calmed down after doing some reading. It was a part of your growing up. Sometimes, my or others' intervention, e.g., punishment, brought out your anger. I don't remember you screaming, but mostly you would not stop when you were told so. Your grandmother told me a few times Ying was the one with a bad tantrum in his childhood. He would kick and scream on the floor, no matter where he was. You grew up in a small family. Your tantrum was hardly needed before you got our attention.

Spanking was not a part of raising a child here. Ying spanked you once, and he said that his hand hurt afterwards. We just laughed. The advice in the book or online is to move the child away from the spot if a child throws a tantrum. I did this a few times to change your behavior when it was needed, such as in a store or among our friends or relatives. Moving you outside or to a quieter place would calm you down, although I might still find traces of your anger afterward. Not every time, I had the patience and time to explain to you why I had moved you away from your activities.

Eva, Bryce and Ranran

The house on Sicard Way was only a five-minute walk away from your junior kindergarten. Wang Nainai took you to school and picked you up after school every day. The little bubble of

Sicard Way served well for children to play after school. You had a few friends your age.

Eva was a girl you liked. You two became good friends after you rescued her from the fallen coat rack. One day, you somehow found Ying's wedding ring and gave it to Eva. Later, Eva's mother found Wang Nainai and returned the ring, saying that it was not something for children to play with and asked her to put it in a safe place. Wang Nainai relayed the encounter to me. I put the ring somewhere you couldn't reach. I said nothing since I did not think you had a clear idea of what belonged to you, nor what wife and husband meant. Maybe I should have scolded you.

One of your friends was Bryce, who lived down the street on McCurdy. He was the oldest of the three boys in his family. You played well with them. You were at his home a few times. I then got a note from his mother asking you to stop going to his house because his younger brothers needed a nap after lunch. Afterwards, Bryce came to our house to play. With Wang Nainai around to keep your activities safe, you had a lot of fun with him. Bryce wanted to spend the night at our house. I called his mother, and the answer was no. He brought his brothers once to play together, but it was only one time. As his mother told me, the family must have relatively strict rules about bringing up three boys. You were in the same EFI class of senior kindergarten with Bryce the next year. He was often late for school and came to class barefoot, holding the snow boots in his hands. He was transferred to another class after a short while. After a few years, the family moved to a bigger house in Stittsville to have more space for the boys to grow up.

Another boy you often played with was Ranran, who had a Hungarian father and Chinese mother. The family lived downtown, and we met at the Chinese school. Ranran was a year younger than you but was strong, like his father. His parents welcomed a peaceful playmate for their boy. His father was a construction contractor and an excellent cook. The meals at his house were always full of freshly prepared meat. We even went camping together once, and his father prepared Chinese instant noodles in his own style. I took you two to museums and parks, sometimes accompanied by his mother. She and I became good friends. Ranran had his own mind and knew how to fight for himself. You were a follower and listened to all his stories. You two got along fine. The friendship lasted two or three years until Ying got into an argument with his father because of cultural backgrounds. His mother and I kept in touch for many years. Ranran was strong on the soccer field and later became quite good at playing chess.

Chinese Nannies

In Chinese, "Nainai" means grandmother on the father's side. When it is prefixed with a last name, it becomes a respectful way to call an old lady from another family. It differs from English naming, which often uses the first name such as "Grandma Alice" or "Grandma Pat".

I hired four Chinese nannies after we moved to Ottawa, and we called them "Nainai" with the prefix of the last name they told us. In Ottawa, I had a full-time job, and you needed full attention from a toddler to kindergarten. These ladies were around sixty-five years old when they were with us. They had been retired in China before immigrating to Canada to stay with their children. The cost of a living-in nanny wasn't skyrocketing in those years, but the weekly pay was very good pocket money for them to keep and spend later. It worked well with three of them, and we kept in touch with them for many years after they stopped working for us.

Qin Nainai

Qin Nainai was the first nanny I hired in Ottawa. I found her contact information on the bulletin board at the entrance of Loblaw on Baseline. She lived with her daughter, and her house was only a five-minute drive from my home. Her son-in-law worked for Statistics Canada. He was quite knowledgeable about the hiring and payment system. The three of them came over for a chat and had a look at our apartment at 1800 Baseline Road. The negotiation was friendly. Qin Nainai was to stay at my place for six days a week. She would take care of you when I was out working and would not attend to you at night. We would share the chores around the home. It would be my responsibility to pick up and deliver her back home every week. The pay for her work included her room and board, and a weekly salary.

Qin Nainai worked as an office clerk on the army base where her husband was an officer. During the Cultural Revolution, her family moved to Beijing because of her husband's new role in the cultural bureau. Later, her family became civilians when her husband retired from the army. While her husband was busy fulfilling his commitments, she kept the family together and raised her son and daughter. Her son joined the army and then worked in a government office. After many years, her daughter met her would-be husband and left China for Canada.

After she was widowed, she lived with her son in Beijing and took care of her grandson. After her grandson started going to school, she immigrated to Canada to stay with her daughter. By that time, her daughter and her son-in-law had bought a house and a second-hand car. The couple had worked hard and already paid off the mortgage on their house. Her son-in-law had a stable job with the government. Her daughter went to adult school, trying to complete the high school requirements so that she could go to college. Qin Nainai was a great help around the house. Her expectation was to take care of any grandchild, but the couple had no children after trying for many years. Qin became bored with the comfortable life. In our conversations while she was with us, she was never shy about expressing her dislike of the lifestyle at her own home, especially the cat. The cat left its hair everywhere in the house, and they had to cover all the leather furniture with bed sheets to avoid its claws. However, the cat was her only companion on the weekdays while the couple was out either working or studying. Therefore, she posted a note to offer babysitting services. She appreciated the opportunity for a paid job away from her home.

She was very serious about getting the tasks done. Her focus was finishing the quota every day. It means that you should have at least three bottles of formula daily. She also cooked some rice soup or poached egg for you from time to time, although I always had jars of baby food stored at home. You were well fed. The tradeoff of her determination was your table manners, such as eating in the highchair and eating only at mealtimes. The rules that were firmly adhered to by Jiang Taitai and followed by me in Toronto were soon forgotten. She would crawl under the table to find you and feed you one more spoon. For a toddler crawling or learning to walk, you had a lot of fun with her feeding style. Pretty soon, the patterns recommended by Dr. Spock were no longer important.

She wasn't a skilled cook because there were always canteens when she lived in China. She liked my cooking and always helped to clean up the kitchen or bathe you in the evenings. Therefore, she worked overtime on a lot of days. After you were in bed, Qin and I sometimes chatted into the night. She liked to talk about her life instead of asking me for details of my life. I listened to her stories and found them new and interesting to me, because I had left the country more than a decade ago. She was very proud of her grandson in China and showed me his pictures whenever she received one. I got to know the life of a completely different social branch, which contained an army base, Sichuan province of China, and female clerks in the army offices, etc. At night, you were at my bedside, and Qin was in the other room to have a peaceful sleep.

Since I was new to Ottawa, I often used Saturdays to take Qin and you to explore the city and suburbs. We were at Dow's Lake for the Tulip Festival. The tulip fields were not blocked off in those years, and you liked to sit on the edge of a flower bed. We went to Parliament Hill, where Qin and I sat on a bench while you had a long stretch to run safely. I have a picture of you standing still, shocked when the bell in the Peace Tower tolled on the hour. We went to the Canada Day fireworks on the hill once. You were scared when the fireworks cracked in the sky. I never expected such a surrounding impact, and I had to cover you with your coat and then somehow block your ears with my best effort. We never tried again until you went back there with your high school peers after many years. We were in Perth and other small towns for the local festivals. You had your first taste of cotton candy and experience of the play structures temporarily up for the fair. There was no cell phone or WeChat in those days. I made sure that Qin Nainai was safely home with her pay every Saturday afternoon.

Her family welcomed the opportunity to play with a little boy. You played with their cat when we took Qin Nainai home or went to pick her up. Her daughter came to visit often. She either played with you or chatted with her mother. Her husband was from a traditional Cantonese family that never lived in mainland China. Therefore, she and her husband occasionally had conflicts because of their different cultural backgrounds. Qin Nainai and her daughter often shared with me their complaints about the man. However, my observation was that the man was a very serious statistician and didn't know much about taking care of his family. On the days when Ying was in town, we sometimes had gatherings of the two families. Ying and the statistician got along well and had long conversations every time.

Qin Nainai stayed with us for almost eight months before your first trip to China in August 1994. When we came back from China, her daughter and her son-in-law contacted me and came to our place to discuss the procedures to report Qin's income. I signed the forms they had prepared, so Qin became my employee for the time she worked for us. They sent away the forms and paid for the required fees and insurance. In that way, Qin could collect employment insurance for a few months, and her income became part of the deductible when she filed the tax in the following year. It was good for her family. In 1995, I also learned to file a Canadian tax return for the first time instead of being fully exempted in the previous years.

When you were five years old, Qin Nainai worked for us again to fill in the last few months of your senior kindergarten. You did not listen to her all the time. You two had a fight when she tried to get you down from the kitchen counter. She told me she liked the younger you better. Regardless of the conflict, she stayed until the end of the summer when you started grade one, which was a full-day school program.

As for Qin, without a grandchild at her home, the relationship between her, her daughter, and her son-in-law deteriorated. Qin often had to buy groceries with her own money and carry them back home to cook for the family. She told me that her son-in-law expected her to contribute because she had income in those months. The Continue Education of the Adult High School in Ottawa for her daughter, who was already in her late thirties, was more like a social opportunity. She graduated with her best effort, which included Ying's tutoring in her math courses sometimes. Instead of going to college, she started her involvement with some business opportunities.

Over the years, her son-in-law became distant. He sold his car, which was rusty and expensive to fix. He bicycled to work and expected the other two to either walk or use public transportation for all the chores. Qin later moved to the senior housing in downtown Ottawa. I visited her there from time to time and listened to her stories about her family. She was happy to have her own space, and her social benefit was enough to pay her monthly bills. Her daughter would come to stay with her sometimes. Her son-in-law retired and liked to travel with his wife or alone. His own family was in Toronto or even in Hong Kong, and therefore, he was away often.

Luo Nainai

Luo Nainai was introduced to me by Qin Nainai when we lived in the rental townhouse in Kanata. You started junior kindergarten in the fall of 1996. A month into the fall term, you developed pneumonia from a cold. After you started antibiotics, I got bronchitis, likely from a similar virus. I was just too busy. You got sick, I believed, because you were no longer well protected by the healthy environment of the daycare. After both of us recovered, I felt that our family of two became fragile and challenged. Hiring a live-in nanny was a justified option to stabilize your daily school and my full-time job. With you going to school during the day, the chores were a lot less demanding than what Qin Nainai had. Reliability was important.

Luo lived with her daughter in a government-subsidized apartment building in downtown Ottawa. Back in China, she was a middle school teacher for many years and then a clerk at the university where her husband worked. Her daughter first came to Canada as a graduate student and found a job after her graduation. She sponsored Luo to Canada after Luo's husband passed away. Luo then sponsored her son to come over. When I contacted her, her son had just started his journey as a new immigrant to attend school and pursue a new career. The family of three adults relied mainly on the single income of her daughter and the government aid for new immigrants. The nanny opportunity was indeed beneficial for the family in need of money.

Having been a professional in China, Luo declared at the start of our negotiation that I should not expect her to be a servant in my house. Since I came from the same system in the same country, I knew what she meant and agreed. She would work from Monday to Friday. Her responsibility was to take care of you whenever you were out of school. As usual, I would make the trip between downtown Ottawa and Kanata to pick her up on Sunday night and take her home on Friday evening.

With Luo at home, I could breathe a little easier between my work and your flexible school time at the junior kindergarten. When I was busy, I could pick you up from school, leave you at home and go back to work since my workplace was only a 10-minute drive away. Luo Nainai didn't like chores around the house, so I did whatever was necessary to keep the house clean. I would cook dinner and clean up afterwards. On a normal day, I woke her up in the morning before I left home with you. Compared with Qin Nainai, Luo was good to you differently. Her focus was on education. She often folded old newspapers into all kinds of carts and vehicles and made some long stories about them. You just sat next to her and followed her, moving around. When I came home from work in the evening, I often found you two sitting on the carpeted floor with a line of paper models. The focus was on her storylines and your imagination, not any basic skill in origami.

Luo had the drive to learn English and the lifestyle in Canada. She listened whenever I explained to her about household cleaners, food, and seasonings that are not Chinese. She liked to go shopping with me. In the evenings, the three of us often went out, and you had some fun riding in the shopping cart once we were in a store. Soon, she had her own shopping list so that she could take it home on the weekends. On some trips returning her to her downtown apartment, we made stops to shop for her needs or pick up medication from a pharmacy. However, she never invited me (and you) up to her home. Therefore, we never met her daughter or son.

She started working for us before Thanksgiving. Naturally, the first lesson I gave her was Thanksgiving celebration. On one outing, I bought a frozen stuffed turkey. I showed her where the cooking instructions were and explained the steps. Two days before her weekend, I thawed the turkey in the refrigerator and then cooked it. For the Thanksgiving dinner, I got the minimum: turkey, dressing, gravy, and cranberry sauce. She watched me when I scooped out the stuffing from the turkey and cut and carved it into piles of white and dark meat. The dinner for the night included warm buns, corn, and carrots (for you), boiled greens (for her and me), turkey and turkey soup. It was the first time she had turkey, and probably one of the few times she had food fresh out of an oven. The next day, I sent her home with several aluminum foil packages. The leftovers were more than enough for us (including Ying) on the weekend.

It was Halloween afterwards. I invited the Bulgarian visiting scientist, who was working with me, to observe the trick-or-treating in Canada. She cooked her traditional potato soup, which was made with boiled potatoes, butter and salt, but it was very delicious. It became your favorite soup, and I have used her recipe for years. Later, we took a picture together. You were in your pumpkin costume with a little pumpkin lantern. Luo took you to trick-or-treat in the neighborhood. I took a walk with my visitor on several streets. In those years, there were still many school-age children in the houses on Clarkson Crescent and Pickford Drive. The houses were mostly lit. People were all prepared for the trick-or-treaters, regardless of whether the visitors were a group of children or a pair of a kid and the grandparent. Luo was very impressed with the abundance of snacks, candies, and fancy costumes.

Luo was very reliable when needed. During her time with us, I had to go on a quick business trip to a navy base in California. Before my trip, I discussed her duties (including the extra pay) with her and asked her about her thoughts on the matter. She was confident. I generated a to-do list and printed out a copy for her. Ying also got a copy so that he could check a few times remotely. I informed the school that you would be absent for a few days because I was away. I filled the refrigerator with what you two needed, as well as some household stuff she brought up in our discussion. On my return, I was overjoyed to find out that everything at home was in order and you were happy and healthy.

The workload and responsibility during the days of my business trip probably tired her and made her rethink her options. She said one night that she was needed at home so that her daughter could work, and her son could study full time without worrying about meals and housecleaning. However, she promised to look for a qualified replacement. She left before Christmas after staying with us for three months.

Years later, I had a few tickets for a show by a group of Chinese artists. The show was at the Bronson Center, which was within walking distance of the senior housing. I invited all the nannies.

I met her again, and she told me that her daughter had gone to the States and that her son had been hired to work full time. She lived in senior housing and no longer needed to worry about her children. Later, I was told that Luo worked with the local publisher on some booklets, helping older people to learn English as a second language.

Sun Nainai

Sun Nainai was introduced to me by Luo Nainai. Luo probably looked more at the intellectual stature for educating you when she provided her replacement. In addition, my reputation was not bad in the small community of Chinese grandmothers who had tried or wanted to work as live-in nannies.

Sun Nainai was a professional journalist and editor of a newspaper before she retired in China. She and her husband immigrated to Canada to be with their daughter. Her daughter's family was one of the typical small tech families in Kanata. Such a family contained a couple, who worked full time for high-tech companies, and a child. The couple often sponsored a pair or occasionally two pairs of their parents to come to Canada. The visiting parents took care of the child and the chores around the house. For Sun, she and her husband came to Canada to help the young family when the baby was born. Her granddaughter was less than a year old when I contacted her. Being away from home to explore was probably her goal instead of any income. She did not need me to pick her up, and therefore, I never knew where she lived. We did not meet until the day she started working for us.

It was an adventure for her, and her duty was to attend to you during my working day. It was a full-day workload because your school was closed for Christmas Break. You were four years old, running around definitely with your own mind. I showed her where the things were. She was familiar with the operations in the kitchen. I then left for work. At the end of her first day, she told me you did not listen to her. I could imagine that taking care of you, in contrast to a well-attended baby girl, would be a big transition for her. I reminded you that Nainai was there to help us because I needed to work, and that you should be nice to her. It did not work. When I came home on the evening of her third day, she said that you had no respect for her. The incident was that she burned the hotdog when she prepared lunch for you, and you refused to eat the burned hotdog. She said that it was a waste of food and that you were spoiled.

I don't argue with people older than I am. Other than my respect for older adults, I have always believed that it is hard to train, and that any discussion would be endless if I started one. I just prepared dinner, and we did not go back to the topic at the dinner table. Later in the night, she came to me, saying that she was leaving. As she told me, she was a professional, and she was younger than my age when she got married and had her child. Her child was brought up by her mother-in-law while she always worked. Therefore, she never had much experience dealing with children. I asked her to work until Friday to give me the weekend to look for a new nanny. Besides, it was almost Christmas time, and Ying was coming home.

So, Sun Nainai stayed for about a week. Ying came home, and

I had a few days to look for a nanny again. After a year or two, Sun Nainai and her husband moved into the senior housing in downtown Ottawa. She was still a professional, although retired; she was active in organizing older people for the local ethnic celebrations and other festivities.

Wang Nainai

Wang Nainai was introduced to me by Qin Nainai. Qin told me that Wang and her husband lived with their son. Wang only had a few years of education back in China, but she brought up her three children through a lot of hardships. Wang would like to try, since she wasn't doing much at home.

It was before the New Year of 1997, and as usual, the Christmas shutdown of the companies would end right after the New Year. Ying needed to go back to work in Chalk River soon. The lesson learned from working with Sun Nainai taught me the importance of a prior assessment. I put you in the car and went to visit. The family lived in a townhouse compound in Nepean, about a twenty-minute drive from our Kanata home. We received a big warm welcome when the door opened. The old couple were very nice. Her son was a software engineer, and her daughter-in-law, who had been an accountant back in China, was attending school to start a new career. Her granddaughter, Shelina, who was already in elementary school, immediately became acquainted with you. The old couple did not have a boy among their grandchildren, so you naturally fit in. We agreed that Wang Nainai would start after the New Year. I would drive between Nepean and Kanata to drop off and pick up on Friday and Sunday evenings.

The family came from Shanghai. Wang was originally from Suzhou, a city in Jiangsu province of China, and her husband grew up in a rural area of Suzhou. Many years ago, she went to Shanghai to marry her husband, who was a highly skilled worker at a leather factory. The couple had their children in Shanghai. Because of the strict population control in Shanghai, her husband volunteered to send his family to their hometown. As a result, Wang brought up her children in a village in rural Suzhou. Her son vividly remembered growing up around the rice field. Wang transitioned from being a city girl of Suzhou and Shanghai with a monthly ration of supplies to a peasant who worked in the field to earn the rice on the table. Financially, her life in the countryside was still better off than that of the normal peasants nearby because her husband sent her money often. The family reunion was at least once a year. However, they lived apart for many years. She assisted the families of her in-laws and took care of her children mostly as a single parent.

In the words often used for evaluating coworkers in the industry, Wang Nainai was proactive, a fast learner, and had both hard and soft skills. She settled in our home and quickly learned to take care of you. It did not take long for me to let her manage everything around our household. She was up early in the morning. By the time I woke up, she would wake you up, feed you, and get you ready for school. We formed a very efficient routine in the morning. Sometimes, she volunteered to pick you up after school so I could stay at work longer. However, I tried to avoid it because she always carried you all the way from your school to home, which was at least five bus stops.

Life with Wang Nainai was smooth. She thought ahead most of the time and arranged everything. You trusted her and followed her orders. In the evenings, dinner was ready or almost ready when I picked you up and got home. This was quite different since I had always cooked all the meals at home with or without a nanny around. I liked her cooking as well since the Suzhou flavor, which insists on adding a little sugar to almost every dish, brought back nice memories of the food I had as a child. Your time after school was often used for a game of learning that involved everybody. In the game, we passed a ball around while saying the next alphabet or number in Chinese or English. She was excited about learning. We took turns cleaning up at night. She never seemed tired, but she would doze off on the couch when we started watching TV. It would be her bedtime and your shower time.

We took her home on Friday evenings. The occasion was sometimes like a family reunion. Wang Nainai often insisted that we go in and have dinner with her family. She even asked her son to move his car a few times so that I could park mine. Her husband, the grandfather, with a big smile on his face at the door, helped take off your shoes, coat, and snow pants and led you inside. Her daughter-in-law had already prepared dinner for the extra people. One time, the grandfather noticed that the stripe of your snow pants fell off. He got out the big needle and thread and fixed it. I was deeply moved because I felt not only his kindness but also the hard life the old couple had endured when they were apart. Shelina always came to play with you so adults could have conversations peacefully. At dinner time, you usually had a pretty good appetite because Shelina's mom was an excellent cook. After you were fed, you often crawled under the dinner table or ran around the house until Shelina finished her dinner.

Although you were quite spoiled there, the family had quite strict rules. I remember that Shelina once asked her father for a Game Boy when you got yours. Her father just said bluntly, "It is a Game Boy, not a Game Girl," which ended her request. The family was very well-mannered. Following Shelina, you learned to say hi to older people whenever they were around. You learned to chat quietly with her and later with others. When she graduated from high school, Shelina was the valedictorian of the well-known Lisgar High School in Ottawa. Her goal to become a medical doctor was set early on because she felt the pain caused by the sickness of her grandparents and others. After attending U of T and Queens, she accomplished her goal and then went to Newfoundland with her boyfriend for their medical residency. Many years later, we all gathered at her wedding in Toronto.

Wang Nainai was fundamental in my house hunting and later moving into our new house. I often shared my encounters with her, and she was a good listener. She was sympathetic, but always positive. I had to go out many evenings to look at a house with a friend or an inspector. She never complained about her additional chores. She was all for it when we settled down to buy the one on Sicard Way along McCurdy Drive. The closing day was in early spring. After I got the keys, I took you and Wang Nainai to inspect the new house. I had to manually pull down the garage door because the chain had come off the rail. The kitchen was a mess, especially the oven. The basement, where the son of the previous owner stayed with his girlfriend, was smelly. Wang and I worked out the strategies for cleaning the new house. We made many trips to clean and throw out garbage. I had to stop her from scraping and washing after she accidentally sprayed the oven cleaner on her face. Once the cleaning was complete, she helped me ship the items that could fit in my car into the new house. She selected and bundled the items during the day while I was at work. For the evening trips, you just tagged along, sitting in a tiny space in the car during the short ride. It was your outing before bedtime for quite a few days. The new location was ready and clean before our major move. When I brought her to the new house to spend the first night on a Sunday, she walked everywhere and was all smiles, saying repeatedly, "Great, great!"

She enjoyed our house as much as we did. A few small patches of the flower beds were soon cultivated to become her veggie garden. She brought the seeds from her own garden, which was quite substantial and well attended to by her husband at home. Shortly after, we got the greens from southern China on our dinner table. After she left, I tried to grow vegetables outside the house as well, but it lasted for only a few years. I had big tomatoes, and the fresh cuts were tasty. You and I went out in the dark with a flashlight to see the wiggly worms going in and out of the fruit. It was thrilling but messy. I had a cluster of rhubarb inherited from the previous owner. After downsizing it and distributing it among friends for a few years, I gave the entire stock to our neighbor, who loved rhubarb pies. The chives I grew from seeds from a Canadian Tire were the most successful ones. They grew from as skinny as regular grass to very chive-looking foot-long and flat-leaved perennials. They became too much for our family and a nearby Chinese family to consume. I dug out the entire 2'x3' field and shipped it to my friend when she had just bought her new house. Lacking enthusiasm and time, I had a short stint growing veggies, although there were frequent seed and baby plant exchanges among my friends.

Wang Nainai stayed with us throughout the second term of your junior kindergarten and almost your entire senior kindergarten. She left before the end of the spring term of your senior kindergarten because of her husband's health problems. I got to know some of her Chinese friends when she was with us. There was a couple from Wuxi, a city in Jiangsu province. When they came to visit Wang Nainai at our house, they walked several kilometers from their son's house in Bridlewood. Later, they came with the husband riding a bicycle and the wife sitting in the back whenever they felt safe. I drove them home at least once when I came home from work. Walking such a long distance was unthinkable for me. The lady, Qian Nainai, was a devoted Buddhist and had given free haircuts for decades in China and then in Ottawa. She and her extended family became quite close to us. Shelina, Qian's granddaughters, and you played and chatted whenever the families were together. For years, when her hearing was still fine, Qian would call me from time to time to get me over to her place to give me a haircut. Instead of being paid afterwards, she often sent me away with her homemade dessert or meat.

A few years later, Wang Nainai's family moved to Kanata when a house nearby became available. The house is a three-minute walk away from ours and is in a different bubble named Patch Way on McCurdy. It is built on a cliff and, therefore, has four levels with a backyard entrance. It was large enough to take in two pairs of grandparents: Wang and her husband, and the parents of her daughter-in-law, who were also immigrated to Canada. In 2001, your grandparents came to stay with us for the entire summer. We invited Wang's family when we celebrated your grandfather's 80th birthday. We had pictures of three sets of grandparents. It was a lot of fun. In the years following, Wang and her husband moved to the senior housing, as did the parents of her daughter-in-law. New immigrants, families of Wang's second son and daughter, and the sister of her daughter-in-law, stayed in the big house with them at different times. They moved on to start their new lives in different trades.

Her son's family and ours were good neighbors for over fifteen years. We helped each other with babysitting, home repairs, and car repairs. Wang Nainai and her daughter-in-law made authentic Chinese snacks. Mooncakes were for the Mid-Autumn Festival; dumplings, pancakes, and leaf-wrapped sticky rice are for three other events after the Chinese New Year. We often enjoyed the freshly made delicacies from either downtown or down the street. I tried to host a dinner, at home or in a restaurant, for the two families and relatives once every year to show my appreciation. The close tie of the two families made you and Shelina become close friends and game buddies. The friendship lasted from your grade school years until she went to college. Before Ying and I moved to Toronto, our two families got together a few times every year. Wang's husband, the nice old gentleman, passed away quite a few years ago. Wang stays mainly in the senior housing, playing mahjong almost daily with a few friends.

I am forever grateful to these Chinese nannies who helped me through those years. They are all very kind, especially towards children.

BOOK TWO

Preteen, teenager,
college and beyond

Preteen School Years

I have told my friends many times that kids will grow up, anyway. However, what I did was probably the opposite. For a long time during your elementary school years, your parents were actively involved in finding a better fit for you. All that we went through with you was difficult, but hopefully worthwhile. You survived and grew up amidst the choices and trials.

Senior Kindergarten

In the fall of 1997, you started senior kindergarten at the public school Castlefrank Elementary. To understand the bilingual education, I talked to the teacher for Early French Immersion (EFI). She said that a child growing up in a multilingual environment with English and different dialects of Chinese would be very welcome in her EFI class. I was a little worried that I knew nothing in French, but it would be a good exposure, I thought. Your friends from junior kindergarten were also going to EFI. So, you were in EFI class for your senior kindergarten.

For the distance between our house and the school, you were qualified to take the school bus. There was a school bus training session in the summer. You went and learned the rules on the bus and how to check traffic after getting off the bus. The senior kindergarten was half a day. The school time alternated every few weeks, and therefore, your school could be in the morning or the afternoon. As a routine, Wang Nainai took you to the bus stop in the morning and made sure you got on the bus. After school, she waited at the bus stop (on a different side of the street) to pick you up after you got off the bus. She never called me while I was at work and was quick to rearrange things wherever necessary. Therefore, she was always there for you and never had an accident in the kitchen or anywhere else, even if your bus was sometimes delayed.

Days went by smoothly, and Wang Nainai was punctual for the school bus. Once winter started, the edge of the sidewalks was often filled with snowbanks of different sizes and heights. I reminded you and Wang Nainai to stay on the house side of the snowbank and to avoid the snowbank after getting off the bus. One day, Wang Nainai told me that people in the house behind the bus stop complained about kids running up and down the snowbank. The activities led to blocks of mixed ice and snow falling back onto their driveway. I went with you to the bus stop the next morning. Indeed, the children ran up and down the snowbanks near the neighborhood's driveway. It was not safe, and they showed no respect for private property. I guess I never told you not to play on the snowbank. I tried to stop the running in vain. It was such fun to run wild during the few minutes before the start of a school day. I thought it over at my work. When I came home in the evening, I asked you to go with me to clean up the driveway at the bus stop because you messed up. You realized the nature of the problem and refused. I started dragging you out, but Wang Nainai intervened. She said that you knew right from wrong and that you would not do it again. At the end, I went to check the bus stop alone. The driveway was clean, and I only cleaned up a few blocks near the snowbank. The running up and down on the snowbank stopped afterwards.

With you in EFI, I started learning French. I could manage a few words in French from my days of doing research with the scientists in Grenoble. However, learning the alphabet and numbers systematically never came to mind. It was fun to learn from you after your day at school. You have sharp ears, and I could still imitate, although my "R" was never perfect. I could manage the alphabet and numbers. Besides the French content, a large part of your work at and after school still involved arts and crafts. For the spare time at home, we added French content to our "Say and Catch" game. When the three of us tossed the ball, we would go over the English, Chinese, and French alphabets and numbers. You helped Wang Nainai on her turn if she became "wordless." Wang Nainai could count to three in French. She always repeated after you filled in for her. I was not a quick learner in French either. We laughed and moved on.

Early French Immersion

I did not dwell on options for long when choosing your elementary school for grade one and beyond. Sending you to private school was an option, and some of my coworkers do so. Kanata had a few private schools with relatively poor facilities and limited space. Montessori school was an option among private schools, but Kanata did not have one. I visited two of them that were relatively close to Kanata. The class size was small, and a classroom setting might accommodate several grades at the same time. It was a unique style of learning that heavily relied on the initiative of the individuals. Based on my schooling, I believed in the qualifications and dedication of the educators who provide evaluation and guidance at school. It is especially crucial if there is differentiation. I thought it over. I was not sure if Montessori would do you good and was not sure if, financially, I could afford to pay throughout your elementary years. Therefore, you continued in the EFI class at the same elementary school.

School changed from half a day to a full day. Unlike the schools in the States, the elementary schools in (at least Ontario,) Canada did not have a cafeteria, nor did they offer lunch days for students to buy. Children would bring packed lunches to school, starting from grade one. I took you grocery shopping, and we picked lunch meat and snacks. For a while, the Lunchables boxes were your favorite. In winter, you had semi-warm pasta in a thermos for lunch when I had time to cook in the morning. The worst lunches were those before school was out at the end of June. It is usually hot and dry in Ottawa by the end of June. Besides, the heat wave may hit before the end of the school year. I remember the days you came home hot and thirsty. I could imagine the taste of the room-temperature sandwich with soggy cheese, ham, and lattice. The best I could do during those years was to have a box of ice cream bars or sherbet in the freezer and a few bags of snacks in the cupboard. Luckily, you already understood the sequence of a day: your portion of the snacks should not be big because the dinner is in two hours.

You did fine in grades one and two in the split-grade EFI

class. The comment from the teacher was always that you are a smart and happy child and that her advice was always to pay more attention to the teacher in the classes. I could still manage your dictation every week. There was more French, English, and math content in the classes. However, there was still more than enough craftwork by individuals or in group settings for events or themes. In grade two, you were one of the two best students in reciting poems in your class. The teacher told me later that you intentionally did poorly in the second round of selection because you did not want to be in the school-wide competition. Something clicked in my mind: the drive to be the best. The lack of competitive spirit was probably the default of a single child who was always tended to by caring people at home. On my side, other than introducing you to different branches of knowledge, I had the concept of the "favorite" instead of "best" in whom, what, or which. Being the best student to me sounded quite remote, although it was painfully needed in your new world.

You had a new teacher, Mme. King, and a separate English teacher in grade three. Mme. King was keen on keeping in touch with parents. Her message at the beginning of the term was that in grade three, the students would be seriously focused on knowledge learning. The subjects such as math and science were taught in French, resulting in an increase in French content. When learning about different geometric shapes, Ying and I were concerned. You were given the names of the full set of shapes in grade three; the concept of these named shapes would be gradually introduced in several rounds, from elementary to high school. The fact then was that the grade three students were to memorize the names of everything round or with corners in both two and three dimensions. This made math become a course of memorization. In addition, I did not agree with the teacher on the definition of a cone! With the split-grade class of grades three and four, you were just picking what they liked from the content of both grades. You were doing fine, but I felt that the continuity of learning was falling apart.

Around the same time, feedback from Mme. King was that your vision might be a factor affecting your focus when she was instructing. Indeed, we went to the optometrist on Kakulu Road, and you got a pair of glasses. You should wear your glasses in class when you have trouble seeing the writing on the blackboard. It stopped your wandering around in class for a short while but did not make you become interested in the classes. I took you to the Oxford Learning Center to be evaluated to find out from the professionals if you needed any specific help. The report of the assessment showed that you were well advanced in your reading and comprehension skills. Even your French was adequate. Based on your class setting and your behavior in the class, I concluded that the split-grade class was just not the learning environment for you.

Grade Four

I talked to the school about putting you in a class without split grades, even though you did well in grade three. You switched from EFI to English because there was no other choice. In schools in Kanata, English classes are usually larger than the EFI classes, even the latter are mostly split grades. The reason is that families were mainly English-speaking. In addition, the public schools were required to admit all children of the proper age, except the few defined as requiring special education. The year of your grade four was the time we had conflict with school on identifying you for the gifted program (Chapter: Gifted Identification).

The English class seemed to be easy for a student transferred from EFI. Your English was good after a few sets of Kumon English and a bunch of Pokémon game time in the previous summer. Grade four was taught by a single teacher, Mrs. Rockburn. There were helpers, including parent volunteers, when needed. She had to deal with a few children who frequently disturbed the class while carrying out her general teaching tasks. In her view, a good student was probably first well-behaved in class, listening to her instructions and responding when asked. She said that you were not listening. She was particularly annoyed that you were often doing other things in her classes, although you knew the answer almost all the time when asked. To improve your effort in her class, she paired you in activities with the worst student, who was transferred to a special school before the end of the term. I was concerned about your behavior, too.

To improve your class behavior, she and I agreed to allow you to read other books, provided you did not bother others. It worked for a short time until you brought to the class a book that others liked. We then agreed to give you some other related work, such as enrichment, to work on during the classes. By then, she and the special education teacher at the school were probably fed up with me, a parent asking for too much while her child was not a problem in the class. The parent should be set straight. Mrs. Rockburn soon failed your entire test because you could not write number 6 properly. For the enhancement, she gave you a math workbook and told you to only work on it during her class time and not take it home. Without helping you at all, she complained about your lack of effort towards her extra assignment.

You started having discipline problems. One time, you got a warning because of throwing gravel on the sidewalk of Castlefrank Road outside the fence of the school. You were one of the last few in the crowd to stop. Another more serious warning came when you wrote a little rhyme to mock the problem child whom you often paired with. You showed it to your EFI friends. Your rhyme was heard among the children during the recess and made the problem child upset. You vented a little of your own anger, but the schools have zero tolerance for such things.

You soon got your first and only detention. The incident was that you went online on the school computer to show others a game. The content of the game included comic figures from the infamous leaders in the Gulf War. It was defined as a racist game by the school principal. You got banned from using computers. I had a serious talk with you about the difference between adult and children's content. There are plenty of reasons for schools not allowing outside information besides class material. I wrote a letter to the principal explaining the source of the video game. I apologized for your behavior but expressed my concern about her over rating the incident, even in terms of political correctness.

Grade Five

Grade five was probably the best year you had in your elementary school. The process of gifted identification finally ended. You were enrolled in the special education program available at the public-school board. What was more important was that you had a male teacher for grade five, Mr. Hackman.

Grade five was the senior grade of the school. For a school that had students exceeding its capacity, the grade five classes were in portable classrooms. The outside of a portable classroom looked like a trailer house, and its inside had the setting of a classroom of reduced size. Portable classrooms were sometimes too far for the students to reach the facilities inside the school building when the class was in session. The weather factor also played a part in the portable classroom. Its thin walls with cracks were poor at shielding the winter cold and summer heat.

Mr. Hackman won the trust and respect of his students, including you. He cared about his students and got his class together. Therefore, he could direct his class quietly into a spare room inside the building when it was too cold. He made exceptions to allow students to wear their hats and coats during his instruction if it was cold. Occasionally, in summer, he carried out his class in the shade on the school lawn when it was too hot inside the portable classroom. At the parent-teacher interview, he apologized for the not-too-good condition of the portable classroom. He praised the students' cooperation.

Mr. Hackman signed your IEP (Individual Education Plan) form for gifted education. Your special education plan included the regular class session and the pull-out program. Twice a week, you and two other students had activities with the school's special education teacher. The purpose of the pull-out sessions was to work on some enrichment material in a small group of similar students. I don't remember if the special education teacher ever provided any feedback on your behavior during the pull-out session. I never went back to visit any school staff except Mr. Hackman. You liked the pull-out sessions, as you told me. For a while, your answer to my question on the session content was "stuff." So, I stopped asking as long as you enjoyed the small group meetings. You managed the work from both the regular class and the pull-out classes very well.

At the end of grade five, you got an A in almost all subjects. Mr. Hackman told me during the parent-teacher interview that you liked to chat and that he enjoyed the conversations. He said that you were a bright child and that your ability to learn was amazing. I thanked him because you finally had a good year at school. For grade six, you already had a spot in the special education class for the gifted.

In a few years, Mr. Hackman left the school to take the position of vice principal at a different school in Ottawa. I checked Castlefrank Elementary online from time to time. It became a school with both English and EFI from junior kindergarten to grade three. The portables are no longer needed.

Grade Six

You were finally in the gifted class for grade six. Unfortunately, to your disadvantage, it was a split-grade class of grades five and six. The class was held at Glen Cairn Primary School, which was a lot larger than Castlefrank Elementary. You took a small school bus every day to and from the school. My chauffeuring was only needed on special occasions or in bad weather. After school, you were old enough to stay at home alone until I came back from work.

Mrs. Adele, the only teacher for the split-grade gifted class, had a degree in child psychology and training in special education. She was obviously well qualified for both the students and their parents. I was quite impressed by our first parent-teacher meeting, which was mainly her addressing the parents about the plan and purpose for the school year. She was well-mannered and confident.

Occasionally, the parents were given the opportunity to observe the class if they wanted. I put my name down. The opportunity was to observe at least two classes, including the recess of the day. It was the first time I got to see what other gifted children were like. As I expected, more than half of the students were knowledgeable and active in class. Some of them were obviously excellent students, no matter where they were. You were there to address your deficiency, and there were a few with other problems, likely having difficulties in a normal class. One boy caught everybody's attention most of the time because he was frustrated and constantly (but politely) asking the teacher for help.

It was a dilemma for a single teacher to hold together a group of bright children and the disruptive few. The scene in the class was not pretty. The teacher had to address the frequent requests of the boy before he became upset. Keeping her communication with the boy, she masterfully stayed on her planned instruction to separate grades. However, the difference between the gifted and normal classes often came into play. The class was not quiet; the children, who already knew the content, questioned her instruction often. She answered their questions patiently as best as she could. She remained calm in facing even some ridicule from the crowd. I was concerned after observing the class and asked for your opinion. You said that it often happened and that the students had the correct answer or broader view of things. You enjoyed the class because of the atmosphere and the tolerance, while I was worried about the loss of respect for the teacher or older people.

Your grades in the class were fine. At the parent-teacher interview on one of the PD days, the teacher did not have any complaints about you other than improving your quality of the work. I reiterated my hope of addressing your deficiency in gifted class. The teacher did not see it as a concern. She emphasized the importance of peers, which I agreed with wholeheartedly. Her responsibility was to fulfill the curriculum, and she had (volunteer) helpers in class sessions occasionally. I had a more-in-depth discussion with her about the goal of the special education class. I asked her about the special education program for grades seven and eight. Her answer was that it would still be a split-grade class, but the subjects would be taught by more than one teacher. At the end of your grade six, I called the school to ask for a visit to the class of the ongoing grades seven and eight, but the answer was no.

Peers in the gifted class were indeed the bright side of special education. Gradually, I noticed that a few children were from the families of my Nortel coworkers or your computer or badminton camps. However, there were no neighborhood kids. You started having small or large weekend gatherings. You were at several large gatherings. At a gathering, six or seven students played electronic games, sometimes with heated discussions. The host family often prepared some snacks. I was there only to deliver and pick up. There were several projects throughout the year, and you were in quite a few small group gatherings to work on projects. Occasionally, you brought one or two friends after school to work or play. Their parents came promptly to pick them up before dinner. I felt that you really grew mentally with the class setting and peers,

Chinese School

Saturday language schools, which include Chinese ones, are a tradition among diverse ethnic groups in North America. The multiculturalism policy of Canada encourages this activity. In Chinese schools, Mandarin or Cantonese is taught and supported by people from various regions. In Ottawa, when you started grade school, the Chinese school at Broadview High School was managed by teachers from China. The existence of such a school had been passed on verbally by the parents. The textbooks were shipped from China or just sheets were handed out in class. However, all the teachers there were professional teachers when they were in China.

When you started grade one, I took you to the Chinese school on its first school day. I put your name down and bought the textbook. The first year of the school focused on Pinyin and simple spoken Chinese of words and phrases. It was easy for you because the Chinese spoken in class was short and from everyday life. Pinyin is composed of the English alphabet, which is pronounced differently. You did very well in the first term. You also did very well in the second term, but you worked seriously and did my drills whenever you had time, especially the night before the final exam. The commitment on my side was to take you to the school every Saturday. While you were in class, I often went grocery shopping. The length of your class was long enough to either go to Chinatown or a nearby supermarket that carried an extensive selection of vegetables. In the extra time waiting for the class to be dismissed, I had opportunities to chat with other parents or some grandparents.

You moved on to grade two the next year. Writing Chinese characters became the primary task. There were dictations almost every week to check if the students remembered the characters learned in the previous session. Inserting any work to practice Chinese during the week was challenging. You were simply not interested because you were the only Chinese in your normal EFI class during the week. Since the school was every Saturday, you and I needed a session on Friday night to review what you had learned. With our combined effort, especially at the end of the term, you still did well on your final exam.

When taking you to the Chinese school every Saturday, I envied the people who regarded the occasion as a family activity. The family came in a van and left the child to study while grandparents chatted with their peers. The young couple then went shopping or ran other errands. Handling the half-day duty as a single parent made me feel a bit overwhelmed and lacking justification. I asked Ying if he would come with us or alternate with me for your education in Chinese. This could be a family activity to support both you and me. Ying asked me if you liked classes and learning Chinese. My answer was that you were not very interested but were not behind in learning. His decision was simply to let it go if you were not interested. He did not feel the need because there wasn't much opportunity around to speak Chinese, anyway. So, our Saturday trips to Chinese school stopped. Later, when questioned about your poor Chinese, Ying and I, or you and I, came back to this point several times. What is missed is missed forever.

Several years later, you attended a session of the summer camps offered by the Chinese school. The school no longer enforced exams, although it continued Chinese lessons during the summer camps. Some children were there for the entire summer. Without knowing many Chinese words, you were there to listen and observe. You enjoyed the lunch available at the camp, but you mentioned you saw a teacher punishing a student with a ruler. I told you about the old masters at the schools in China, where a special ruler was indeed a tool for teaching.

Over the years, the Chinese schools flourished in Ottawa. By the time we left Ottawa to live in Toronto, there must have been close to ten Chinese schools with additional Chinese after-school programs. A student who finished the Chinese class of grade six and beyond could claim the high-school credit for foreign (the third) language. Saturday schools extended from half a day to a full day. The afternoon classes included painting, choirs/dances, and chess playing. A few Chinese schools borrowed the auditorium for the families to stay. There were activities such as forums and short courses for adults, too. From time to time, individuals set up stands for haircuts, sales from pastries to insurance.

Kumon and French

In the summer between grades three and four, I enrolled you in Kumon, which was a well-known enrichment or remedial program for children. My original intent was to help improve your English so that you would not feel bad when you started grade four in a pure English class. To my surprise, your English was already at a grade five or six level, while your math level needed some basic training, although grade appropriate. You had a full summer of Kumon English and Math. The daily sets of English and math were not challenging.

Doing the Kumon sets became a moment in the evening for you to sit down calmly after a day at camp. Gradually, I felt that the English in Kumon learning was very similar to learning English as a second language. It could become a diversion from how you learned at a normal school. I removed the English content at the end of the summer. You continued Kumon Math because you did not mind. In addition, both Ying and I felt that the repetitive exercises were good for laying down a solid foundation of number sense. We went through all those drills throughout our elementary school years in China.

It took four years for you to complete Kumon Math. The

skills, which resulted from repetitive practice, made it easy and quick for you to correlate with the math you were learning at school. Ying and I both admit that common sense in math at your age still requires class instruction. The last few work sets are on basic skills in calculus and related coordinate systems. Your work sets were marked and sometimes sent back to you because your work did not show all the steps in the answer book. After many repeated sets with errors, I negotiated with the center to let you take the exam without turning in the sets every week. The reason was that you were already in high school and spent three hours on the bus every day. Ying guided you through the last few rounds of the assignment. Ying, an instructor of college physics, knows derivatives and integrations inside out. He tried to make it intriguing when he explained the transformation between algebra and geometry. I felt that Kumon at that level was too methodical instead of conceptual. You were obviously lost on how to improve. The final exam was not very difficult for your quick mind. You passed it within the limit of allowed errors and only two-thirds of the allowed time. Years after you started college, I found a few Kumon work sets under your bed when I was getting your room ready for hardwood flooring.

Besides Kumon, you needed help in French from time to time. However, the help was short every time because your grade usually went up quickly with a little help. I hired a tutor once for conversation. She was a college student living in Vanier. Another time, you were in a French after-school group in Bridlewood. After a while, the owner of the group said that you could come back next term to be a learner and guide at the same time. We never went back. After you started high school, a French-speaking family became our neighbor. The lady was a substitute teacher for French and other subjects. You were practicing French with her and her children. The children came to our house many times to admire your magic tricks and the abundance of your electronic games and gear. Learning an unfamiliar language was probably never your favorite subject, but you survived.

After-School Care

Schools were usually out at 3 or 3:30 pm every day. An important task for a working family was to arrange after-school care for the child to stay until 5 or 5:30pm. By law, a child cannot stay alone at home until the age of ten. Between ages ten and twelve, the child can stay home for only two hours. Ying's first job was in Chalk River, and his second job was in Iroquois near the St. Lawrence River and Highway 401. Therefore, I was acting as a single parent in the first few years of your elementary school. For my 7.5- or 8-hour working day, my pickup time after work was no earlier than 5:30 pm, after I sent you off to school in the morning. After-school services that allowed a child to stay until 5:30 pm were hard to find.

Wang Nainai went home to take care of her husband before the end of your senior kindergarten year. Qin Nainai came back for a while until you became a full day student. At the beginning of your grade one, I tried one or two home cares. It turned out that picking you up at 5 pm was too strict for me, and I just couldn't make it every time. I investigated the after-school program offered by the school. The pickup time could be as late as 5:30 pm. It was in the school auditorium, and the children of different grades sat in groups or a circle to work on their own homework. There weren't any organized activities, although there was always a teacher or helper to monitor. I thought it would work for us and planned to discuss with you about things to do in the after-school setting once you settled in. However, before I could do it properly, you got kicked out as a bad influence. The incident was that you, with two or three other kids, walked in and out of the auditorium and exchanged the *Toy Story* quote "What's up, dude?" When you were outside, your voice was overheard by a senior teacher. I could only blame my catch-22 mode. I explained to you the broader meaning of a dude and why people could be sensitive to these words. You knew you were in trouble, and I had to look for other options. At home, I reminded you of the famous line by Thumper in *Bambi:* "If you can't say something nice, don't say nothing at all." Isn't this what we all try to follow to keep the peace at school, work, or even home?

On the day of the incident, you went back to your classmate's home after school. His mother, who was a volunteer at the school, was quite sympathetic to my situation. When I went to pick you up, she told me you could stay at her place after school until I found someone. It was very generous of her since I often walked in to pick you up almost at her dinner time. Families with multiple children often have extracurricular activities after dinner. In a few days, I found Carol among the ads of childcare in the Kanata newspaper. She lived a five-minute walk from your school and a two-minute drive from our house. Her husband worked for a high-tech company and therefore, her dinner time was after 6 pm. She had two sons, Guy, who was a few years older, and Andrew, who was younger than you. Guy also went to Castlefrank Elementary. She didn't mind if I came to pick you up around 5:30 pm.

Before I hired her, she went to pick up Guy every day with Andrew sitting on a snow sledge. For many days before you could walk along with Guy, she had Andrew on the sledge on her way to school and you and Andrew both on her sledge on her way back. Once back at her home, she gave everybody a cup of hot chocolate and a cookie. After that, you and Guy should do the homework first and then play. All three of you played along fine. After the first week, I was quite grateful for the opportunity. There was no rude language and no more crowds causing trouble. Her English was the one from an area near London and taught as standard English in China.

Carol was very punctual and never missed picking up the children. We were on very polite terms, i.e., never talking about anything that was deemed private. Your friendship with Guy lasted many years. He was at your birthday parties. Being the older brother, he was the most well-mannered child in the family. He later went to Algonquin College and then went to England to explore. Many years later, Ying and I were shopping at Home Depot in Kanata and noticed that Carol was working there. We had a long chat to catch up. All her children grew up, and she liked to work and felt worthy that way.

Summer Camps

The preteen school years were the time when you spent the summer or even March Break at camps. The main reason was that you were not old enough to stay at home alone for an entire day. Luckily, the companies I worked for always had Christmas shutdown, which mostly aligned with your Christmas break. My vacation days were carefully distributed to cover your PD days and to extend a family vacation. A Christmas trip could be ten days; a trip to China would take longer than two weeks. Still, you were out of school for many days in summer, Christmas, and March breaks when Ying and I needed to work. Attending camps to learn something outside of the school curriculum was a better option than sending you to home care. The camps were offered by the community, universities, YM/WCA, sports centers, and companies. The content of the camps was different, and you were in three types of camps: the regular camps, specialty camps, and sports camps. As I remember, the max number of camps you went to for a summer was eight!

You attended many regular camps offered by the community or Nortel. There were a lot of children like you with parents at work. These camps have daily or weekly themes. A camp day has theme-related activities in the morning and different sports in the afternoon. The camp usually serves one or two snacks and requires the children to bring their own lunch. You attended such camps at the community centers in Glen Cairn and Beaverbrook branch of the Ottawa Library. In the morning, I packed you up with lunch, water and a set of clothes for changing. Swimming pants were required sometimes, but your participation in the afternoon swim was not enforced. In the evening, I picked you up on my way back home. Nortel, the company I worked for, organized summer camps for the children of its employees at both Carling and Skyline campuses. You attended one at each site because of my working locations. You came with me to work in the morning, and I took you to the campsite, which was usually inside the gym. Like some other parents, I sometimes went to check on you during my lunch break. It was fun for the children to be around the camp guides, who were a lot younger than their schoolteachers. The guides were enthusiastic and inventive. I was told once that you led the entire group and leapfrogged the entire gym room. The Nortel camp usually ended at four in the afternoon. I brought you to my cubicle every time so that I could get my things done for the day before going home. My coworkers often came by to chat and tease. Many years later, one of my friends still remembered how you and I walked, holding hands, to the parking lot after work.

You were in the Bright Math camp at Ottawa University. The instructor at the camp was a professor at the university. The class period included math work at various levels and constant evaluations, which were likely data collection for the sake of her research. It turned out to be a chaotic, super multi-grade class. You were fine in the first half of the day, but you drifted away in the second half. It was probably your first time in a class where the knowledge of the material was interesting but overwhelming. You also felt that some others were quite competitive and eager to get attention. The professor said that you were too young for the environment. It made me think that the summer should be fun without class-type camps. Two years later, I signed you up for the science camps offered by the engineering departments at the same university. The camp was more like a show-and-tell of the instructor at some departmental laboratories. The content was a step further from what was available at a science and technology museum. You were bused to and from the university. You had opportunities to tour different components of the university.

The computer camps for children were at their beginning stage. They were offered by a software company in town. I enrolled you at least twice. The content was selected from some game programs created in the BASIC language on the DOS platform. Your first session was to learn computer skills. While playing games, you learned the layout of the keyboard, mouse operation, and file saving. As the parent of a camper, I was invited to the last class on Friday. The head of the camp explained the activities of the specific class and the outcome. As did by other campers, you showed how to send a document to a printer and print out a nicely formatted document. The second class was the beginning of robotics, and the company provided the software and the model. The students learned to pick the commands, insert them into the operating system of the model, and operate the robot. On Friday, I saw the program package installed on the computer and the actions of the robot with updated software. You were quite proud of what you had accomplished.

You went to several sports camps when you were in grades four and five. You were in the swimming camp at Kanata Wave Pool for a week. It gave age-appropriate swimming instructions in the morning. You learned everything that did not require submerging your head. For a while, you took tennis lessons with a short racquet at the tennis courts outside the library in Glen Cairn. You were old enough for tennis camps, and therefore, you went to tennis camps in Stittsville and Turnbull School in Nepean. After two years, you moved on to playing badminton, which became your sport.

I told my friends that I raised my son on piles of money. It is true. Without grandparents or relatives at home, you were out of the house most of the time. Were you enjoying the camps? Probably not, compared to a child who only had one camp booked per summer. You never complained, and we were never late for a single day. For the long summer of quite a few years, it was a pattern that you were out with me in the mornings and back with me in the evenings.

Friends

You always had a few friends, probably because you had wit and were never the center of any conflict. From time to time, you told me that the class was divided into different camps while you didn't want to belong to any when friends came and talked to you. I supported your stand because the school was for learning knowledge. However, as a bystander most of the time, you might have missed the exposure and growth in leadership and conflict handling.

As a parent, I learned to host your friends in the house and keep a watchful eye on the activities. Silly things happened a few times. I could hear you running around in the house in the late hours or tiptoed into the master bedroom to set booby traps. One time, you and your friend were curious about the amount of money in your piggy bank. You agreed that you two would split the treasure if there was a way to open it. Another time, on my return from work, you and your friend were competing to see who could make the highest mark on the wall with a water gun in hand. It also happened once that one kid became upset and wanted to go home. I had to call his parents. As did other families, I booked your birthday celebration outside the house to prevent any problems with food or cultural differences. The safe and age-appropriate entertainment venues such as Kiddy Kart or Midway were popular. You were at the birthday parties of your peers. Buying a birthday present was an item on my shopping list many times in those years.

Brandon and Connor were friends for many years. Both lived nearby, and spending a night at a friend's house was often. Both were invited to spend the night a few times. More often, you had one of them over to play and chat. Brandon was from a French-speaking family and was allergic to peanuts. Our place was probably the first friend's home where he spent the night. He came with an EpiPen. Since I couldn't guarantee a peanut-free environment in my cooking, I searched online for a peanut-free breakfast. I went to McDonald's the next morning and bought breakfast. You were at Brandon's house many times over the years. When you were learning karate, Brandon followed his brother to the martial arts school, and was in the same karate class with you for a while. While his brother went all the way to the black belt, Brandon did not like discipline and left to pursue his interest in the arts. Occasionally, I would bump into his mom while walking on McCurdy, and we exchanged updates. Brandon went to Queen's University in Kingston with his brother and became an engineer.

Connor was the middle child of an English-speaking family. He had an older brother and a younger sister. Besides birthday parties or occasional sleepovers, he preferred gentle conversations with you. He would often walk over to visit you and either talk or play games. Later, his sister started following him on his visits, and we would walk them back to make sure that they reached home without detours. I remember that his mother was a very elegant English woman, and the lawn and flower beds outside their house were always well maintained. However, Connor was often lost and unhappy, probably because he did not get the attention that he thought he deserved. I don't know if he went to a university to study after high school.

Over the years, we had a few good friends in Ottawa. Like Ying and me, they left China to pursue advanced degrees, worked in other countries, and then settled in Canada. We had a lot to talk about whenever we gathered. The parents of one family got a doctorate degree from Germany and worked separately in Germany and the States for a while. Canada was the country they could immigrate to and finally stay together as a family. The wife was Ying's coworker in Chalk River when her son, Jiankai, was brought from China to live with her. He was starting kindergarten. You acted like a big brother to help him when they were over at our house and out at a restaurant. It took a few years for the family to settle down in Ottawa. We were close friends, and you and Jiankai were always together when we met or were out in the park or restaurant. Jiankai loved his grandparents very much. They took care of him in his early years and then took turns visiting Ottawa and staying for months sometimes. He spoke perfect Chinese and tried hard to be an obedient son and grandson, as well as an outstanding student at school. You impressed him with skillful maneuvers in game playing, but the two of you were never close. He went to the University of Toronto to study finance, and he is now an accountant.

Charity and Donations

After we moved into our own house on Sicard Way, we started having people knocking on the door for donations. Words like non-profit organizations and charity campaigns were new to the entire family. They did not exist in China when Ying and I grew up. We were excited at first whenever there were unexpected doorbells or knocks on the door. As a child, you knew not to open the door, but you stayed nearby. During my conversation with the visitors at the door, you sometimes ran upstairs to bring down your piggy bank. I was impressed and allowed you to take out up to five dollars at a time. The visitors were from organizations like the Red Cross and Harvest House. The conversation with the visitor could last five to ten minutes. Gradually, I learned to get receipts for my tax return. I also learned to check the credit of the organization online to be selective in writing cheques.

We learned to canvass for different activities. I was recruited by the Arthritis Society of Canada during a call. I canvassed door-to-door in the designated neighborhood. After two years, I was given a list of the canvassers' names to do follow-ups from time to time. At the end of the campaign, I drove around to collect donations and sent the money to a person responsible for an even larger area in the management chain. For you, the school had fundraising activities, and you brought back chocolate to sell. I followed you on a tour of the neighborhood. Later, you went around the neighborhood by yourself. Honestly, neither of us was very convincing in door-to-door activities. I took the candies to work and asked my friends to contribute as I did to their Girl Scout's cookies. At home, as expected, we had students coming over for fundraising, too. The organization could be a school, a sport team, or a music band. Gradually, we got used to seeing cadets selling chocolate and the Salvation Army ringing the bell before Christmas. More than half of my mail came from non-profit societies. It is a world that keeps reminding people that their kindness to needy people is appreciated without conflict of interest. I only got unhappy once at Halloween when the trick-or-treaters asked for a donation.

After years on the learning curve, I finally cleaned up my mailing list and learned to say no to a few when the doorbell rang. I kept contributing to World Vision for many years. We sponsored a child in Peru for many years and then a child in Brazil. At the beginning, I asked the organization for a child in grade school, like your age. I got a younger one because of the structure and target of the program. We finally met the child when we visited Peru. For my home country, I got involved with campaigning for education in rural areas of southwestern China through my schoolmate from Taiwan. It lasted for thirty years. The activities included summer English camps for the local students. I planned to put your name down for the camp season so that you could see with your own eyes without your family around. However, it was hard to arrange. Over the years, the organization was successful, and I paid for one or two children every year from elementary to high school. Some of them went on to universities.

I have my own guidelines on these activities. I told World Vision that I would sponsor a child in a region that is not at war. For education in rural China, I stopped supporting the organization when it started taking care of war children in Cambodia.

Plan for Junior High

At the end of your grade six, I was deeply concerned about what you would become after two more years in a split-grade class for junior high. Your reading skills and overall comprehension were already equivalent to grade eight when you were eight years old. I was quite interested in the idea of acceleration to target your attitude towards learning. Acceleration was not allowed in public schools, and you were not a perfect student. I started calling private schools that had grades seven and above. To my surprise, some of them invited you to stay for a day for evaluation. We visited three of them. The first one was 100 percent French. The second one invited you to enroll, but the principal stood firm on the condition that you should start from grade seven and then grade eight.

The third school we visited was Road College, which was on Chapel Street next to Ottawa University. The school was new and trying a new concept of learning. It was small and had only grades seven, eight, and nine. It had a very flexible curriculum to introduce the students to the outside world, such as factories, farms, senior centers, and national parks. The principal was very sympathetic to your situation because she was homeschooled when she was young, and she was a believer in acceleration. After observing you for a day, she and the vice principal (the Monsieur) agreed that you could have mixed grades of seven and eight content for a year. I told them I might pull you back to the public school after a year because only the public schools have the proper lab setup for high school courses. They agreed and said that they would provide honest recommendations when necessary.

You started your long journey to school after the summer of grade 6. Bus rides from Kanata to downtown or even further continued for five years.

Gifted Identification

"**S**tudents with gifts and talents perform—or have the capability to perform—at higher levels compared to others of the same age, experience, and environment in one or more domains. They require modification(s) to their educational experience(s) to learn and realize their potential."— National Association of Gifted Children[2].

The process to identify you as gifted ran from the last few months of your grade three, the entire length of your grade four, and the early part of your grade five. It was painful for our family and for the education professionals who were involved in the identification process. We challenged both the process of gifted screening at your school and the criteria of gifted identification set by the school board. The school board yielded after we sent the case to the Ontario Special Education Tribunal. The board adjusted the gifted screening process to be more flexible soon after this and other cases and the related effort of the parent group.

Chronology of Gifted Identification

There were formal meetings and interactions between our family and the educators. The list below shows the timelines of the events in this long process.

---

[2] The text is from the website of National Association of Gifted Children, an organization in Canada focused on the needs of gifted and talented children.

General gifted screening when you were in grade three.

- November 2000. You were two months into EFI grade three. The grade three students took the CCAT (Canadian Cognitive Abilities Test).
- December 1, 2000. I took you to the Oxford Learning Center to see if any help was required. The evaluation was one-on-one and created a report.
- Early 2001. I filled in the Parent Information Form. I sent the school a letter that included the form and the Oxford Assessment Report.
- Early 2001. After my letter did not get any response, I inquired about your test score. I was told that you did quite well.
- Before the summer of 2001. I inquired about the result of the screening. I was told that you were not identified as gifted and that you could try again next year.

Efforts to address your special need when you were in grade four.

- Early October 2001. I called the school, requesting a retest. I was told that your file showed you should be given a psychological evaluation if your parents wanted you to be identified as gifted.
- October 17, 2001. I took you to a psychological clinic, and you were given the WISC-III (Wechsler Intelligence Scale for Children) assessment by a psychologist.

- Early November 2001. I presented the report of the WISC-III test results to the school. I was told that you needed to take the CAT/2 reading subset test to get 95 percent or better to get the one point to meet the 12-point gifted profile.
- November 16, 2001. You were given both level-14 Reading and Language subsets of the CAT/3.
- November 20, 2001. I called the school and inquired about the test results. I was told that you did not get the point because your score was 89 percent.
- November 21, 2001. Ying and I went to your school and looked at the test results. We raised our concerns about the content and format of the test set.
- Late November 2001. We investigated the test materials and pointed out the inconsistency in evaluation. We did not get any response.
- November 26, 2001. I sent in the IPRC (Identification, Placement, and Review Committee) request.
- November 28, 2001. I got the letter from the principal rejecting an IPRC.
- November 30, 2001. I replied to her letter explaining the rights of parents.
- December 3, 2001. The principal suggested a case conference, and we agreed.
- December 14, 2001. The case conference was held at the school. Attendees were your parents, the school staff, the board special education support teacher, and the ABC representative.

- December 17, 2001. I sent a follow-up letter to the principal requesting a response to the CAT3 test and EQAO results. We did not get any response.
- December 19, 2001. I received the input of the board psychologist passed by the school principal. I emailed the psychologist an email, asking for a meeting after the holidays. She never replied.
- February 3, 2002. I sent the principal a letter asking to proceed with IPRC. I attached the document of parent's recommendation.
- February 4, 2002. The principal replied, saying that the school could retest you with CAT2. She also sent your EQAO results.
- February 5, 2002. We rejected the school's offer to retest you with CAT2 and asked to proceed with the IPRC.

IPRC, IPRC appeal and Tribunal

- February 7, 2002. The principal contacted us via email about meeting time slots.
- February 8, 2002. The principal emailed me, saying that IPRC is not needed and therefore no appeal.
- February 21, 2002. IPRC was held at the school. The outcome was that you should stay in the regular program. Retesting you with CAT/2 was offered again, but we declined.
- February 25, 2002. We sent in the IPRC appeal.

- March 20, 2002. The names of the parent representative and board representative for the appeal meeting were confirmed.
- April 3, 2002. The board provided documents on OCDSB gifted screening and identification procedures.
- June of 2002. The stack of material for the Appeal was sent to all the parties. The stack included a cover letter from the board dated June 20 and information sets prepared by the board and the ABC representing the parents.
- September 9, 2002. The IPRC appeal meeting was held at the Confederation High School. At the meeting, the board introduced a new document, "Appeal Information" to be read. The appeal did not change anything.
- November 5, 2002. We mailed the Ontario Special Education Tribunal a letter to request a Tribunal hearing.
- November 15, 2002. I received an email from the secretary of the Tribunal acknowledging our request for a hearing at the Ontario Special Education Tribunal.
- November 21, 2002. I got a call from the school board, saying that the board agreed to identify you as gifted.

Why Gifted Identification?

From grade one to grade twelve, a child spends a lot of time at school five days a week for nine months every year. To make the school time worthwhile, I believe schools should provide a child with a suitable learning environment. Time spent at school is then to nurture attitudes towards knowledge and methods of learning. The level of knowledge to be achieved at a certain age is less important because it differs across regions and countries worldwide. This mindset is related to our cultural background. In the classrooms of primary schools in China, all the desks are set in the same direction and all the students sit straight when the teacher is instructing.

The purpose of identifying you as gifted was to address the problem with your attention span. From your toddler days, you were focused whenever you wanted to do something. You could listen or watch for more than an hour by yourself or in almost a one-on-one setting. However, your short attention span was obvious unless you were interested. You were quick and observant, with good intuition, but you were not following well, especially in a group environment. You had no patience for repetitive instructions and were easily distracted. When instructions were given to different groups in the same room, you would pick up whatever you were interested in. Along the same lines, you never liked team sports.

Your short attention span was exposed as a problem in your classroom behavior when you were in split-grade classes of EFI from grades one to three. The students usually sat in groups; each group sitting around a large rectangular table (sometimes with storage sections for each student). Students of different grades in the class took turns listening to the teacher. When the students of a specific grade were not being instructed, they were expected to review and practice quietly with what they had just learned. You seemed to pick up whatever you liked. The rest of your class time was spent playing with other students sitting around the same table. At the end of grade two, your grades are composed of fifteen As and three Bs. The teacher commented on your report card, "A knowledgeable little boy, James demonstrated that he could accurately analyze and assess the value of information." "He is such a quick study but frequently did not listen for instructions … Next year, James must focus on listening to the teacher." I became concerned about your behavior in the classroom when the learning became more serious in grade three. As advised by your teacher, you got your first pair of glasses so that you would not wander past other tables to get closer to the blackboard during classes. But the teacher still had to remind you often to work on your assignment.

I felt you needed help to improve your focus. I took you to the Oxford Learning Center in Kanata to get an evaluation when you were three months into grade three. My intent was to find out which subject(s) at school you might need help with. The result was surprising and did not call for any help. In the Oxford report, your reading was at the grade ten level and comprehension was at the grade eight level; none of the other skills was below grade four. Compared to all "Above Average," the only "Average" pointed to the "auditory attention-span and distractibility." Even for French, your skill was "grade-appropriate." The only help the center might offer was to boost your confidence in speaking French. The test report included a tester's observation of your participation to confirm the validity of the result. This was the first time I read a report outside of my profession. I welcomed the results because they sounded scientific. The outcome was also reassuring because in the back of my mind I always believed that you might be smarter than the norm, but with some deficiencies.

My assumption was based on the readings on the offspring of older parents I had done from the day I knew I was pregnant.

I found you a tutor in French. In addition, I felt it was important to provide you with some enrichment or even acceleration. For me, reading many books or finishing a Harry Potter book overnight was good, but you should always, or at least often, be interested in what you learn at school. Otherwise, the "boring classes" might lead to laziness in learning while wasting time at school. The goal of elementary school should be to establish a good learning pattern. The pattern would benefit the students in their spare time, not the other way around. Was it too much to expect? If the student, as an individual, could not learn well in the school environment, it was the parents' responsibility to figure out how to improve.

I informed the school about your Oxford Assessment Report, asking about the possibility of any enrichment. I did not receive any response. During the gifted screening in grade three, I wrote the school a letter that included the required Parent Information Form and the Oxford report. You were not identified as gifted. In grade four, I transferred you to an English class to ensure you were not in a split-grade environment. After the encounter with the confusing French definitions in the grade three math, Ying was relieved that you were finally in an English class. He was convinced that my initiatives were aimed at improving your education experience, and he supported me throughout the process.

In public schools, the EFI is always optional but more challenging. English classes at a school must be provided to all age-appropriate children. The teacher of grade four soon noticed that you were not listening during her classes. I asked the teacher to provide you with some extra work so that you would not be bored while catching up on what you did not know. My actions, which were targeted to improve your focus in class, were probably viewed by the educators as abnormal and contradictory.

Gifted Criteria and Your Scores

Your school board, the Ottawa-Carleton District School Board (OCDSB), had a 12-point gifted profile for gifted screening. A gifted student must have a minimum of twelve points at the end of a three-stage assessment. Stage 1 was a group assessment. The students were given CCAT in class. The CCAT had three subjects: Verbal, Quantitative, and Nonverbal. A student who scored 98 percent or better in each subject earned twelve points. If a student had eleven or ten points, Stage 2 was the teacher's recommendation. The input of a teacher should be based on his/her judgement after he/she processed information in the Parent Information Form filled in by the parents. The teacher's recommendation could bring in one or two points. If the point could not come from the teacher, in Stage 3, the student could take the CAT/2 Reading Comprehension test and achieve at least 95 percent to get the needed point. To summarize, the gifted students thus identified had the potential and performed well during the single test; the few that had been identified through Stages 2 and 3 were well-behaved at school with very supportive parents or already excelled in English.

For the CCAT given to the grade three students, you had the best scores among the EFI students. The Parent Information Form was sent home after the test. There were twenty-six items in the form. The parent was asked to rank his/her child as compared to a "typical child in your neighborhood." The ranks in each category were "lack", "less", "compare", "more", and "to a high degree." There was no space for "not applicable" or "don't know." There were categories that were not applicable at home or required a professional-level opinion. Confused but honest, I ranked you "to a high degree" on intelligence, vocabulary, and curiosity, etc., but low on the few related to attention span to show your deficiency. In addition, I sent in the Oxford assessment, hoping it would add some weight to the gifted identification. It did not happen because none of the EFI students were qualified. As I learned from other parents later, I should have given you the "to a high degree" in all the categories in the form as a very positive input from the parent. However, my input did not matter; it turned out that your grade three teacher, as she told me later, never saw the Parent Information Form of her students before, after, or during the grade three gifted screening process.

An alternative to CCAT-based gifted identification is the clinical IQ-based test. The board had its own psychologist, and other clinics in town had qualified professionals as well. A well-recognized assessment at the time was the WISC-III test, which provided an IQ evaluation on Verbal, Performance, and Full Scale. The report of the test included the tester's opinion on how the individual behaved during the test and, therefore, whether the test result was valid. School boards in Ontario, such as the

Toronto or Niagara board, handle these test results independently. For example, a 99 percent in the "Full Scale IQ" would be identified as gifted if either "Verbal" or "Performance" was above 97 percent. The criteria are in line with the compilation of the test results because the Full-Scale IQ is a composite of the Verbal and Performance. However, OCDSB aligned the WISC-III results to that of CCAT. The mapping between WISC-III and CCAT is found in a table on gifted criteria published by the board. In the table, the WISC-III Full IQ score is no longer composite but is equivalent to CCAT non-verbal. Therefore, gifted identification for a student who underwent the IQ-based test follows the same 12-point criteria. The student must score at least 98 percent in each category of WISC-III to be identified.

Following the school recommendation, I took you to a clinic to be evaluated by psychologists. You were given the WISC-III. The result was that your Verbal Scale IQ and Full-Scale IQ were 99 percent and Performance Scale IQ was 97 percent. The summary from the psychologist was "… a very bright student and in most educational settings, he would be eligible for the gifted program." Once again, the scores and explanations in some categories pointed to your auditory weakness. The school or OCDSB could have done the right thing at the time to identify you and provide you with a special education program to address your deficiency. It did not happen because of the mapping between the WISC-III and CCAT in its gifted criteria.

You were missing one point, and the point would not come from the teacher. So, Stage 3 was offered. Instead of the Reading Comprehension test of CAT/2 Level 13, you were given the set of reading and language tests of CAT/3 Level 14. You were confused because you had to deal with the new way of writing the test and did not do well. At a much later time, the school offered to retest you with the proper level of CAT/2. We did not take the offer because things could go wrong again (un)intentionally. Therefore, your scores did not meet the gifted criteria of the board.

Association for Bright Children

The Association for Bright Children (ABC) is an all-volunteer, provincially incorporated non-profit organization. It provides information and support to parents of bright and gifted children and adolescents. Support and advocacy are available through newsletters, networking, an annual conference, and local workshops. Ottawa chapter is one of the few across Ontario. It was a gathering place for parents who have children with higher-than-normal IQ. Most of them often had concerns about their smart but troublesome children, some of whom really needed help from normal or special education. The chapter held parent meetings and seminars to discuss common topics. It also had the Take-Off sessions in the spring and the fall school terms to offer weekend classes for the children. The classes varied from story writing, painting, dissection, LEGO, magic, astronomy, to bird watching.

The ABC Ottawa chapter submitted its input to the board's special education plan. Its input focused on gifted screening and education. The fact was that the number of gifted students was down by 30 percent after the updated screening strategies came into play. The criteria (12-point gifted profile) excluded students who were gifted with certain deficiencies. Its input analyzed the 3-stage screening process. It pointed out that not all students would perform at their best effort during the single CCAT group assessment in Stage 1. In Stage 2, some items of the questionnaire and their ranking for parents required background knowledge. The eventual input from a teacher would require certain professional training. The CAT/2 Reading test in Stage 3 was for the evaluation of achievement unrelated to a student's cognitive skill. ABC input also criticized the board for its handling of the results from the IQ-based tests, such as the WISC-III tests. The disaggregated mapping between the WISC-III and CCAT was a shortcut and lacked scientific support and was only done at OCDSB.

I found the website of the ABC Ottawa Chapter from an old email, which was from the professor who offered the Bright Math camp for children every summer. I inquired online and soon I connected with Elizabeth. She was the representative of the ABC Ottawa chapter at the Special Education Advisory Committee (SEAC) of OCDSB. Conversations with Elizabeth were encouraging. She understood my dilemma well and had strong opinions on the stages of gifted screening at the board. Clearly, I was not alone, and my attempt to improve your school environment was on the right track. She introduced me to similar cases in Ontario, and she sent me some links to learn the definition and history of giftedness and the related education. In turn, I produced a document that provided details of your giftedness and expressed your parents' wish to address your auditory deficiency in your future education. Elizebeth introduced me to Liz, who was the chairperson of the ABC Ottawa chapter. Liz could represent the ABC Ottawa chapter if needed. Our goal was to ask the board to identify you as gifted and hence provide you with the enriched or gifted program, which was a part of the special education of the board.

In the few months that followed, we went through a case conference, an IPRC, an IPRC appeal, and pushed the case to the Ontario Special Education Tribunal. It was tough in terms of confrontation and humiliation along the way. However, I had Elizabeth and Liz on my side, guiding me to move on and discuss why after every defeat. At the IPRC appeal, ABC was present on our behalf and prepared a document to support your giftedness and your need to be in the special program. ABC sent its feedback after the failed appeal to review the process and express its own opinion. Coming from a very different cultural background, I could never imagine that it was possible for an individual (family) to persist on the opposite side of the system.

In the years that followed, you and I took part in the activities of the ABC Ottawa chapter. You certainly benefited from the Take-Off classes. You attended the magic classes offered by Jean-Luc Dupont. In his classes, you learned to present yourself as well as provide proper critiques while becoming more and more interested in magic. You attended other classes such as dissections and bird watching. In line with your usual behavior, you quit one or two courses because you disliked the content or the organization. You and one of your friends went to the Take-Off session to volunteer when you were in high school. You went back to Monsieur Dupont's magic class to help. Being a class assistant was to fulfill your IB CAS (Creativity, Action and Service) hours.

I was the chapter's secretary, with a single duty of generating the minutes for every gathering. For several years, until you were well into high school, I volunteered almost every weekend during the Take-Off sessions. I did these activities for fun as well as to keep myself up to date on the matter.

At Odds with the System

My initiatives in improving your learning environment at school put our family at odds with the educators at school and on the school board. As a parent, my goal was to address your short attention span so that you could focus on learning in class. After a few fruitless rounds with your in-class enrichment, the only way out seemed to be the special education offered to the identified gifted. However, major changes or any serious interaction between the parents and the school rarely originate from parents. Normally, the school contacts the parents when their child is deemed troublesome. The school orders an assessment of the student, and the board has its own psychologist. Based on the assessment by the psychologist or a similar professional, the school (or board) produces a plan to either solve or eliminate the trouble. As for you, you were a fine student, learning whenever you were interested. You were far from being categorized as a troublemaker by the educators.

Your homeroom teacher played an important role in the entire process. I had meetings with her at the beginning of your fourth grade. I asked her to let you read other books, provided you were following the class. Obviously, she did not like a student who could answer questions without listening. I then asked her if you could be given some work as an enrichment. The purpose of these meetings was to improve your behavior in the class, e.g., to better focus on your own work. She was polite and distant every time we met. She never provided updates on your progress in the enrichment. It turned out that she was quite negative about these parent initiatives. Her anger reflected on the sheets of quizzes you brought home for me to sign. You were bothered by being paired up every time with a classmate known to have learning problems. You were also bothered by some incidents. For example, she mocked you when you made an error in a dictation, and the entire class got a good laugh out of it. She called you "Potter" in front of your class. For the enrichment material, she did not provide any guidance when you were stuck solving a problem. She wrote a note on the page that you need to ask your father, while her rule was that the material should never leave the classroom. She never relayed the situation to me during any of my follow-ups. Her note on the page was presented at multiple meetings as evidence that you did not have the drive to study. Another piece of evidence she collected was the bad marks in your science duo-tang. We looked through the duo-tang afterwards and found that your work was marked with smiley faces, "well done," and grades C and D. The "C" and "D" were presented as evidence at the meetings. The inconsistency in her grading made me wonder if she intentionally put the letter grades there.

The special education at the school targets students who need help outside of the normal school environment. The Special Education Resource Teacher (SERT) at the school was a teacher with extra training in special education. In my case, accommodating a parent's request for a student certainly fell outside of her normal duties. She provided your homeroom teacher with the enrichment material, but probably as a gift instead of a serious educational component. There was no help or even follow-up. So, you were lost. While testing you with the Reading subject of CAT/2 Level 13, she provided you with the CAT/3 Reading and Language sets of level 14. To follow the rule of Stage 3 screening, she could have omitted or crossed out the Language set as only the Reading part was required. But she gave you both sets and administered the test in two sessions, before and after her lunch, at her convenience. I noticed the wrong level of the test after I checked online. In addition, the test materials of Level 14 included a separate test booklet and answer sheets. It was your first time. A question and its multiple-choice answer set were no longer in a group; you had to go back and forth to locate them when filling in an answer. Ying and I met the SERT for the first time when we went to school to question her about the test level and the answer sheet. I was sad to see filled circles and smudges in the answer column showing your selections and corrections when she showed us your test. You tried. We questioned whether the test result was valid. She bluntly answered that the supposed CAT/2 test was not available and that the test was valid. Much later, at the IPRC, we heard a verbal comment that the previous test was a mix-up. In the entire process, the school offered to retest you with CAT/2 twice, but we declined.

The decisions in the long process were mostly made by the principal of your school. She had worked for a long time in a French or French Immersion environment and was quite proud of it. She was not confrontational at the beginning but became patronizing early on and told me in her emails about her experience at the French schools. The implication I got was that the non-English and non-French parents should appreciate and accept the difference. When we insisted and the board got involved, she organized the preparation for each meeting. The information generated by the school every time was quite negative. Instead of a fair presentation of your grades and class behavior, their collection contained only your sloppy work on a test and worst grades in your work. Verbally, their summary listed your not-so-correct interactions with the teacher, some of which we never knew before. She blew up once when we insisted on going through the IPRC. She was angry in one of her emails that was never mentioned at any meetings. "Since the IPRC purpose is to identify an exceptional need, and James does not fulfill the criteria to be identified as gifted, I cannot hold an IPRC meeting. An appeal is a parent's objection to a label or identification of their child's needs. Since James is not identified as exceptional, or as requiring special education, there can be no appeal." Her misunderstanding was cleared away by the ABC SEAC at the board by the end of the day.

The major contributors, such as your homeroom teacher, the SERT, and the principal of your school, were on the opposite side. Therefore, the outcome of the meetings to address your education was a failure of unexpected humiliation. At the case conference and later the IPRC meeting, our intention was clear, and we sent in our information beforehand. The school staff surprised us with a stack of your poor grades and sloppy work. One of them summarized your behavioral problems as evidence of your laziness and lack of interest in study. After we clarified with the principal about her rejection of IPRC in her email, we finally set the date for the IPRC. Two days before the IPRC, we were told that the school could offer the proper CAT/2 to retest you. The IPRC was held after we declined the CAT/2 offer. The outcome of the IPRC was that there was a mix-up in the test level and that you could take the CAT/2 with the proper level to gain one point. We declined the offer again because we had no confidence in these specific educators. Instead, we submitted our appeal.

For the appeal, the two sides were given ample time to prepare. A thick (stapled-together) stack of materials from Exhibits #1 to #3 was mailed to the participants. It included: (1) the information provided by the school board, (2) documents of gifted screening and identification procedures, and (3) documents prepared by ABC as the representative of the parents. The document prepared by ABC started with a cover letter by ABC clearly stating our request and the overall process. It contained a series of publications, such as ABC analysis on the OCDSB gifted program and cases of gifted identification. Our case was one of them. On the day of the appeal meeting, the school/board brought in new information; the new document, "Exhibit #4 Appeal Information," was introduced. The document was a chronology of events and so-called facts about you, showing that the school board stood its ground. Instead of a fair presentation of a student, the goal of the document was clearly to enhance the answer "NO" in identifying you as gifted. Even the mix-up in the test was rebranded as "more of a ceiling for the bright students". The document was read out at the meeting instead of going through the previously distributed information. There were three of us, our representative, Ying, and I, facing eight to ten educators at different levels. We were outnumbered. The appeal meeting went through the due process. We were informed formally that there would not be any change in your education plan.

The appeal concluded our confrontations with the educators. It was left to Ying and me to decide if we should move any further. All along, you were very cooperative. You tried your best whenever a test was needed. I don't know if you still remember anything in those months. I wonder from time to time what you had in mind to survive in the class. Life at home was as normal as possible. Other than asking you how you did at school or on a test, Ying and I did not show any frustration or discuss what happened at those meetings when you were around.

End of the Journey

Ying and I were angry because we were mistreated at every meeting. We sent in our input for every meeting beforehand. They always used only their own information by giving a speech or introducing a new document while our input was ignored. We, as the parents of a student, were just there to listen and be humiliated. However, should we take the last step — a hearing at the Ontario Special Education Tribunal? There were very few tribunal cases over the years. In the twenty-some years I was in North America, I had not even been to court for a traffic ticket.

Ying and I talked about it over and over. We could not accept the outcome; it was just wrong. The logic and process handling were against all the science and scientific methods we had learned in our lives. At a higher level, we (and ABC) felt that moving forward could bring some changes to the criteria of gifted identification on the school board. We generated our recommendations for the school board. Two major points were: (1) to use the WISC-III result independently and directly, like the practice of others, and (2) to remove CAT/2 as a component in gifted screening. Specifically, we asked the board to identify you as gifted and to assign you to the special program for the gifted. It was the last week of the 60-day grace period after the appeal when we mailed out the letter to the Tribunal.

Ten days after our mail to the Tribunal, I received an email from the secretary of the Tribunal. He acknowledged our mail and informed me he had sent me the must-read material in the mail. Subsequently, we had a few email exchanges to explain to him how far we had gone before we mailed him the hearing request. Less than a week after his initial email, I got a call from the head of the OCDSB. The board had a new response: (1) the school board realized you were very close to meeting the criteria for the gifted, (2) if procedures were handled a little differently you could have been identified as gifted, and (3) the school board would like to hold an IPRC to identify you as gifted. The good news was shocking! I called Ying, Elizabeth, and Liz to share the news and joy. It was a victory for a pair of stubborn parents and advocates who were determined to argue about fairness. After so many sleepless nights, the end of our journey was quick and sweet!

As was shared later by Elizabeth, the board was waiting for any action by the parents after the appeal. All along, the educators hoped the parents would give up. They hoped the parents were angry enough to transfer the child to a private school. If not, you were a fine student with good grades, after all. Our persistence in asking public education to address the bias in gifted screening was not common. Once they became defensive, the school and the board did not really adhere to the guidelines for the educators. Throughout the long process, they could have done things differently on one or two occasions to identify you and end the matter. The board quickly backed down when it had to choose between giving up one point or preparing for the Tribunal hearing. The tribunal hearing did not happen, and we did not loudly and clearly criticize the board's bias on gifted screening. However, the standards changed quickly afterwards. In less than three years, I was told that a student with 98 percent in one of the CCAT subjects plus teacher/parent recommendations would be identified. By that time, parents who wanted to get their child into the gifted program also learned to use the top ranks in all categories when the Parent Information Form was sent home.

Later, at one of the ABC gatherings, I was asked by a parent, who was a medical doctor, "Have you thought any further about making a human rights complaint?" I never did, probably because the multicultural society was new to me. The communication between the educators and the parents was mostly professional and "politically correct." There were two kinds of unfairness or mistreatment. The first one was towards Ying and me. It was the self-righteousness of the educators. My voice in English, which is good enough to argue or explain in writing and training others, was never heard or even asked at those painful meetings. Their attitude at the end of the process was that the matter could have been "handled a little differently." There was nothing inappropriate. There was no apology. The other unfairness, which was towards you, likely reflected the frustration and bias of the few individuals. It was just human. Again, there was no apology. It reminded me of what my professor in Wisconsin said: "Apology is for your soul," although justice and charity are a part of the western virtues.

It didn't really matter if we had a language deficiency and were not familiar with the education system in a different country. It was a long learning process to experience how far an individual can go. In contrast to the world in which we grew up, there was enough information and respect for individual rights. Along the way, I found ABC, where similar people could freely share their experiences and work on an issue. I am very grateful to Elizabeth and Liz, who advocated wholeheartedly for the children with higher-than-normal IQ as well as deficiencies. There were always options in the way an individual could or had to choose. We opted to work with the public education system. Soon after your identification, we had to choose between the pull-out enrichment and special gifted class. In the years afterwards, we had to choose between public and private education twice. In my mind, the intensity of the small class and acceleration finally nurtured your habit of learning.

Getting you identified as gifted was the biggest battle with the system in the life of your parents. We achieved the goal of providing the Canadian in our family with what he deserved. However, to voice one's differences is a lifelong experiment for us immigrant. Among educated adults, such as in the working environment, it is a part of the soft skill set.

Teenage Years

From Road College to Colonel By Secondary School, you started as a homebound boy and grew into a relatively independent young man. It was hard for you sometimes. Instead of spending two years in grades seven and eight in Kanata, you were on the bus to Road College. It was a step towards Colonel By, which was a very good school environment to get you ready for the independence of university life.

Public Transit

Road College was set up in the hall and some rooms of the All-Saints Anglican Church of Sandy Hill at 317 Chapel Street. It was safely in the vicinity area of the University of Ottawa.

The closest bus stop for the express bus between Ottawa and Kanata was at the intersection of McCurdy Drive and Maple Grove Street, less than a five-minute walk from our house. The express bus goes to downtown Ottawa in the mornings and reverses in the afternoons. In the morning, its last stop in Kanata is at the bus transit on Eagleson Street. Therefore, the backup plan was to drive you to the bus transit if you missed the express when it came near home. Once out of Kanata, the bus made a few stops before it reached downtown. One of its stops near the university was across the street from a local bus stop at the intersection of Nicholas Street and Laurier Avenue. Two stops on the local bus take you to the school at 317 Chapel. It was relatively straightforward, provided both buses and you were punctual enough for you to make the transfer. The frequency of the buses in Ottawa was only a fraction of that in Toronto. In the afternoon, the express bus went in the opposite direction to bring people working downtown back home. You took the local bus first and then the express to go back to Kanata.

You got your first cell phone. I asked the school for a letter about your need to take public transportation. We went to the big bus transit in Lincoln Field and bought you the student bus pass. Before school started, we did a test run, which was the first time on public transit for both of us. We collected bus schedules after we noticed each bus carried its latest schedule. We noticed the local bus on Laurier was going in a loop with different routes in different directions at different time periods. The actual stops on Chapel and Laurier at different times became a question for you to sort out once the fall bus schedule started. Back at home, I learned to check updates on the bus schedules on the website of OC Transpo. My busing coworkers told me that the arrival time of the next bus could be checked by phone. You used your cellphone and made a call for the time of the next bus. I was glad that the school year started in the fall instead of winter.

On the first school day, I took time off to accompany you on the bus to school. On my way back, I skipped the local bus and walked the distance from the school to the express bus stop. It was about ten minutes. I took the normal bus back to Kanata. Walking home from the local bus stop was a lot longer than five minutes. It was late in the morning by the time I arrived at work.

To ensure your safety, you would call me three times every day. Your first call was when you arrived at school in the morning; the second call was after you got on the express bus after school in the afternoon; the third call was after you reached home. Your calls usually came as expected, although my call reached you first a few times when you were waiting for the bus. My coworkers were amazed by the details of the arrangement between a mother and her twelve-year-old son.

Ying or I walked you to the express bus stop every morning. You were cautious and probably scared a bit at the beginning, but the daily trips back and forth were uneventful. You told me once that the driver on the express bus stared at you and probably thought you were underage. I agreed because you were barely twelve years old then. You were punctual throughout the year. To reach the school on time, you walked the distance from Nicholas to Chapel along Laurier a few times when the express bus was delayed, and the right local bus was gone. On the way back home after school, you figured out that there were two buses, both having different routes at different times. You walked with the heavy school bag quite a few times to catch the express bus to Kanata on time. You told me you often walked with your schoolmates. The stop of the express bus coming back to Kanata was closer to home, but across the street. You were confident of crossing the street safely by then because of your years of experience on the school bus.

Road College

Road College only existed in Ottawa for less than five years. Major factors that could have contributed to its short lifespan include its unique education program and lack of primary grades. All the teachers at the school had at one time belonged to the public-school board. They worked together because of their determination to accomplish more than the content that was offered by the normal school system.

The school had close to ten students with diverse backgrounds. There were two other students in grades seven and eight. One of them, Tristan, came from the States and had been identified as gifted. He came to Road College because he could not get the equivalent at the public schools. He was in grade eight and looked more mature than you. The other one was from the embassy of a Middle Eastern country. He was catching up with the content in grades six and seven, since he had a different school system back in his home country. He had a bodyguard and was chauffeured to and from school every day. The other students, including a girl, were of high-school grades. Because the school used space in the church, the last task of a school day was to rearrange the desks and chairs to set the place ready for its next function.

Your learning at the school started with Grade Eight English and French and Grade Nine math. The feedback from the principal was positive when I asked at the end of September. The math teacher was the one who brought the Math Kangaroo program from Eastern European countries to Canada. She was promoting the program at the time and, therefore, she fully understood what content you would need to learn math. The school required a minimum of one and a half hours of homework time every night. I don't recall you ever needing an hour and a half. You still had plenty of time for games and other readings. There were a few times when you ran off to catch the bus after school, forgetting to tidy up the room. It led to an extra assignment as punishment, such as copying the school rules or something similar. The consequence was more constructive than a detention or a note to the parents. I could feel that you fully accepted the unique school style and that you were trying hard.

This was the time you started carrying your bag into your room after you got home and to work independently. The quality of your work improved under close supervision in the small group instructions. You always packed the bag for the next day before you went to bed. It was a very good habit from your time at Road College. I asked about your day at school from time to time, and your answer was always fine. I was informed about all the school activities from the principal's weekly letters. Her letters contained a lot of details about the school and extra activities of the passing week, as well as those planned for the coming week. Unavoidably, quite a few activities required additional fees and parent response.

The bedtime was strictly observed because you had to catch the express bus at 7:30. Once in a while, you would jump into my bed on your way to your shower before bed and say, "Do I have to go to school tomorrow?" Or when I woke you up in the morning "Do I have to go to school today?" My answer was always a simple "You do" and followed by an "OK" from you. The journey to school continued. Your school was no longer just classes and textbooks. It included catching the bus, building close relationships with a few peers, and properly talking to different teachers. It was the norm of the family, where the parents went to work and the child went to school every day.

Handle Defeat

Being in an unlocked building, the school lost things from time to time. In early October, the main classroom was vandalized. Your brand-new school bag with its contents was stolen while other students lost one or two items. When I picked you up from school, you were quiet. The bus pass, cell phone, and Walkman became your new favorite items, introducing you to a new level of responsibility as symbols of growing up. You were very proud of having them. I could imagine that you packed your bag neatly so that you could run out to catch the bus after school. Unfortunately, the thief thought it was a nice bag with nice things in it. You have been very good at taking care of your own belongings since you were a baby. I remember you in a stroller, holding a baby spoon when we shopped in the big-box stores. You never let it go. You probably never thought you would lose anything. The feeling of defeat could be more damaging than the missing school bag. The thought almost brought me to tears.

My focus was to get you ready for school the next day. We quickly assessed the damage and determined what needed to be replaced immediately. I canceled your cell phone service. We went around and bought a new school bag, a cell phone, and some school supplies. We replaced your bus pass at no charge because I had bought the pass that included one replacement. After we got home, I asked you to write a list of missing items, including the progress of schoolwork that was also missing. The list included the textbooks, your wallet, the Walkman, your lunchbox, and the house keys. To be on the safe side, Ying and I discussed and arranged changing the house keys as soon as possible. After you left for school the next morning, I wrote the principal a letter providing the list and asking if the disruption of your schoolwork could be minimal. Her response was very positive and helpful. The teachers would manage the missing textbooks, and you would have new binders filled with what you need. Life was back to normal after two days. The bag was never found. Your wallet, which was emptied, was found in a ditch near the school after a few days.

The school improved its strategy to protect the students after the incident. Students were assigned locker-type cabinets to keep their own stuff. You kept your belongings well despite frequent outings and several trips throughout the school year.

Knowledge and Exposures

A major part of the schooling at Road College was outings, which I think was very impressive. The teachers, especially the principal, worked hard to introduce the students to their social environment. She intended to fill the days with what she had missed when being home-schooled and what she could not do while teaching at a public school.

In the year you were there, there were two-day seminars

— one on conflict resolution and the other on negotiation skills. The students attended and were later certified in an Ambulance First Aid Course. In the music workshop, every student composed and played a song. In an etiquette course, the students learned table manners at an upscale restaurant. The course also covered interview skills. Among the outings, the students visited a nearby retirement residence, as well as all the major museums in Ottawa. For physical education, the students went to the gym and playground nearby. The winter sport was badminton, which became your favorite and continued as a hobby. In the fall, the parents were asked to ship the bicycles to school, and the students had a few bicycle rides.

The biggest activities were the excursions, of which I really appreciated the effort the teachers put in before and during the trip. At the end of September, the students traveled to the Stratford Shakespeare Festival for a culture excursion. To learn classic English, the school attended three plays at the festival. Another goal of the trip was to build bonds between teachers and the students, as well as bonds among the students. It was well planned, and after-class activities included discussions, card games, and dart throwing at night. Arrangement with the chocolate factory and the theaters of the Stratford Festival made the trip very smooth and full of content.

The leadership camp at the MacSkimming Outdoor Education Center happened at the end of October. The group spent more time onsite instead of traveling. Besides a lot of hikes, the students learned how to use a compass and "rescued" Monsieur from the woods. They also prepared meals, set and cleared the table, and cleaned dishes and the surroundings up to the standard of living in the wilderness. The loveliest scene was the campfire which our family had never had during our few camping experiences. "James with his witty observations, James jumping up and down waving his arms to ask a question, James's dancing in front of the campfire!" These are the original lines from the principal's letter.

Before the Christmas break, the school prepared a play and invited the parents. You were the narrator in the play, and the play was on the stage of the church, almost professional. In the spring term, you started studying the third language — Spanish. Students were quite used to eating out for lunch out, visiting museums, and attending seminars. Compared to a few months before, you became more independent in your work and relatively organized. In terms of your grade level, you were ready for the end of junior high. While studying the content of combined grades seven and eight or even higher, you spent the year filled with other social and skill learning.

When I was volunteering at ABC, I introduced Road College to ABC. The principal of the school was an ABC speaker in the spring. Although most parents expected the public school system to do the right thing, her speech was interesting and raised a lot of questions.

Ready for High School

As she had promised, the principal of the Road College sent your student report to the public-school board. She let you take the entrance exam for the International Baccalaureate (IB) program offered by Colonel By Secondary School. You were accepted. Before the start of summer, I called the IB director of Colonel By, explaining your junior high education and asking if you need to do any catch-up courses. He checked your test results, and told me, "No, I don't think so. He scored above 98 percent in the exams." This completed your journey outside the public school system. Your qualification for the IB program avoided any objections to your acceleration into grade nine.

The summer of 2005 was relaxing. You were in the camps of Soong's badminton school for two weeks. The IB program requires 120 volunteering hours to develop creativity, activity, and service. I contacted the Chartwell Empress Kanata Retirement Residence for any volunteer opportunity. The retirement center is safely within the residential area along Katimavik Road. Because you were underage, you could only volunteer without earning credit. However, it was a friendly environment to have a head start. When I took you there on the first day, I told you that you would see people needing help and that you were growing up and should learn to pay attention to others. You were assigned to read the newspaper or play card games with the residents there. Later, you were "promoted" to set the breakfast table or help to serve breakfast. You were enthusiastic, although you needed to get up early sometimes. You got along well with the people there. At the end of the summer, they gave you a send-off party, and you came home with a big Thank-You card and some small gifts. That was a rare opportunity because security or criminal checks were soon added to the process of working at any volunteer positions.

In the summer, we practiced the bus route to Colonel By. It

was still the same morning and afternoon express bus route, but the journey was all the way to the east end — Blair station. We then took a local bus at the same bus terminal to school. The time each way is an hour and a half. I felt it was a little cruel for a child to spend three hours on the road to school every day. You did not complain because Colonel By would be another new adventure, a good choice for the high school in town. Without the year on the bus for Road College, it could be even harder for you to get used to the long bus ride.

Colonel By Secondary School

The Colonel By Secondary School offered the only IB program of the public-school board from 1997 to 2019. The school is near the residential area of Gloucester. Many of the students are from Orleans, and students in the IB program come from all places in Ottawa, such as Barrhaven, Central Point, and Kanata. Compared to other high schools nearby, the school has a very good academic atmosphere and good music groups and sports teams. There were no students smoking around the campus during recess, and not a lot of students walking out to malls during lunch breaks.

In the afternoon, the buses of OC Transpo come to school to pick up students at the end of the school day. Sometimes in the morning, a bus goes to school to deliver if most passengers are students. In the four years you were there, the worst was when OC Transpo went on strike. We found the second family in Kanata with a child going to Colonel By, and carpooled. The father was a very skillful driver and delivered you on time every morning. I did the pickup in the afternoon. The streets near the school were packed with cars. To be on the safe side, I always parked my car and went to the school to pick you up. Occasionally, we had other riders. Many times, on my way back, I had to try a different route, hoping it would have less traffic during the rush hour to get you to your lesson or training on time.

The school has a cafeteria that mainly provides lunch and breakfast. The cafeteria even lets the students use microwave ovens. At first, it was really a treat for students who went through years of elementary and junior high with packed lunches. You were excited and had a few pleasant lunches with peers, and lunching together was fun. However, there were more and more club and team activities during lunch break once school started. You asked me to pack a lunch for you because you would not have time to enjoy lunch anymore. In contrast to your laid-back attitude, you put your name down for a few clubs and teams. Badminton was a seasonal sport at school, and you really looked forward to qualifying for the school team.

High school obviously had more fun and freedom to a certain degree. Shortly after school started, you brought home a certificate that showed you were #1 in staying on the wall. The certificate was from a peculiar competition during the lunch break. The lightest students were selected and taped to the wall. Being probably the smallest and lightest among the new students, you volunteered. You stayed for the longest time before the tape became loose. You had fun and got attention from some big brothers. It was a silly thing that had the flavor of the activities in the college frosh week. You told me that the end of the school year could be fun, too. In the days before graduation, the school allows the senior students to play a trick. One year, the graduating seniors brought three piglets and marked them with numbers 1, 2, and 4. The entire school spent a long time looking for the Number 3 piglet.

IB Program

The IB program was challenging. As usual, you were not interested in being the best and therefore, your life balanced out all right. You told me once that the number of gray hairs was proportional to the marks of a student. Obviously, some of your peers were working extremely hard, leading to the interesting conclusion about gray hairs. Other than the few nights when you needed to finish a project, your bedtime was kept at around 11:00 pm.

In your first year at Colonel By, Ying and I were worried that you were young and might get sick in the winter cold. For the second term of grade nine, we rented an apartment unit, which is about a five-minute walk from the school. We could see the campus from our apartment. I stayed with you in the apartment most of the time. In the morning, you walked to school. I drove across the city to Kanata for work. On the days without after-school activity, you walked home. It was relaxing in the apartment. You were focused on your schoolwork or other readings, and I, hopefully, arrived home before dark and made simple dishes for a dinner of two. Without a TV at home, both of us did a lot of reading those days. It did not take long for me to realize that driving on Highway 407 at a speed over 120 km/h is a waste of gas, especially in the winter months. I also learned to park my car facing south with windshield wiper up in the parking lots. As I noticed later, several other families bought or rented space near the school because of children in the IB program.

In the final two years of the IB program, my signature on your schoolwork was no longer required. The only help I could offer was to run off to get the paper and other supplies for your projects when needed. I would ask you about the book assignments and French class. However, I believed you were getting more and more from your teachers and peers. What was more important was that you got the spirit of the school. Ying would ask about your math and physics from time to time. He prepared pages of diagrams and practice problems to help you when you were learning geometry.

Besides the report card, the teacher-parent interview on the PD days was a very good setup by the school. In grade nine, we were informed about the homeroom of the student and were given a brief speech by the homeroom teacher. Some teachers had welcome sessions at a fixed time. Many teachers had booths in the auditorium for visitors. The school made sure that the teachers of all subjects were available when the parents of certain grades came to school. Both Ying and I tried to attend the events on a PD Day each time. We might have missed some speeches, but we always went to the auditorium and stood in line to meet the teachers. Over the years, your math teacher (Mr. Whitlock) and chemistry teacher (Mrs. Pall) appreciated your wit and potential. Mr. Whitlock was the sponsor of your magic club. Mrs. Pall liked you showing her tricks and commented that you were calm and never panicked, ready to handle everything. In return, I felt her dedication to her profession and her love and excitement with the youths. Your French teacher in the last two years was very helpful, and she set up a time window outside her classes for any student to practice French with her.

I still heard complaints about your discipline problems (now at a high level). The technology teacher was old-fashioned; he did not like students doing anything other than completing the work and sitting quietly in the room. He asked you to go around helping others if you finished your assignment. You did, but once or twice you were in your Heelys roller shoes. He was firmly against wearing those on campus. Your social science teacher gave you the worst mark in his class. When I asked, he said that the class was graded based on class behavior. You could not stay steady for the entire class period, and sometimes you spread cards on the desk before the end of the class. Those two subjects were short courses, each lasting for only a term or a year. Therefore, any discussion after the teacher-parent interviews did not improve your marks. Regardless, I warned you that your cards should only be out outside of class. It took a long time (four years) for you to grow into a young man with a somewhat academic mind.

As it is said, the IB program is a well-rounded program. Besides IB courses, the volunteering requirement encourages new ideas, organizational skills, and teamwork. I really appreciated it. You were canvassing with others after school and looked for ideas with me to fulfill the requirement. The short music courses, volunteering at ABC and other places, eventually filled up and exceeded the required 120 hours.

Routine of the Family

After Ying came back to work in town, a routine on weekdays was formed for the family of three. I usually left home early and came back early. Ying worked in Nepean or Ottawa downtown, and he went to work after 8 am and came back home during flexible hours to avoid traffic. My activities after work and before dinner often involved picking you up and taking you to extracurricular activities. The express from downtown was not always on time. You were not always on the express because of your activities. Our cellphone communication was well used and my calculations on your arrival were correct most of the time.

For picking you up on the roadside, I became pretty good at parallel parking for a while. I went to pick you up near Kanata town center once because the bus changed routes. It was raining. You were already off the bus at the stop along Katimavik. You saw me and started running towards me with your little umbrella. I remembered that big smile under the swinging little umbrella for a long time. Many times, I picked you up at the corner of Castlefrank and McCurdy because you took the regular bus instead the express. A few times, you got off the bus at the other end of McCurdy and took a shortcut to walk home. I found you in the little forest on the side of Castlefrank. It was a pleasant surprise for you and a relief for me on the dark and cold winter evening. Still, you were calm and told me you could wake up as soon as the Kanata-bound bus made its turn after getting off the highway. After the transit station at Centrum was completed, I went there to deliver and pick you up many times because of the bus schedule.

The kitchen in our house had a dining area with a glass door leading to the deck. We always had dinner in the kitchen when there were no guests. For many years, you ate from your own plate with a fork, spoon, and maybe a knife. Ying and I were in the Chinese style with chopsticks, making trips between the dishes and our own rice bowl. It wasn't my intention to train you in western style. The main reason was that you were never keen on Chinese greens and well-cooked brown meats soaked in Chinese sauce. To provide you with food from different groups, I prepared your plate and asked you to finish the food on it. Your nephew stayed with us for three months when he immigrated to Canada. He improved your skills in using chopsticks and trained you to share a bowl of instant noodles with him. To my surprise, you didn't mind.

Your plate was always clearly divided into several portions. The content was nutritious and tasty to your/my standard. The portion of the meat could be chicken or fish strips, sometimes a piece of steak. Options for veggies were corn, carrots, or broccoli. The starchy portion included macaroni, rice, or potatoes. You finished your plate properly more than half of the time. Occasionally, I made spaghetti or potato soup so the whole family could have the same dinner. Ying's comment on dishes like spaghetti was usually, "I like it once in a while." You were the only one to have a glass of milk next to your plate on the dinner table. Like every other family in town, we had a large BBQ on the deck. Barbecued mild Italian sausages, chicken or steak were alternatives to the meats for the family in the summer. Later, we added small and finer grills for fish fillet and rotisserie vegetables.

I made your dinner plate after I finished cooking. Once the dinner was set, I called you and Ying. You usually rushed down from your bedroom upstairs. Ying came at his own pace because he might be in the middle of writing an email. You finished your plate quickly without paying attention to the other dishes on the table unless I added something to your plate. Many times, by the time Ying came to the table, you had put your plate and silverware in the sink and were in the rush to go back upstairs. I don't remember we discussed much about your school days at the dinner table. Only Ying and I sat at the table, catching up with what happened in our days. Ying did the dishes most of the time. He taught you how to wash dishes. He paid you a few coins if he asked you to clean all the dishes or take out the trash.

Ying took his nap after dinner. Later in the evening, I got the fruit ready, and either called you down or took the plate upstairs. I often knocked on your door and sent in the plate, while having a peek at your work. Sometimes, a piece of the test required a parent's signature. We looked through the pages together to go over what you had missed in the test, just to make sure that you knew the correct answer. My comments could be a little harsh if we agreed that your carelessness was the key problem. My opinion was that you were still aligned with the class if your mark was around 90 and the errors were understood after a test. You were probably lost in the course if your mark dropped to around 80. I discussed my opinion with you quite a few times. I expected you would try to get good marks in the courses you liked while passing everyone. It was quiet in our house during those hours. I went back online to work or watched TV for the rest of the evening. Once you had completed your homework and packed your bag for the next day, you came down to the big room above the garage where you had all your game gear. It was sometimes my job to remind you to end the game and go to bed.

For a short while after you started high school, you were still working on the last part of the Kumon Math assignments. The content already extended to Calculus, including flavors of different coordinate systems. Ying, after his nap, would check on you, and if you were available, work with you on the logic and transformations. The pressure in the house was high quite a few times. Kumon gave you the same sets repeatedly until you could do the set without errors. Ying was frustrated because he had patiently explained the same problem multiple times. Your understanding obviously was not improving. I was glad that it was over after you passed the last exam.

Choice of University

You grew physically and mentally over the last two years, which was the real IB program. Playing on the school badminton team, you gained team spirit. You had your own magic club that was sponsored by your math teacher. Without my close supervision, your GPA was well above 90 percent in your senior year, suggesting that you were finally aligned with the academic content.

It was time to set up your path for college study. You selected your major before going off to a university, although it took years of decision-making. Early on, because your friend Shelina set her mind on medicine since elementary school, medicine was the first thing on your mind. We had a paperback copy of the complete medical encyclopedia from one of the medical societies. It was about three inches thick. You told me once that you would like to read about medicine on the bus if I could split the book into three. I did some cutting and sewing. You read the books and finished, although I warned you not to read when the light was dim. The knowledge led to your decision not to become a doctor. When Mr. Whitlock was your math teacher, you told me that being a high school math teacher was a wonderful goal. Based on my experience in teaching and training, I commented that the nature of the job is quite repetitive. The job requires a love for interacting with others, especially children. Eventually, you settled on chemistry, possibly encouraged by Mrs. Pall, your chemistry teacher. Ying's father was in math all his life, and Ying was in physics. He thought you chose chemistry to avoid any connections. After you picked chemistry, branches of material science or engineering, I believed, might be practical. It would be complementary to the fast development of the telecommunication industry.

I pushed you to take the SAT and thought you might apply to Cornell University. Working for Corning, one of the best places for research on materials, would open a new world for you to explore. However, the sentiment in the family that year was anti-America. To check on Canadian universities, I took you on a tour of McGill University in Montreal during its open house. We visited the department buildings and the dorms. It was a beautiful campus on a slope almost in downtown Montreal. On the way back, you simply said that it is too French. The Department of Materials Science and Engineering at U of T invited you for an interview and lunch. You attended and had lunch but did not accept their offer. I guess that by that time you had already made your decision based on plenty of discussions with your friends. Your choice was to go to Waterloo with a few of your peers. You also chose Co-op Chemical Engineering. It turned out to be an excellent decision.

Girlfriend

News about your girlfriend came from my coworker. She stopped me in the hallway at work and asked about you. Her daughter was your age and was a grade behind you at Colonel By. Her close friend probably became your first girlfriend. The girls came from a French Immersion background and, therefore, were in the same French class with you. My coworker said that you and the girl were often seen at the bus stop, which was on the way to the girl's home. Obviously, it was known at school that you two were together. I asked you about it and you acknowledged it.

I never saw the two of you together sometimes when picking you up from school. After a while, you went out with her to a movie in the evening. I asked you not to turn off your phone so that I could reach you. I called you before the start time of the movies in the evening, just to check which movie you were going to and how long the movie was. Yes, your phone was on, but you were not answering. I felt tricked. As usual, you called me after the movie for a pickup. I went to the movie theater, noticing that the girl was still there. I could have said hi if I had been in a better mood. You told me that her parents were coming, and we left the girl there. For the first and the only time in all your school years, I grounded you for a month. You did not protest because you knew what you had done. On the last day of the month, you confirmed with me promptly that you could go out again with her or other friends.

During the following Christmas break, we were on the Pride of America cruise in Hawaii. Before the end of the trip, you told us that the girl invited you to a church retreat for the weekend after our trip. There wasn't any requirement for parental permission since you had already accepted her invitation. I asked a few questions, but you didn't know if her family would go or what a retreat was. This really sounded like the first experience of spending a night together with the girl. Ying and I were concerned. Upon returning home, we communicated with the other family and received some simple answers. You got in the car of the girl's family with your backpack and sleeping bag. You returned on Sunday afternoon and told us about the activities at the retreat. It was an enjoyable experience.

After you started college, I was updated by my coworker about the girl. She left the IB program and transferred to a different school to finish her last year of high school after you left Colonel By.

Friends of Colonel By

It did not take long for you to make some friends. In your IB classes, most of the students were high achievers. Some of them were from Chinese families that immigrated to Canada from different parts of China, even the rest of the world. You heard them speaking Cantonese interchangeably with English among themselves. Some of them spoke Mandarin. You asked me why you could not speak Mandarin well. I told you we gave up because you were not interested in going to the weekend Chinese school. You said that I should have forced you. After the Chinese nannies in your toddler years, there wasn't a time in our house when you had to speak Chinese. In contrast, many of your friends grew up in larger families, including grandparents, who preferred their first language. We had you in our forties, and you never lived with your grandparents other than for a few visits.

Some other students in the IB program were from families that were originally from Eastern European and other Asian countries. School buddies and small gatherings often had the flavors of diversity. Regardless, students were relatively open to different cultures. When going home after school, a lot of students took the same local bus to the Rideau Centre and then went on different buses to go home. You got your shopping experience from your peers wandering around the shopping center. Once you bought a T-shirt and a pair of shorts, neither of which really fit. It turned out that you wandered into a store where one of you was working, so everybody bought something from the store. This was your first-time buying clothes yourself. To give you an orientation on shopping for clothes, I took you to the Bayshore Shopping Center on the weekend. We toured Gap, Bay, and Old Navy, whose products were popular among students or their parents. I gave you a lesson on the male and female sections and different sizes. After a few years, you and I went to explore the outlet mall in Los Angeles during your first year of university. You were a veteran in shopping for your own clothes by then and superseded me on named brands.

My GPS became handy during the years you were at Colonel By. You were invited to quite a few birthday parties or Christmas celebrations by the families, most of which were in Orleans. At the Christmas party of one of your friends, I learned from the host that Hanukkah is the day Santa Claus starts his yearly journey from the North Pole. One time, I had to warn you about playing mahjong after I picked you up twice from the mahjong table of a family. When the snowbank was higher than halfway up the stop sign, driving on the non-major roads in the residential area could be tricky. There were a few times when the GPS brought me to the back of the house, or the GPS did not even have the address. I thanked my independence and driving skill built up in my days of field work deploying seismometers.

In my mind, people in Orleans were less techie like us in Kanata because a lot of them worked for the government, while we worked in industries. Pretty soon, you were used to more hugs (and even kisses). We were surprised by the closeness at first when you met your schoolmates in the restaurant where we were dining with our friends. The birthday present became more practical for the high school students. You sometimes put in your share for a relatively expensive piece that the birthday boy wished to have. At the end of your high school, your friends, IB or not, had a party for you at the Rideau Centre and took you shopping around. The reason was that you were at their birthday parties over the years, but you never had a birthday party yourself to receive gifts. You came home with some money and gifts that day, and I was moved. I asked you to remember to treat your friends at least to lunch in the mall whenever you gather again.

Your high school friends kept in touch for many years. Throughout the college years, gatherings were arranged whenever people were back in Ottawa. I offered our home for a gathering. But most of them happened in Orleans or in the center of the city. You often took a bus to the gathering yourself. Once or twice, you drove to Orleans. You had two close friends, Kenji and Susan. Kenji was a quarter Japanese, and you occasionally spent the night at his home when the gathering ended late in Orleans. He introduced you to systematic gym exercises. He studied nanotechnology at Waterloo and later went to Japan for graduate study. Susan was from China. Among the Colonel By IB students, she was one of the few who worked part time during her high school years. She studied accounting in Waterloo. The two of you were shopping and experiencing off-campus life during the spring term of your first co-op. She was like an older sister to you while you had a girlfriend. After you got your car, the three of you rode together between Waterloo and Ottawa. Kenji married a Japanese girl who was a distant relative. Susan married one of her classmates, I believe. You and your girlfriend were at their weddings.

Years went by. You grew into a young man who preferred discussion among your peers. Instead of being supportive and providing guidance, we, your parents, were only informed of your big decisions. I still had in my mind the picture of your big smile under the swinging little umbrella when I was fully trustworthy. Think back, we, a family of full-time workers and a student, never learned to have family meetings, not even the proper dinner table conversation.

Away from Home

You left home for university. It seems children who leave home for college education mostly settle elsewhere instead of coming back. Among our friends in Ottawa, most of their children settled in Toronto. Academically, you studied and worked very hard in the co-op program. However, postgraduate study did not happen because it was neither a part of your plan before Waterloo, nor a likely creation out of your busy life of study and co-op terms. You were mentally ready to earn money and become independent by the time you graduated with your bachelor's degree.

Ready for University

In the summer before you started at the University of Waterloo, we went to the traditional Open House of the school for new students. It was our first trip between Kanata and Waterloo because we did not visit it during the decision-making cycle in the previous year. We drove around and all of us got a first look at the school. The school covers a large area, but it is a kind of plain. It does not have lakes and city streets going through the campus like the University of Wisconsin-Madison; it does not have the huge downtown area surrounding it like the University of Toronto. The dormitory buildings are decent. However, you were assigned to the Ron Eydt Village, which is in the cluster located farthest from the department buildings. The campus is large, implying a lot of walking. Several cafeterias are located and shared among the dorms. There is a student center with shops to buy books and daily supplies. A large part of the campus was filled with buildings of different departments. We found one library, and I hoped that this was not the only one on campus. We explored the student center to find out where to buy textbooks and other supplies. The auditorium next to it was where the Open House was.

I vividly remember the key points in the speech given by the vice chancellor. It is the only time parents are invited to school until the graduation of their children. Do not call the school to discuss your child, but ask your child to look for help instead, if needed. Stop helping your child with the schoolwork if you did so when he was in high school. Your child may be a straight-A student in high school, but he should expect to receive A, B, or even lower grades. Therefore, neither your child nor the parents should be surprised. Leave your child with the university for them to figure out their future and how to be independent. I felt the sense of reaching a milestone, although you were relatively independent already. Besides, ten or fifteen of you from the Colonel By IB program were going there.

The end of the summer had quite a few goodbye parties. You told me that one of the computer science majors was already working in Waterloo. I ordered a laptop of your choice. I also shopped around for things like bed covers and a laundry bag for dorm life. You did not want a personal refrigerator because you preferred a simple life and were confident that you would like the cafeteria food. President's Choice had a branch office at the student center in Waterloo. You and I went to its booth inside Loblaws and set up a co-owned account, and you got your first credit card. The fees, which included the tuition, room, and board, were a direct transaction from my bank account.

The student card had functions on campus and could also be used for public transportation, going to many other places around the town. Therefore, your credit card was really your pocket money. I switched your cell phone service to Koodo because it had a good deal in Waterloo. It is crucial to have a good cellphone since the landline was not available by default in the dorm. The cellphone package was soon extended to include unlimited messages after I noticed the number of your messages was in the thousands.

Ying and I traveled to Waterloo with you and your packed luggage before the beginning of the frosh week. We were required to arrive within a fixed time window so that the traffic in front of the dorms could be managed. Your dorm room was simple, with a good bed, desk, and chair. Your roommate was from Brampton. The dorm was co-ed, and the co-ed arrangement even applied to your floor, e.g., your room was a few doors from a girls' room. We met the floor master, who was a junior year student. He emphasized the study environment but also mentioned the occasional floor or building parties of boys and girls. There were several large study areas on the first floor of the dorm. While moving you in, we passed the girls' section and noticed that the girls had a lot more stuff, and a few rooms were already well-decorated. We walked to Village 1, where the nearest cafeteria was located. We also found where to do laundry, and I reminded you again that the pillowcase and towel must be washed every time to avoid eye infections. Before driving back to Kanata, we drove to the strip mall close by. It had quite a variety of dining choices besides popular fast-food places. As usual, we tried Chinese food. The price was reasonable, and the wait was acceptable. Ying and I were on our way soon after dropping you off in front of the dorm. We felt a sense of accomplishment, although we were not cheering like the empty-nest parents in the TV commercials.

Parents of a University Student

For the first two years, relatively frequent trips to Waterloo were necessary. Checking out and in of the dorm at a certain time must be strictly followed. Before the first summer, we bought a mattress and spring box set for you to live off-campus. Over the first three years, several trips were made to move you in and out of different rental locations in Waterloo or co-op locations in different cities. It took a bit of experimenting to figure out the best way and the best time for the trip. It is a five-to-seven-hour drive, depending on the traffic. Gradually, we learned to avoid rush hours when driving across Toronto. In addition, the stretch from Toronto to the Cambridge-Kitchener-Waterloo area could also be congested. The routine Ying and I worked out was to leave Kanata early, get off Highway 401 to have a dim sum lunch on Shepherd Avenue in Scarborough. We then went back on Highway 401 in the early afternoon and stayed in the first left lane of the express, or the normal highway, until the exit for Waterloo. On our way back, we usually spent the night in Toronto to have lunch with friends or relatives. After lunch, we shopped for Chinese groceries and then spent the afternoon on our way back to Ottawa.

It was a new style of communication — one-way follow-ups with a university student. Later, whenever I was asked by the coworkers when their child started university, my advice was to have a backup among his or her friends. Obviously, I had learned my lesson. I could have paired you up with one of your Colonel By friends. In that way, there would be less anxiety, which turned out to be unnecessary most of the time. We agreed you would call home every other week. You promised, but it really didn't matter. When the time came, it was the parent making many calls to check if the child was fine. In 90 percent of cases, the child was fine. When you finally picked up, the tension could be high. You were out; the phone was muted when you were in the library; it was too noisy. Maybe the string attached was an embarrassment in front of your peers or just a noise from which you could not get any help you wanted.

You let me know a few times when you left the phone in the office during your co-op terms. I really appreciated your notice, thinking you were finally growing up. Your phone was broken once or twice, and you made good choices for the replacement. The only times you called were to ask for post-date cheques and sponsor signatures. Otherwise, as your mother was always thinking ahead of you, trips, your bank account, or RESP were arranged. I called and gave you the instructions. It took a long time for me to realize that all these were a new list of changing chores when you left home and became a university student. From a baby to a teenager, Ying and I raised you as a worry-free child, other than asking you to be a decent student. I don't know when or if you ever noticed the list of chores for you when you were away from home. The first item on your list should be "call home".

Financially, the first year was expensive. The bill included the tuition and fees for the two full terms. You were awarded a scholarship from the university, but you were too young to use your RESP. The tuition for Waterloo engineering majors was one of the highest in Canada. However, we were ready for the cost because our mortgage on the house or a car was paid off by then. After the first year, what we needed to pay in the summer and the following years was much less. It was paid partially by your RESP and your co-op term every year. In summary, the cost of your university education was a lot less than those who went to universities without a systematic co-op program.

During the few times you were home, you were more open to discussions about knowledge and opinions. Ying was impressed. However, like your very good appetite right after you came home, your enthusiasm in conversation at the dinner table would die down after a few days. You stayed in your own room most of the time to work on your schoolwork or to play computer games. You also had many gatherings with your Colonel By friends. Most of them were doing fine at school. A few of them got the IB credit from their universities, moving on quickly to postgraduate degrees. Ying and I also organized some gatherings with our friends for holidays. You were the oldest among the children, and they often asked college questions at the dinner table or during game time.

Ying was away in China during one of your visits in the

summer. You volunteered to clean up after dinner. You washed dishes, pots, and pans, and tidied up the countertop. I took you out for your birthday. We went to Best Buy for a birthday present after having steak and sweet potato fries at Montana's. You walked around and around. Eventually, you picked up a $15 MP3 player, which was all you wanted and far below my expectations. I felt you had really grown up. The life of a university student was practical and sufficient. Like your school bag in those years, it contained cushioned sections for a laptop and at least two pouches, one for the cell phone and the other with a hole for the MP3 player. The design was practical and sufficient.

Learning at the School

With alternating school and co-op terms, the University of Waterloo has a school calendar that differs from other universities. An academic year contains fall, winter and spring terms, each of which is close to four months. The only vacation is the Christmas holiday, which closes the school from Christmas to New Year. It often aligns with the Christmas shutdown at some companies that have multiple branches at different places across the world. For you, a student, the additional days to extend the Christmas break between the two terms depend on the time of your last exam and when your co-op job starts. It takes five years to complete the bachelor's degree in the co-op engineering program, which requires a minimum of four work terms. It is a non-stop, five-year program for a young man to grow.

The degree program with co-op had a fixed course distribution, as you showed us at the beginning of the first year. The courses of your major were not offered every term, and therefore, you would be a year behind if you needed to repeat a course. Along the same line, there was little flexibility in taking any required courses in your supposed work term if you had opted out of a co-op term. The school and work terms alternated after the winter term of the first year. It meant that during the school term, a student studied the courses, while looking for and interviewing for a job. Once his job was settled, he needed to look for a rental for his co-op and to sublet his current space at school. Thanks to various pools for jobs and rentals available to the students, you found a job and arranged changes in your life for every work term. Occasionally, we were asked to issue postdated checks to your landlords and move you around. However, there were parents who had to check rentals in Toronto or look for co-op opportunities for their child. It was a long training to become a professional. The goal was to pass each course, get a job, and plan and manage your everyday life. You survived and, in addition, you were good enough to have some fun and make new friends.

As said by the chancellor, your grades were not great, so I soon stopped asking about them. However, you passed every course and even had a full load of courses most of the time to take some electives in business and psychology. On your visits, we had a few conversations about the subjects you took. On the calls, you sometimes told me that a course was hard, but you always had some plans to improve. My warning was that a potential C was bad because you were probably lost. In your major courses, poor performance may lead to potential challenges ahead because your professional skill set is on the line. You understood the consequence. You were doing fine with your survival skills from Colonel By.

Information about your life on campus was sparse from our short phone conversations. The dorm had a large separate space for students to study quietly. Otherwise, dorm life, especially the activities on the weekends, was exciting and good social occasions for everybody. You played the piano downstairs a few times. The food in the cafeteria was fine. In the strip mall within walking distance, you found your favorite dish among the Chinese eateries — a bowl of beef noodle. You went out with friends to try Indian food. To keep fit, you played badminton, and the school had several gyms for all indoor exercises. Other activities included your participation in the magic club at the university. There were career-related training courses to attend.

Your school term was busy. The first half was spent learning the courses, and the second half included rounds of interviews for the next co-op job. We were happy that you were chosen in the early round. We were puzzled by your declining any invitation to go back to the same company for a second term. Later, you became selective in looking for a job. You seemed keen on expanding your experience. I was impressed by your confidence and thought that it was not a bad thing. However, I could feel that you were growing away from any further graduate studies beyond the bachelor's degree. After the job was settled, you were busy with subletting your place at school and looking for a rental near your next co-op. You could find online the students who had previously worked for the same company or at least the co-op location to consult with.

Ying and I wondered how much knowledge a student could master in an education that is extremely career focused. However, the counterpart of this is how much knowledge is really needed for your future career and life. You skipped grade seven to go to the IB program. I skipped high school (in China) completely to finish the doctoral degree. The fact is probably that you can always learn if you need or want.

Co-op Terms

You completed six work terms, the maximum possible. Waterloo is famous for its systematic management of co-op programs. Online, your training could start from writing your resume to going for an interview. Once you had learned the basics, you were in the pool of job postings. The system lets you schedule real interviews with potential employers and sends you their feedback afterwards. The system allows a student to apply for jobs as well as disallows the student to reject a job offer without a good reason. Unlike a few others who had to use family resources for job and rental, you managed well in finding jobs and places to live. After you got an offer from Shell in Sarnia, your fifth co-op job, we gave you a car as required by your work. You organized your belongings into a series of small suitcases and a few boxes. You drove around for your work and school terms. We were no longer needed to move you in and out.

Before your life in Waterloo, you had never been in a paid

job. You graduated from high school before you turned seventeen, and therefore, there was not a lot of time to practice job hunting. Ying and I kept you worry-free so that you could focus on your schoolwork. Finding the first co-op job in the spring term at the end of your freshman year was a learning experience. At the beginning of the year, you needed to ramp up the educational style of the university and dorm life. The course load was heavy. It probably took you another ramp up to get into the co-op mode, while many others in the same or higher years were already in the hiring process. You did not get many interviews, but you were assured by more than one professor of a work term at school. At the end of the winter term, you got an on-campus job with a professor. I regarded it as a wonderful opportunity to get into the academic research environment with a professor outside the class. For the summer, we moved you out of the dorm and into a furnished basement of a house a short distance from the campus. We went out shopping for the basic cooking wares, besides some dishes and bowls we brought from home. You stayed in Waterloo the entire summer, learning the chores of managing your life, thanks to some help from Susan, your Colonel By friend. You had fun with the graduate students working on a project of alternative fuels. By the time we went to Waterloo to move you out for the fall term of sophomore year, you were packed and already checked out with the landlord.

The second work term was in Peterborough during the winter term of your sophomore year. We moved you back home and then to Peterborough. You were to stay in one of the several bedrooms of a house. The washroom, living/dining room, and kitchen were shared. We drove around to check the location of your company and the places where you could eat or buy groceries. When picking you up, we were told by the landlord that you got along fine with the two or three others. From that time on, you learned to plan dinner and lunch, and you packed your lunch diligently every day. From what I heard, you were involved in two or three projects of the company. You learned to work different shifts in the lab until the group finished the experiment. A part of your co-op life was getting up or going back home in the cold and dark winter days.

The third work term was in Mississauga during the fall term of your junior year. You were nineteen years old and got your driver's license for a short while. Leaving you with a car became a good idea because Mississauga is a big place, and the house is in the middle of a residential area. We, especially Ying, shared some of our driving and car maintenance experience with you. We only had one GPS, and Ying and I had never deviated from our route to Mississauga or Brampton on our trips between Kanata and Waterloo. From Kanata, we drove two cars with you and Ying in the old Ford Focus. It took a few turns for us to reach your place in Mississauga after a detour in Brampton. The house was beautiful, with a well-maintained lawn and flower beds. Everything inside the house was of high-grade, including the pillows and bed sets on your bed. However, it was a place with smokers. I guess you learned to ask the smoking question when hunting for your next house. Ying and I left the GPS with you and followed the map to return to Toronto. For me, Mississauga, a fully grown metropolitan, was full of multi-lane streets and highway ramps, including the route from your home to work. You drove fine. You had car trouble once and handled it calmly. At the end of the term, you became a confident driver.

The fourth work term was with Environment Canada in Gatineau in the spring term of your junior year. It was close to home. Ying and I got familiar with the ways to get to the Quebec side of the capital via different bridges. You were home almost every weekend. We bought you a full-size adult bicycle for you to commute to work and your fitness facilities. Thanks to Kenji, your Colonel By friend, who set you up with a well-rounded fitness routine. I was a little worried in the beginning about the big up- and downhills on the road across the river between Gatineau and Ottawa. But you were fine, showing that you had grown up. There were many Waterloo co-ops in town. The students during their work term often had gatherings. Fifteen or twenty of them would visit the museums on the free night on Thursdays or go to sushi dinners and parties for any kind of celebration. We visited one gathering to deliver something to you and felt the powerful networking among the youths. While working with Environment Canada, you learned to access the data sets of the environment and run software to evaluate and forecast. You did a presentation at the end of the term. You also refreshed your French while living in Gatineau. However, you said no when they invited you to come back for a second term.

The fifth work term was with Shell in Sarnia during the winter term of your senior year. You called to ask for a car because the co-op job required a vehicle to go to different locations on site. When I asked what kind of car you might need, you answered, "oh, an RAV4 should be good." I told Ying what you said, and we just laughed. We spent a weekend visiting car dealers and liked a one-year-old Toyota Matrix. It was a size smaller than RAV4, but the hunchback made the interior quite spacious. Being on the small side, the gas mileage was very good. In place of an RAV4, it would be a nice car for a single person with some luggage. So, we bought the third car for the family. I was the owner of the car. I bought the insurance and assigned you as the principal driver. You drove it a bit during the Christmas break. When you left home for the job, you happily loaded everything in and drove away. You called us when you reached Sarnia. For the entire work term, the Matrix served you well.

The Shell at its Sarnia location is a huge multi-functional center. You went through different levels of physical checkup before you got the job offer. During the Christmas break before you started at Shell, I arranged the family trip to Peru with Globus Travel. You were very concerned because you had to be the same healthy person to start with Shell after our trip. You asked me, "What if I got malaria or hepatitis in my blood after the trip?" I explained, and eventually, we allowed you to skip some activities with the Peruvians we had planned to meet. The pay and benefits were good at Shell, and you learned maintenance in the oil refinery. However, working for a big oil company was not your cup of tea, while it is the goal of many others in chemical engineering. In fact, quite a few of your peers went to different oil companies in Alberta after they graduated. A few of them came back to look for jobs during the downturn of the petroleum industry or after the fire in Fort McMurray. We found out later that you set your mind on living in Toronto, a condition for your actual job.

You found your sixth work term with a biochemical firm in Toronto in the spring of your senior year. It was an extra one before two full terms at school to complete your degree. With your car, you took care of the moving. We went to visit you once in the summer. You lived in a small but clean room in a house that was close to where you worked. The company produces some chemicals, and your work was mainly in the lab.

Graduation and the Job

For the last two terms on campus, you stayed in a sublet close to school and the strip mall. You were busy, especially with the project for your graduation. By then, you had mastered the logic and skill of being proactive in a project, product, or your own future. You survived.

In the Christmas break between the fall and winter terms, you drove home for the holidays. It was in the middle of a winter storm with ice pellets. We were nervous. Although you were with Susan in the car, Susan did not drive. You called when you left the school after lunch and then called again after you drove through the heavy traffic in Toronto. It was already evening, and the traffic was crawling. You called outside Kingston around midnight and said that most of the traffic was getting off the highway. It was icy rain, and you were spending the night there. I was relieved that you made the right decision. The sky lifted a bit the next day, and you came home in the early afternoon after sending Susan home. Your car still had an almost complete coat of ice. I hugged you when you came into the house. Was my spontaneous hug, which was very rare, my relief to see that you were home in one piece? Or glad that you all grew up and could make proper choices when needed? Maybe both. As a mother who was calm and prepared most of the time, my hug before that was when you were eleven years old and away from Kanata to attend U of T camp. Right after the New Year, you left for school with Kenji and Susan and her boyfriend. We were happy that you had another driver in the car and put your car to good use as well.

Your messages in the second half of the winter term were often about job hunting. You started looking for an actual job. We had a few brief discussions on the phone. You did not want to pursue a specific profession that is related to your major. Your goal was a consulting job, likely a decision based on your mixed experience in many co-op positions. The job should be near or in Toronto. It would not be easy for a young fellow with only a bachelor's degree. I hoped that the many co-op experiences would be a big plus on your resume and in your interviews. The good news came on the day we arrived in Waterloo to attend the commencement. You were hired by an established industry consulting firm in Toronto. You were quite relieved and told us that landing the job was after four rounds of interviews and evaluations. It reminded me of Ms. Pall's comment: "James is calm and never panicked."

The commencement of the School of Engineering was held in the auditorium next to the student center. It was my first time at commencement. I got three degrees in the States, but the diploma always came in the mail after I moved on. It was exciting to listen to the speeches of the Chancellor, the Dean, and the graduate representative. Ying took the camera, running around and trying to take the pictures when you walked across the stage. I had my iPad, using it more like binoculars. There were cheers and screams in the crowd of their own. It took a while to exit the building afterwards. I found you in the crowd and Ying went to buy a bouquet for you. After that, we only got five minutes of you to take pictures before you left for different parties with your friends. It was your big day, and you got a good job in Toronto as you wished. What a monumental accomplishment!

You only had a few days between the closure in Waterloo and the date to start the new job. The car turned out to be handy with your new job because the first batch of companies you were assigned to were at three different locations. You found a one-bedroom apartment in a residential compound in Mississauga. It was a short drive to reach the Xerox Research Center, where you were to spend more than half of your time. It must have been quite tiring at the beginning. However, Mississauga is a nice place to find various groceries and eateries. We visited you to check if you needed anything. We were amazed that you cooked for yourself most of the time. To my surprise, you could live without a microwave! You happily walked us outside the Xerox Research Center. Your daily activities included providing training sessions and working on projects with different groups. Later, you were into Scrum Master training on streamlining processes when it was adopted by many industries. I felt you moved away from your profession. However, project management, which you seemed on track for, is another layer of skill and knowledge on top of basic science. Why not?

After three years, you left the company for a smaller firm

downtown, and then you moved to another company (also downtown) for a software position. The reflection that came to my mind much later was that you worked and waited for the girl to graduate. Subsequently, you moved and changed career for the girl you eventually married. In the year she was finishing her bachelor's degree in Waterloo, you often drove on the weekends between Mississauga and Waterloo. I had to guide you out of an accident in Waterloo once since I was the owner of your Matrix. It was also for the girl. In the end, you sold the Matrix, and settled well in the life of downtown Toronto.

Girlfriends

At the end of the winter term of your freshman year, we went to move you out of the dorm. You met us after we brought the car to the loading zone of the Ron Eydt Village. You told us that your stuff was all packed in your girlfriend's room. Her name was Rachel. All your stuff was packed nicely in the proper size for carrying around. Soon, Rachel came down, carrying two of your packages. So, you introduced your new girlfriend, and she was already helping. A decision that came to my mind within thirty seconds was to invite Rachel for lunch.

On the way to lunch, Ying and I were happy to see you and Rachel chatting all the time, walking behind us. We had lunch at the Mongolian BBQ in the strip mall. Rachel was active but polite in the conversation and in handling the tea for everybody. Wow! What a treat. Rachel was on track for medicine, but not to become a doctor. She came from a family near Windsor. She had a younger sister who was more into technical schools and learning a trade. Under her influence, you carried a Rubik's cube around. She was going to her first work term off-campus. On our way back to Ottawa, Ying and I talked about Rachel and your relationship. Yes, the girl was likely a high achiever who could outshine people nearby. Ying and I agreed she was a good influence but did not know if you would fit into her shoes. It was nice that you had a girlfriend, one more friend to talk to and share the pressure of college life.

At the end of your spring term, you asked me to issue a set of postdated cheques for a rental place. It was a flat with five bedrooms, one kitchen, and two washrooms. You were sharing the flat with Rachel and her friends. Somehow, you ended up living with four girls. Before the fall term, we went to Waterloo to move you out of the summer rental and onto the second floor of the two-story house. This was the time we bought you the mattress and spring box set. The kitchen was big enough for five people and already had enough cooking utensils. We did not see Rachel but were told that she had already moved in.

Over our calls in the fall, I learned everybody was very busy with schoolwork. You all went to buy the weekly supply on weekends, and sometimes took a bus to the mall when there was a sale of household items like detergent and toilet paper. We visited you once in the fall, and the flat was amazingly clean. We had dinner with Rachel and you again, and you told me that your duty on weekends was to clean the washrooms. You sublet your room when you went on your second work term in Peterborough. After Peterborough, you went back to Waterloo and stayed in the same house for the spring term at school. When we came to Waterloo at the end of the summer, you found a place to store your bed and loaded your stuff into the car. Your fall term was a co-op in Mississauga. While moving you out, we came across Rachel's parents. However, we were not introduced. Later, you told us you and Rachel split.

When you were back in Kanata, we went out driving sometimes for you to get more driving experience. I asked you what had happened between you and Rachel but did not get any answer. I didn't know if you were sad. You were probably not a good match for the girl, who could obviously manage her life and others very well. Somehow, without knowing who wanted to split and what the key issue was, I was on your side. I told you to look for a kinder girl next time. You asked me how to tell a girl is kind. It was a good question. I did not have a suitable answer. I told you jokingly to find a girl with a look like Shelina, who was Wang Nainai's granddaughter and was a friend to you since preschool.

We were told about your next girlfriend approximately five years after our last conversation about Rachel. She eventually became your fiancé and then your wife. We visited you in downtown Toronto. After Ying and I exited the elevator outside your apartment, you informed us you were living with your girlfriend while unlocking the door to let us in. She was out visiting her relatives. The room was filled with her belongings, including the cat and an abundance of cat hairs. The girl was obviously into arts and crafts, with stacks of containers besides the amount of clothing, usually for a girl. She was getting a master's degree in arts from Ryerson University (soon to be Toronto

Metropolitan University) close by. On our way back to Kanata, Ying and I talked about you and the girl quite a few times. We had hints about your new girlfriend before. In the previous years, we got a picture of you holding a cat and another picture of Kenji and you with two girls in Vancouver. The girls were Kenji's girlfriend and yours. We just didn't get it. Your detective mom wasn't functioning because the thought of "one after another" never came to mind. I was bothered because the two of you only had one bed, which was narrower than queen-size. There wasn't another place in the unit where you could lie down because of the cat. I made a bank transfer to your account with an amount more than enough to buy a proper couch. I was old-fashioned, messaging you that you two should probably get married or sleep separately. You said that you would wait for the sale to buy a new couch or bed.

The girl is kinder, and we finally met at Shelina's wedding. She was polite, not eager to please anybody. Your presence at the wedding was a big and happy surprise for Wang Nainai, who took care of you for almost two years when you were in kindergarten. We learned that her younger sister was already married and moved to Europe. The two of you came to Kanata once on a snowy day with a terrible windchill during the Christmas break. You stayed in the hotel although we made spaces for you two to stay. You arrived late the night before and came to our house for a quick visit the next morning. To be away from our other guests, Ying and I took you out for brunch and took a picture together. Kanata was obviously too cold for her. We visited you the next spring. She was at home. She did not go to a dim sum with us because she was a vegetarian. At dim sum, you told us you were going to propose to her soon. In the months that followed, we asked several times whether we should meet her family and even offered to meet them in Vancouver. It never happened. By then, your communication with Ying and me became sparse. Your wedding took place in Vancouver, and you married into her family, I believe. I painfully realized that people with a "Chinese" prefix are diversified. We not only speak different dialects but also have imprints of different regional history and social structures. I could only hope that you had made the right decision and were happy with her or her families after your marriage.

The years you were away from home marked a transition from being a student to a professional and then to a family man. There must have been quite a few choices to make and learning curves to encounter. I admit I knew very little about your transition. I trust that you, as a survivor, have the drive to manage well your professional level and family matters.

Hobbies

It took years for me to notice that the community, as an entity of our social structure, provides ample opportunities for children. A community usually has an activity center for parents to bring their children to organized group activities. It also has a library for children to sit around and enjoy story times. A child without siblings can learn and explore in group activities that are available at the community facilities. Working full time, we could not take you there because these opportunities mostly happen during normal working hours. For the same reason, I did very little for the community other than paying taxes. However, Ying and I always have in our minds that you are the only child and need some friends. We started paying for group activities quite early so you could connect with other children. Along the way, we expect some activities to become your hobbies as you experiment and discover others.

When You Were Little

The first attempt to set you up in group activities did not work out. I enrolled you in an indoor soccer class when you were barely the age for soccer. I thought it could be a good start, since more than half of the kids are on various soccer teams these days. The class could be a good exposure for you without outdoor factors such as rain, heat, or insects. The indoor soccer field was a school stadium the size of several basketball courts. You were assigned to a team and listened to the instructions. However, once the practice started, you set your mind to follow the referee, who was the only adult on the court, instead of staying with your team. Cute in the new jerseys, you were such a strange sight on the court. After being told not to, you stayed away from the ball. The coach told us you were probably not ready for this. After that, you lost interest when the real soccer season began.

However, you were surprisingly good when alone with an adult. When you were three years old, Kanata Music Academy had a "Talent Quest" class for children of age before kindergarten. The content was to introduce a child to a different musical instrument in every class period of thirty minutes. The ratio of the class was one-on-one. I enrolled you to just listen to some distinct sounds of music since we did not have any at home. You were never shy about going into a class with a stranger. In return, the teacher was so impressed by your focus, quick learning, and feeling on tempo and beat, especially for the piano and drum lessons. I was present for one or two sessions and was also impressed because my childhood was entirely different. You were quite happy after lessons. But the lessons were moving on to learning music notes, which would require a bit of practice and review at home. Neither of us was ready for it. I pulled you out.

After you turned four years old, a teacher at the Academy called me, saying that you would fit well in their individual piano lessons. I declined because I didn't know if the piano was the right instrument for you. The teacher told me about the "Music for Young Pianists," where the parent and the child were learning piano together. The class was not one-on-one but in a small group. I bought a keyboard and other accessories and paid a visit to a setting in Kanata. The garage-based music classroom was of good size and could accommodate six to eight pairs of parents and children. I told the teacher we would try. It only lasted for two visits. There were four pairs in the first lesson and the learning was basic. We were fine. There were six pairs in the second lesson and the class was more involved. For the simple beat and a song, we were asked to stand up and walk around with the music. You stopped getting up after two rounds. We had to get out of the class after you became the obstacle of the merry-go-rounds.

Your behavior in these activities led to my concern that you might have a bit of a problem in a group setting. However, you were still growing, and Dr. Spock mostly encouraged free form activities at these ages, except for eating and sleeping patterns.

Karate

The early soccer encounter reminded me of the importance of knowing beforehand. Instead of trying new activities, I took you to watch team sports or training classes. One time, we were outside the Douvris Martial Arts school in the Walter Baker Recreation facilities. You watched, completely captivated, and would not leave. The school offered separate classes for children under twelve for a junior black belt. You really wanted to join. We talked to the owner, who was a senior black-belt sensei and good with kids, and I signed you up.

You were happy and committed while you were getting the

stripes and belts of different colors. You were small but artistic and could accurately follow and remember the stances. At a few competitions in town, you came back with medals, and you were proud to be one on the team. One highlight in the club was the visitors from a Shaolin Temple in China. The school had a little gathering where both Douvris students and Shaolin monks showed their skills. You were thrilled to be around with some real and young Shaolin monks. We went to their show at the Central Point Theater.

You enjoyed karate as an art. The training made you healthier. You were still skinny but no longer getting sick often, especially in the fall. For a long time, you really liked it and did not mind complicated changes of clothes before and after the class and the hard training. The attendance became three times a week when the stick fight (Rokushakubo) lesson was added. You were learning to manage time. We were only late for your lesson once, and you were upset, refusing to enter the room until the sensei noticed and came out to let you in.

You made some friends. One of them was Shawn. He was a child from a broken family. He could easily get upset and was on medication for ADHD (Attention-Deficit/Hyperactivity Disorder). His mother was bilingual and worked for the government. I liked to listen, and we became good friends. She told me a lot about raising children who visited parents in separate places. Shawn came to our house to spend the night a few times. You also went to his place to play and spend the night. His younger sister, who later also joined karate, adored you. Shawn later transferred to a special school where individual students could receive help if required.

For karate, combat was unavoidable. Things took a turn after the orange belt. Combat skill training was added in half of the classes, and students were paired up to fight. The competitions also required students to enter both their skills and fights. You were certainly not used to fighting. To qualify for the green belt, the student was required to fight against a sensei. You passed, but you stopped volunteering for any competition. After discussions with the instructors, I learned that a milestone in karate training was to overcome fear and handle defeat. You were not ready for that, while other students of your age probably had the cultural background or encouragement from their siblings. However, you were well liked among your peers, and the instructors there expected that you could be one of the young black belts by the age of twelve. You wanted to quit, but the school refused. After a few rounds, one instructor said you could be allowed to quit if you declared you hated karate. You wrote a letter, including a line "I hate karate."

This was the end of your karate. I supported your decision in the end. Life went back to normal afterwards. Time would heal, I thought, since you were just a kid. If I had the time, I could have spent a bit more time with you so that you would learn to talk about your frustration and anger.

Piano

When we visited Disney World in Florida in 2001, we became familiar with the musicals. I asked you to consider learning a musical instrument except the drums. We discussed and settled on the piano. I bought a second-hand real piano, a Winchester with a solid wood frame but without a lid. It came with a matching bench. I asked Shelina, who was already in grade eight of piano, to give a test run and the keys worked well. I paid for the "piano without lid" and subsequently, paid for the special mover to ship it home. The piano served you well and was tuned every year. It stayed in a corner of our living room until we sold our house in Kanata.

I took you back to the Kanata Music Academy for your piano lessons. Since you were no longer a very young child, you breezed through the Conservatory Grade 4 piano books in a year and a half. You practiced and were in rehearsals with fellow students for the holiday season celebrations. You took the first piano test of grade four, and you did fine. I noticed that the progress in your piano skills relied heavily on your reading speed. Sometimes, you have a good ear. Therefore, learning the piano at that level was not very difficult. I was with you for most of your evening practices at home.

For more advanced grades, we had to find a professional piano teacher. We visited the Bells Corners Academy of Music, which at the time only had several studios and teachers with contracts. The piano teacher was a woman with a Russian name and accent. She had two pianos side by side in the room so she could play together with the students or provide short training tunes. You played, and she corrected you. She took you in after a few rounds. Her comment was that you had a good ear and could correct quickly, although your technique was mostly wrong. You were impressed by the environment and her skill, but you were a little overwhelmed as well. I signed you up for her 45-minute lessons, which were expensive.

You worked hard on her assignment and were encouraged by her. Home practice became a challenge since the scores were getting difficult with the progress. I could feel that you were frustrated sometimes. There was a Jack Li movie called *The One* at the time. You called her "The One" and told me from time to time that you were scared. Since she did not offer lessons in the evenings or on weekends, my commitment was to pick you up after school and chauffeur you to the location on time. The lessons continued, and she was never impatient while you were scared. The learning under her lasted a year, and you passed the Conservatory Grade 7 exam. It was also the end of her contract with the school. She went back to midtown Ottawa to teach, preparing for her maternity leave. She left a few names with me to continue your piano lessons. You were relieved.

We found a new teacher in Glen Cairn, Kanata. She had taught private piano lessons for two or three decades. Although she couldn't play well, she got very good ears. Her opinion was that the music lessons should be fun and should explore a person's preference in different music categories. Coming from a Russian teacher, your skill was certainly impressive. She was excited to introduce you to different things. After a few lessons, she settled you on the blues. Besides the books for Conservatory piano lessons, I bought some Jazz and Blues piano books. Besides the few sheets for your next exam, your lessons included the fun time of playing whatever jazz or blues you had picked. You were one of her senior students at the rehearsals. You passed the Grade 8 exam before the summer.

We left her at the beginning of the summer because you needed to get ready for the band class of your high school starting in the fall. I also thought that your level of piano was enough for you to have a lifelong hobby to explore music. Indeed, I remember you played the piano in the dorm from time to time during your freshman year.

Other Musical Instruments

In the summer before high school, we were told that Colonel By Secondary School had string classes and that you could choose the string class in place of the band. We agreed that learning strings would be more interesting than anything in the band because you never had the band activity in your junior high days. You had a summer of violin lessons at Dominic's Music on Hazeldean Road, and we rented a violin for your size. The instructor was a retired member of the Ottawa Symphony Orchestra, who enjoyed teaching children. You learned a lot in the summer and in the fall term. However, the school did not offer a junior string class for the fall term, and you had to take band.

In the band, you were assigned to play the flute. You told me it was the only wind instrument you could make a sound when you tried. We rented the flute from the Kanata Music Academy. At least, you had learned the musical notes well in your piano lessons. You practiced by yourself to learn the instrument. Soon, you brought home a checklist where I needed to put a check mark for the days you practiced. The practice was for the band to play at the Christmas celebration. For the occasion, you got your first pair of dressy shoes. Ying and I attended the celebration. You were a member of the crowd of the junior band on the stage. Throughout the celebration, I could feel that the school had the spirit to excel in every field.

The rental flute broke before the band requirement was complete, and we had to go to the store to exchange the rental once. Later, I went through your band involvement in my mind a few times, although you never complained. You were already behind in the band experience when you started, and you were also short and skinny in getting the air through. I could have bought you a brand new one to add some encouragement.

You wanted to have a guitar after the band requirement was fulfilled. We agreed it should be a classic guitar instead of any electric ones. Feeling a little guilty about my support in your learning of the flute, I took you to Dominic's Music and bought you a brand-new guitar. I also enrolled you in the guitar class offered by the same gentleman, who was your violin instructor. The guitar case was big and heavy, but you were happy to carry it in and out of the car, the store, and the house. You learned the basics of playing a guitar from the few lessons. The guitar stayed at home for a while after you went to college. However, you took it with you to school on one of your visits. I hope you still have it and play it sometimes.

199

Badminton

Your acquaintance with badminton started when you were attending Road College. The school was in an old church. With the large space in the hall, the indoor physical education was playing badminton. Probably because of the mini ping-pong we had at home, you had the feel of where the birdie would fly. You quickly learned, and Monsieur was impressed by your reflex and enthusiasm. You liked it, and therefore, I bought some racquets from Canadian Tire. We started playing outside our house or at the Nepean Sportsplex. I took you to the Kanata Badminton Club, which gave kids playing time slots every Friday night. You really enjoyed it.

There were two major badminton facilities in town for youths: Song's and RA. We visited both and received a warm introduction at Song's. The school was close to Ottawa University and Rideau Centre. Mr. Song was a well-known professional player, especially in Southeast Asian countries. He managed the school with his wife, Janet, who also played badminton and was well liked by the students. We settled on Song's. With the training, you improved quickly and made some friends at the school. Song's badminton became one of the camps you went to during the summer, spring, and winter breaks. I learned to appreciate the stores in Rideau Centre, ByWard Market, and the books in the Chapters at the corner of Sussex and Wellington Streets.

You went to several competitions, as encouraged by the instructors. I soon ordered a professional badminton racket for you. These occasions gave you experience in games. By that time, I bought my first GPS so I could pick you up from different friends' places and take you to different tournaments. You were selected to be on the school badminton team in your junior year. You were very proud to be in school jerseys. I was especially glad that you finally grew up and got the team spirit and even some brotherhood. You had to miss some classes because of the tournaments, but you handled well with your peers and team members.

You took the racket with you when you went to Waterloo. Once or twice, you told me you still had time to play badminton with some friends at school.

Other Sports

When you were growing up, we tried to skate, ski and swim, three popular sports or survival skills as regarded by many. However, none of these activities lasted long enough to become your hobby.

Skating was, by default, a part of the winter physical education at elementary schools. In grade four, it was required in winter to bring the skates to school from time to time. We learned it together because it was common for you to say, "I won't do it if you don't do it." We went to the skating rink inside the Walter Baker Recreation Center. You got the basics after a few times when I was still shaking and all sweaty. Later, you were good enough in the class and went out to skate with friends a few times. However, I was not brave enough to take you to skate on the Rideau Canal.

Another winter sport is skiing. We started out when we visited Mt. Tremblant in 2000. As usual, you would not go downhill if

I didn't go. I've never tried downhill skiing in my life and was an observer all day when my friends took me to the Alps outside Grenoble. In addition, we did not have the right jackets and pants. We tried cross-country skiing. Your cousin turned out to be the best. Your balance, like Ying's, was better than mine. It was fun. However, we never had the time to ski often in winters. Later, because of my osteoporosis problem, I tried not to fall, especially when restricted to ski gear. Ying liked the sport and bought the equipment. He never skied much, though, especially with you.

Swimming is a popular sport in summer, but you started late. You slipped into the fishpond of Marineland when you were three years old. Ying rescued you, but you kept the fear of water for a long time. Regardless of the fear, you were in different pools, probably since you were four years old for birthday parties of friends. I enrolled you in a swimming camp one summer. The feedback at the end was that you were fine if your head was out of the water and that you refused to submerge your head in water. I am allergic to chlorine and therefore never learned to swim. Ying took you to swim a few times at the Kanata Wave Pool or during our vacation at different places. Eventually, as I remember, you learned to swim when you spent a week with college friends in the Dominican Republic.

Magic

Magic is one of your hobbies. The activities to learn and show sometimes could be quite involved. You often kept a deck of cards in your pocket, doing your own research and practice. You had a magic club when you were at Colonel By.

Like many boys, you always enjoyed tricks and magic shows. However, it was the classes at the ABC (Association of Bright Children) that really started you in doing magic. The magician, Jean Luc-Dupont, was a high-tech engineer who had worked at Nortel for many years. He hosted shows at night clubs on some nights. ABC invited him for its Take-Off sessions because he liked children and teaching. For me, the most important aspect among all the little tricks was his teaching on presentation and critique. These two may be big words for pre-teens, but it is what magic is about in the end. Mr. Dupont usually explained and showed a card or rope trick at the beginning of his class. For a class of less than ten students, he asked the students to practice, and each student then came to the front to present. While one was presenting, the others patiently watched and then commented. After one or two classes, everybody learned to demo as well as provide feedback with the right attitude and proper language. I remember that his magic class was always one of the few that got filled up first on the Take-Off registration night.

Besides the magic class at Take-Off, you went to a two-week camp for bright children in the summer to attend the magic and another class. The camp was at the Mississauga campus of the University of Toronto. When it started, I settled you in the dorm and made sure that you got to know your roommates. For the weekend you were at the camp, I drove to Toronto to take you around and have some fun. You enjoyed the magic class, although it was not as good as the one in Ottawa. When Ying and I picked you up at the end of the camp, you gave me a big hug — you certainly missed home.

There was a minor incident related to magic. It was with Walter, your classmate in the gifted class at Glen Cairn. For a show and tell in the class, you prepared a magic trick. Before the show, Walter came to visit. You showed it to him, and he was excited. You explained the details of the trick after he promised not to tell. However, he used the trick as his own at the same show and tell session. You were upset. I could only tell you something like "What has happened, has happened." It was probably your first exposure to the betrayal of a friend. A painful lesson to learn magician's rules. Later, you told me that Walter apologized.

Magic brought you a lot of confidence and some friends. You told me you would play a trick in your hands while walking in the corridors of the school during class breaks. You had two friends who were as small and skinny as you were. Three of you would walk together, showing tricks as a team. By your junior year at Colonel By, you had your math teacher as the sponsor of your magic club. Your chemistry teacher liked your tricks. However, I heard complaints about you spreading the deck of cards on your desk during a class. We had a discussion. Your deck of cards should not be out at all before a class was dismissed. It was at least a sign of respect for the teacher and the class. I trusted you were up to speed in most of the classes, although your mind was on the cards or elsewhere sometimes.

I am glad that you settled on magic as a hobby, thanks to the high-quality teacher at the ABC. Later, you started your research on magic materials online. I certainly paid, thinking they were more worthwhile than the games at EB (Electronics Boutique). You even learned to use my PayPal. Although it's hard to invite, you were not shy when entertaining your cousins, nephews, and children of my coworkers.

Electronic Games

You grew up in the time of electronic games and the rising market for game gear. Technology has brought cultural changes, especially for the young generations of many households.

Early on, we played ABCD games because I always have at least one computer at home. The advertisement section of every education CD usually had a few old-fashioned jumping or shooting games. You were not interested because the games required proper finger coordination and the graphics were poor and repetitive. The first game you played was *Pokémon* in the summer after you completed grade three. It was the first role-playing-game (RPG) I looked at seriously. I was amazed that a game full of text and instructions could attract so many kids. It was summer, and you got the game from Shelina, who completed grade six. I listened to the conversations and watched the two of you in front of my computer. Like the Harry Potter books later, these products, I felt, were a lot more powerful in driving the reading initiatives than conventional school. You just read faster and faster so that you could adventure further in your game. Like many parents, what followed was that I had to limit your playtimes for the sake of your eyes. Once school started, I had to remind you to manage your time among your schoolwork, other chores, and game playing.

Pokémon brought you the first game gear, Game Boy. Honestly,

I didn't mind watching you figure out how to play and then play. Soon, *Pokémon* cards and balls came to stores, and the *Pokémon* movies in the theaters. I limited the supply of these toys and had to settle with you on which set of cards to buy or skip inside a store a few times. I was firmly against card trading when I noticed. After *Pokémon*, it was *Digimon* and then a flood of after-school cartoons based on Japanese comics for boys and girls as well. I sensed the strong cultural influence of combat and violence in the setting of boys and girls. They were welcomed by groups of your age because the characters were children or youths instead of adults or super beings of adults.

I was glad you did not dwell on these cartoons and moved on to more complicated RPGs, such as the *Final Fantasy* series. We bought the PC version first and installed it on my computer. The game was rich in colors, and Shelina came over to play from time to time. You did not shy away from the skills, tools, and magics of the characters, which I was not interested in at all. So, I bought game guides for you. It started your reading habit with game guides, game magazines, and later, online information. The consequence, as I later thought, was probably the level of understanding while the brain was overwhelmed by the huge inflow of vocabulary. Instead of understanding every detail, you learned too early in your life to grab only what you need and move on.

We got the PlayStation at home soon. I was and still am very impressed by the Sony color. The dedicated game console was superior to the PC game playing at the time. Our game area was in the room above the garage, half of which was already taken by the large assemblies of the office desk for Ying and me. The game area had a large TV in an entertainment assembly, coffee stands. and couches. I bought a thick piece of carpet to cover the cables from the console to the controllers near the couch. It was a nice setup enjoyed by you, as well as the visitors of your peers and the children of our friends. I often sat on the floor to watch both you and the game. The room was far enough from your bedroom where you did most of your schoolwork. The life pattern then was that you exited the game area when either Ying or I needed to take care of office work after dinner. You played until bedtime sometimes. Over the years, PlayStation was upgraded to version 2. Wii Fit was added to the game area. Later, I bought my own Xbox since I never liked Nintendo graphics. The TV was upgraded to 36-inch before LEDs came along.

We followed the *Final Fantasy* games until the characters became 3-D images. The faces in the first 3-D version had motionless eyes and mouths. It made me think of my choice in presenting research results in 2-D or 3-D. The truth was the 3-D graphs might not add value if the tool was not ready. Other than *Final Fantasy*, *Monster Hunters* was another RPG you played for a long time. It was humans against monsters. It was grand and colorful, and probably the first game you played with peers online. The games and game guides were mainly made by Square. You played other games by Square, like the *Chrono* series. The Christmas gift or any award at the time was mostly new games.

Gradually, you shifted from RPG to FPS (First-Person Shooter) games when playing games with your peers moved from one house to the next. The shooting and running in FPS obviously required less patience than what was needed in managing power with potions, weapons, and magic. Its terrain was not as complicated and colorful as those in RPG. I disliked gunfire and darkish- or grayish-colored games, but you were a teenager then. The new features in the FPS, though, included small teamwork and multi-section screen. You played early versions of *Call of Duty* and *Counter Strike*. We had to check out *Halo* from Roger Videos once when your friends came over for a gathering.

For the handheld, you got a PSP after the Game Boy became a little childish. We had plenty of Gameboy games and we gave some of them to the neighbors. You loved your PSP, and I believed Sony was the forerunner in the similar industries for high definition. On many of our visits to EB (Electronics Boutique) and Best Buy, we often saw or heard unsatisfied requests in the game sections. In our case, we would plan beforehand so that you always got what you wanted. You were a little spoiled. Did I spend too much money on it? Maybe. It was hard to draw the line. I have an open mind myself to the arts and music and anything related to them. At least, you were never an addict like many parents were afraid of.

Collectively, it was a significant investment to nurture an expensive hobby, given the progress of the industry at the time. You still like it, although you occasionally played board games when you were in Waterloo. Before Ying and I moved to Toronto, all the PS, PSP, and Wii games returned to EB and a game store that collected old games. The game gears were recycled. I brought my old Xbox and its exercise games to the new home but haven't played them. Most of the information I need can now be found on YouTube or other apps for the iPad.

Pets and Plants

The pet stores were one of the places we often spent time at when you were a toddler. It was a place to introduce the names and live shapes to a small child prior to any zoo. In your preteen years, especially after we moved into our own house, having a pet at home was often brought up after we passed a pet store. A pet in the house was a luxury in my mind. Especially, the house was empty during the day on weekdays.

To keep things simple and inexpensive, Ying and I agreed to start with buying a rat. It was the kind easiest to take care of and not easily die. Along with the rat, we bought a cage with detachable pieces for the animal to chew and drink water, as well as pet food and bedding. The rat's home was set up in a corner of the living room. This was the first time I had a pet. The bedding had a fresh smell of a mixture of wood chips and grass. It was pleasant but unnecessary inside the house. It was usually my (or sometimes Ying's) job to change the bedding to maintain a normal smell. Your job was to feed and water. You did well. Ying sometimes gave the rat a bath with your help. We called the rat "Rattie," and it was clean and quite good at interacting with people. Rattie was with us for almost three years, which is quite an old age for a rat. Near the end of its life, I noticed a lump growing on its neck. Rattie was not bothered by it in the beginning. I checked online and noticed that it is one of the ways rats die. I visited one or two pet stores and talked with people working there. Their answer was that it could not be saved, and pets die. We were sad in the last few days of Rattie's life, watching it carry the tumor around and getting harder and harder to move. Eventually, when it stopped moving, Ying and you buried it somewhere in our backyard. I did not attend.

The second pet in the house was a black betta fish. It was given to me by one of my coworkers. She bought the fish, intending to add some color among her goldfish in her fish tank. However, she was told that the betta fish only live with the same kind. As a gift, the fish came in a nice round glass jar. It was pretty, with long and wide fins and tail. It grew bigger after a few months. The whole family went to the pet store in Centrum to search for a fish tank. We bought a fish tank that had light and could inject air into the water. It was overkill for a single fish. People at the store told us not to feed the fish too often. The reasons are (1) fish grow too fast and (2) the extra food may spoil the water. The lonely fish stayed with us for probably three years. It died one day when the tank was not functioning properly. We did not feel as sad as we felt when we lost Rattie, probably because the maintenance of the fish was a lot less than that of Rattie, and its death was sudden.

We bird-sat twice. The first time the birdcage came to our house was when the family, a few doors down the street, took a vacation out of the country. We had birds chirping often for a week. You were in kindergarten then, and Wang Nainai did all the chores. You liked the yellow and almost white birds. When we bird-sat the second time, you were in grade school. You and I walked to the house to check on and feed the birds every other night. The budgies chirped and flew back and forth in the cage when we were there. I started hearing "I want a budgie" afterwards. You ran to the pet store to check on the budgies a few times when we were in a mall. I bought a book on raising budgies. I asked you to read the book first and told you we needed to discuss whether you could take care of a bird all by yourself. You spent a lot of time flipping through the book. I still heard "I want a budgie" afterwards, but it was just for fun instead of a serious request. I was glad that the budgie stayed in the book.

Over the years, in our own house in Kanata, I grew a lot of plants. They grew from a pot that cost 99 cents at a store or a piece given by a friend. They were lined up next to the windows facing south and west and grew freely. I watered them and only added a drop of plant food to the water occasionally. With a little help from you or Ying, I moved a lot of them out onto the deck in summer and back inside the house before winter. I repotted, cut, and rearranged the pots (and redistributed among friends) often. Most of my plants were desert or tropical greens, and there were very few flowering ones. My good feeling was that they were always green and never die. Once or twice when you were in preteens, your friends came over and replanted one or two of my plants. Once, when you were in high school, you called me at the office, and told me, "Your cactus fell. It slid down the bookshelves, and the dirt and cactus are on the floor." I had a very tall cactus then. It was leaning against the window, with its tip less than a foot from the ceiling. When I moved to Toronto, I gave all of them to my neighbor who had taught me how to cut cactus and split lily roots.

While bringing you up, I tried to expose you to different things, hoping you would settle on a few lifelong hobbies. Eventually, badminton is your sport. Magic and games are entertainment for you and your friends, probably even in your small family. Don't know if you still play the piano and how far you have come on the guitar. Music notes from your own instrument sound different from those already in MP3. You found a girl who likes pets and is artistic and crafty. It probably fulfills what you had missed as a child. I don't know if you have plants with little animals running around.

BOOK THREE

Family trips

Timeline of family trips in the chapters:

Summer 1994. Beijing, China.

Summer 1998. Beijing and Zhejiang, China.

Winter 2000. Varadero, Cuba.

Winter 2001. Disney World in Orlando and Fort Lauderdale, Florida. USA.

Summer 2003. Maritime provinces and Quebec City, Canada.

Winter 2003. Beijing, Xi'an, and Luoyang, China.

Summer 2004. Edmonton, Rockies, Vancouver, and Calgary in Canada and Portland, USA.

Summer 2006. Vatican, cities in Italy, France, Switzerland, and United Kingdom.

Summer 2007. Palm Desert, Los Angeles, Sequoia National Park, Yosemite, San Jose, Foster City, and San Francisco, USA.

Winter 2008. Islands of Hawaii, USA.

Summer 2009. Beijing, Nanjing, Suzhou, Shanghai, and Zhejiang, China.

Fall 2010. Los Angeles, USA.

Summer 2011. Beijing, China.

Winter 2011. Mexico City, Mexico.

Winter 2012. Lima, Cusco, and Machu Picchu, Peru.

Travel to China

You have visited China several times. China is the home country of your parents. Although you were not born there, it is the reason for our ethnicity or the prefix "Chinese" of "Chinese Canadian". You also have a less-preferred term: Canadian-born Chinese (CBC). Ying and I have fond memories of our youth and the families we came from. The country has a written record of several thousand years. During each visit, we tried to tour some historical places besides getting together with our relatives and friends.

Beijing, Summer 1994

You went on your first trip to China before you turned two years old. You got your first Canadian passport with a visa to China. I was going to a conference in Beijing in early August. As a child under two, you did not need a ticket. On the way there, you were on my lap from Ottawa to Vancouver. Once on the transpacific flight, you slept comfortably on the floor between the TV screen and my row, thanks to the arrangement of the Japan airline. For a small charge, you got baby food, juice, and toys, and the flight attendant was always ready to help. You had no fuss all the way from Vancouver to Tokyo. In the late afternoon local time, I dragged our luggage and you out because we needed to stay overnight in Tokyo. The shuttle and hotel were both clean and punctual. I just wished I had a bit more muscle to deal with all the stuff I needed to take care of, going up and down. In the pleasant hotel, I spent US$30 for a bowl of Ramen noodles for dinner. We then walked inside the hotel out of curiosity and purchased a bag of snacks just in case anybody got hungry at night. I asked for a wake-up call. The next morning, we had a big breakfast in the hotel dining hall and made it back to the airport on time. The stretch from Tokyo to Beijing was short and uneventful, with you sitting on my lap most of the time.

In Beijing, you first celebrated your two-year-old birthday with Ying's parents, your grandparents. They were so happy to meet the new addition to the family. Your grandmother and uncle cooked a big dinner that night. You were cranky by the time the big cake was brought to the table, so I had to send you to bed. Your grandmother insisted you had to have the first bite of the cake and, therefore, we had the cake for breakfast the next morning. I took quite a few pictures of you, the little active boy, among Ying's family members on the party night.

You had another birthday party with my family, including your grandmother (my mother), uncle, and auntie. Your cousin, my brother's daughter, was an agreeable companion to you. My mother was eighty-three years old that year. She was just happy to see me healthy and still strong because my family knew about the operations that I had gone through over the previous two years. Because of a fall a few years before, she had already had trouble walking. She still attended a lunch that my brother arranged, introducing you to our relatives in Beijing. The picture of the gathering showed I was holding you and she could barely stand. She must have really tried to last the entire gathering.

During my conference, both families pitched in to take care of you. In the heat, you were happy on the summer mat made of straw in the old house of my family. During the day, you checked all the flying and crawling species with your cousin in the small courtyard. There were a few tall trees providing pleasant shade. Ying's family lived in an apartment compound. You were the only one running with a disposable diaper on the paths among the apartment buildings. Ying's sister had to stand outside at midnight so you could go back to sleep. She was counting mosquito bites when I showed up the next day. The plus side was that their location is very close to the Palace Museum and other imperial parks. Your grandfather or auntie took you to the nearby parks during the day. After my conference, we had fun visiting the zoo, of course, to see the panda.

On the way back to Canada, we stayed overnight in Tokyo again. This time, my friend Steve and his wife came by to show us Tokyo. Steve and his wife were in Canada less than a year ago and we had a good time cruising the Thousand Islands. You and their daughter were not strangers. Their present to you was a little school bag. You and their daughter, each having a backpack, had a lot of fun on the express train. Steve carried you on his shoulder in the crowd of Tokyo, so you had a cool and better view of the city than everybody else!

Home Village in Zhejiang, Summer 1998

Your second trip to China was also in the summer. You were not yet six years old. We were going to join Ying's family for a hometown visit in the southern part of China. It was the first time in many years for his family. It was hot everywhere. The temperature could reach around 35°C during the day. Walking on the street, we often got drips from the window air conditioners installed in stores or families. The weather report probably did not include the contribution of urban heat. The first thing people offered us after we reached home, or a friend's place, was clean towels so that we could wash our faces to cool down. Dinner or not, the host often brought out a plate of watermelon from the refrigerator as a snack, for the same reason — to cool down. You were bothered by the heat and not eating well. After a few days, I figured out that you liked the small bags of sanitized milk, plain rice, and fruit cocktails. We always had a few bags of milk in the refrigerator in our hotel room.

Great Wall and Imperial Parks

It was the first visit to China for our three-member family. Being in Beijing, we booked a trip to the Great Wall and Ming Tombs. The bus was air-conditioned, and the Great Wall was not very crowded as it often is now. Everybody was excited as the bus got closer to the site. It was a moment to experience the monumental landscape that we had seen in many pictures become real in front of us. You were excited, too. You walked all the way up. The path between the walls was smooth, with sections of stairs to go up the mountain slopes. Like other ancient places, the height of each step can be around a foot. You tried on all fours and arrived safely at the top, one of the tall peaks for tourists to visit. There was a small hut, and the man there issued a certificate saying, "I climbed the Great Wall." You received your certificate and your picture. At each edge of the wall, Ying held you up to see the view of the mountains and the wall further up to the top of the mountain. It was magnificent!

You gave up walking on the way down. The foot-tall steps made you unsteady with tired legs. From top to bottom, you were on the back of either Ying or me. After the Great Wall, we had lunch at the site of a reservoir that supplied water to Beijing. Later, we went to the Ming Tombs. You took a nap on the bus and were surprised to see so many rock statues at the entrance of the tomb. Once we were underground, the air inside the tomb was damp and cool, and the lighting in each section was minimal. The guide led us to the coffin holder or altar of different emperors. Entirely lost in all the ancient stories, you were scared and stayed on Ying's back for the rest of the tour.

Other than the tour to the Great Wall, we paid quite a few visits to royal parks near Ying's home. In Jingshan Park, where your grandfather took you to climb the stairs when you were two, we went up to the top of the series of pavilions. What you can see at the top is the bird's-eye view of the Forbidden City to the south. It is a huge rectangular maze filled with yellow and red, the royal colors. The yellow at the top is the roof with glazed tiles and the red is the walls and pillars of the gardens and courtyard. My brother, your uncle, worked inside the Forbidden City for three decades. His expertise is in examining the rubbing of inscriptions from monuments and tombstones. Rubbing, a skill of art that likely originated in China, is the process of making ink prints of the inscriptions on a stone. As the palace of several dynasties, the Forbidden City has a collection of rubbings spanning thousands of years in Chinese history.

Another imperial garden we often visited was Beihai Park, which is located northwest of the Forbidden City. We went there to walk under the shade of big willow trees along the lakes. We rowed a boat at least twice to visit the pavilions on the water. Life jackets were not required. There was a short oar in the fixture on each side of the boat. Sitting in the middle of the boat with an oar in each hand, Ying would start rowing the boat while I sat with you in the back. The lake was filled with other boats, big or small. We let the boat drift near the lotus fields, and many times, there were dragonflies among the flowers or pods. A well-known structure on top of the hill is the White Pagoda. It is said that the pagoda stores a chest containing relics of a famous Tibetan monk such as real scriptures, his alms bowl, and even his remains. Off the boat, we took you to explore the large playground for children. Besides the stands for snacks, we had a lunch of royal delicacies once at Fangshan, an imperial kitchen where Ying and I got married many years ago. You enjoyed its small and artistic dishes.

Journey to Home Village

To start the homecoming trip, Ying's family of ten, including the three of us, left Beijing in the evening, taking the sleeper train. It was your first time on a train equipped well for long rides. You felt safe because Ying and I were always around, and you had a lot of fun exploring the spaces you could visit. The overnight journey took us to Hangzhou, the capital city of Zhejiang province. A relative who worked in the city was already there and arranged the lodging for the group. After we checked in, we went to an elegant restaurant, and the brunch started with the locally produced green tea. We had the best local dishes and local rice wine. Deeply influenced by several dynasties in China, the wine and many dishes were named after famous Chinese scholars or local scenic points. We were entertained by their stories.

The relative took us around the famous West Lake and made stops at a few historical sites. It was slightly hotter than Beijing, but with less urban heat. We had an early dinner at a different elegant restaurant. The first round of services was wine and cold dishes, and then the main dishes were served one course at a time, in small cups or huge elliptical plates. Ying had to run down the street once to get something from KFC, and you settled down also for a good meal. After dinner, we took a ferry ride on the lake in the cool evening air. The guide never stopped talking about famous rocks, pavilions, and little bridges visible from the boat. It was late, and you were on Ying's back when we were back at the hotel at the end of our first day. This was my first visit to Hangzhou, and the Chinese culture and history of this part of the country were very authentic. It is the culture of Han ethnicity, which includes Ying and me, as well as over 90 percent of people in China.

On the way to Ying's home village the next day, we visited ea farms near the streams distributed along the hills. The area produces the most famous Chinese green tea, Longjing. Apparently, it was the special soil and the water that nurtured the tea bushes. Evolution over generations led to skills to create different flavors in the brand that is available all over the world. We stopped at a teahouse and then a small restaurant to try the local wines with appetizers. I followed you to a nearby pond filled with lotus. You had fun poking the water drops on the huge lotus leaves swaying in the late morning breeze.

Ying had to help with driving the last stretch to the hometown because one driver was sick. I was concerned about legality. Regardless, he made it. It was interesting to see him driving slowly and patiently to meander among the little pickup trucks, horse or ox carts on the paved or unpaved roads. We finally reached Bamao, the home village, which is set in a sizable flat space surrounded by forested hills. The visitors were divided and distributed to several families for lodging. We learned to sleep inside a mosquito net at night because of the season.

Homecoming

Our homecoming stay was well planned beforehand and filled with activities. We brought gifts for many relatives in the village. There were a lot of visits and gatherings. An important duty of our group was to pay respect to the ancestors, who were buried on separate hilltops surrounding the fields near the village. The locals prepared bundles of incense, bottles of local wine, and dishes of food, snacks, and fruits. Little ceremonies were held at each tomb site. We could not leave you with anybody in the village and therefore, you followed. You were on the back of either me or Ying almost all the time, when we walked up and down the hills. We stood for the ceremonies and bowed as instructed. After the ceremonial tour among the hills, we went to the house of a relative to have a meal. The lady in the house was your grandfather's cousin, and she was well respected. Many dishes were on the table and people were crowded around the table, inside and outside the room. The older generations, including your grandparents, were the center of the crowd. All the while, people were busy fetching new dishes or just standing around with a cup of wine for cheers, or a cigarette in hand. The dining and wining in the packed room seemed to last forever. There was so much to catch up on between your grandparents and the village people.

After the day we visited the hills, the news of our arrival was known in the village. There were gatherings in the restaurants or in the large courtyard of a family every day. Because it was cooler at night, the gatherings in the courtyard lasted for hours until somebody noticed that your grandparents were tired. The villagers, most of whom were relatives, wanted to meet and chat with your grandfather, who left home and became a government officer and scholar. Eventually, our family of three moved into a hotel that had air conditioning because you were on the verge of heatstroke. Ying and I were concerned that you were shrinking because of the heat and lack of suitable food. The hotel was in the county seat, which was a half-hour bus ride to the village. You and I were excused from a few gatherings so that I could feed you properly in the hotel.

Little Foreign Boy

At the end of our homecoming trip, I left for Shanghai on an overnight sleeper bus to attend a business meeting on my family's side. You were left with Ying's family for a few days. Your tour continued to a few more places in Zhejiang province. As your aunties later told me, you behaved most of the time. However, on one occasion, when the car broke down on the shoulder of the highway, you ran along the traffic side of the road to check on the people fixing the car or just ran to Ying. You bit Ying's sister-in-law when she tried to pull you away to avoid the traffic. I asked you about it and you were quiet. My method for handling your tantrum was to move you to a different spot to calm you down whenever you were not behaving. I had to take you away from the crowd quite a few times during the trip. Ying's mother would be defensive, saying that Ying was even worse when he was a child.

As an afterthought, you were probably too young for these activities. You could have stayed with your cousin Le Le and her babysitter in Beijing instead of going on this trip. However, sons and grandsons are important in the family tree in Chinese genealogy. Therefore, your participation was expected. In the years that followed, you were a short and skinny boy for a long time. You always blamed your smallness on the encounters during this trip.

Terracotta and Shaolin, Winter 2003

Your third trip to China was in winter when you were eleven years old. We arrived in Beijing to spend Christmas. We planned a week-long trip before Christmas to visit two ancient capital cities, Xi'an and Luoyang, and the famous terracotta.

Xi'an

Shortly after we arrived in Beijing, we took a train to the ancient capital, Xi'an. Compared to winter in Ottawa, the winter in the middle part of China is warmer. Therefore, traveling in winter is still fun. There are fewer tourists in winter than in summer. The drawback is that it may be cold and less maintained at some tourist attractions during the downtime. Outside the train station in Xi'an, there were crowds of people offering hotel and tourist services. We booked a tour guide to visit the Terracotta Army the next day. We checked into the hotel and then started our tour in the city by ourselves.

Unlike Beijing, the ancient capital still has its city walls and gates in place. Instead of palaces, the places to visit are the pagodas and the Stele Forest, which are clusters of monuments and steles of different sizes. We climbed to the top of a pagoda that was originally built as early as the seventh century. At the top, we could see ancient city walls and other small pagodas and pavilion-like structures. I was amazed that the ancient capital was still intact, bringing back imaginations of a series of covered wagons and herds of camels, horses, and even ox carts. In the popular Chinese folklore, *Journey to the West*, the monks started their journey from here to India.

Stele Forest was less than a ten-minute walk from the pagoda. The inscriptions on the stones in the park could be traced back to as early as the ninth century. The contents were mainly Buddhist scriptures or teachings from different Chinese philosophers. I could imagine the park is an educational site for generations to study different calligraphy firsthand. Others, away from Xi'an, could study the publications that contain the rubbings of the stones in the park. As is said on a bulletin board in the park, the rubbings of the stones are in many museums and libraries across China, and even in other countries around the world.

There weren't a lot of visitors, and even the ticket booths were closed in the late afternoon while the places were open and peaceful. We just wandered among the stones, statues, altars, and trees hundreds of years old, reading the little signs saying their name and age. The glazed yellow, red, and green colors were glorious in the sunset and then in the evening lights. Unavoidably, the ancient city wall was the reason for the serious traffic jam during the rush hour when we were in a taxi on our way back to the hotel. There were streams of four or five cars on a three-lane street. Everybody just followed the flow, being very alert to any zig-zagging cars being driven by the impatient few. At night, Ying and I went to taste the local delicacies. It was a bowl of meaty soup that came with a baked bun that was harder than a bagel. The essence of the meal was for guests to tear the bun into small pieces and soak them in the meaty soup. The process provided the guests with time to chat, and the result was tasty and filling. On our way back, we bought you a meal from KFC.

Terracotta and Tombs

The next day was a big day. The tour guide came in a minivan and took us out of the city. He never stopped telling stories on the way. We first went to Qin Shi Huang's mausoleum, the tomb of the first emperor of the Qin dynasty (200 BC). There was a costume parade on the site when we arrived. The soldiers were dressed in colorful battle suits and equipped with fake ancient spears, bows, and arrows. You marched among the soldiers. I bought a book at its souvenir shop and patiently waited in line to get a signature from the farmer who first discovered the site. We then went into the covered excavation sites where the army of terracotta stood as they were first discovered. They were there to protect the emperor in his afterlife. We were blocked from entering the open pit, but at least we could take pictures while walking along the pit. The atmosphere inside the display was solemn, even though they were all statues. Walking among the real-human-size terracotta inside the pit must be a thrill, I thought. However, my Chinese consciousness is never at peace with death-related artifacts, such as mummies and skeletons, in other places around the world.

On the way to Qian Ling, the Tang tombs, we visited the museum and shops where the Qin and Ming terracotta statues were displayed side by side. The two dynasties were almost two thousand years apart in Chinese history. The Ming terracotta, being more recent (a few centuries ago), was craftier miniatures.

There were a pair of stone lion sculptures outside the museum. The legend said that touching a lion's head, nose, and paws would bring intelligence, power, and love in the future, respectively. A closer look showed that these spots were obviously rubbed by thousands of touches. I let you choose and took a picture of you while your hand was on the head of the lion, likely just to keep your balance.

At the Tang tombs, the guide told us that Qian Ling (Mausoleum) is a huge hilly area that contains the tombs of the empress of the Tang Dynasty and her husband, an emperor. A hill is the dome-like design of a tomb that contains the world of the emperor and the empress, including all the necessities for them to use in their afterlife. The guide briefly talked about the discoveries and the tomb raiders in history. As a rare case, Qian Ling was not opened, and raiders (sometimes large armies) came but its inside was never raided. The grand layout above the ground offered plenty of history for visitors. The guide took us to the high end of the area after a long stretch of a broad walkway. He told us a story about the Empress of Tang, the only empress in Chinese history. When her husband died, she became the ruler. After her husband was buried, she set a monument with inscriptions of several thousand words praising the emperor. She set a monument of the same size for herself also, but with no inscription. Her intent left intellectuals of later dynasties wondering. There were at least two opposite views: her accomplishment was too glorious to be described in words or should not be appraised. As recorded in history, her ruling was cold-hearted, with several internal conflicts and many sacrifices of lives. She invented a new Chinese character to name her ruling. The character is composed of "sun" and "moon" on top of "sky," implying that her ruling would always be bright and glorious.

On our way back, the guide gave us a brief tour of the residences of the local people. Because of the very special red soil, the typical local housing is called Yaodong, which is cave-like houses along the sunny side of a mountain. The front of the cave is carved out of a hillside, while at the foot of the hill is a courtyard. Full of local wisdom, the structure and depth of the caves vary, depending on the individual functions. It is the same soil that made the terracotta and underground dwellings for the dead in the tombs. Strata of the soil is hundreds of feet thick, allowing people to dig tunnels, holes, stairways, and rooms the size of meeting halls. The caves are shielded from the seasonal wind by the hills. The walls of a cave provide effective insulation, keeping the temperature mild compared to the harsh weather outside. From the top, we could see strings of red peppers hanging on the wall and sheets holding corn or similar in the courtyard, bathing in the sunlight.

We skipped lunch or forgot about it, although the guide had made a stop where we could have bought some snacks. Back in the hotel, we had dinner at the Chinese buffet downstairs. RMB 50 (~C$10) per person was considered an expensive meal, but it was worth it because the food was abundant and excellent. All of us, especially you, had a very good appetite.

Buddha Statues and Luoyang

The next morning, at a stand outside the hotel, we bought a stack of freshly made Chinese crepes for our breakfast. We left for Luoyang, another ancient capital city, which existed even earlier than Xi'an in Chinese history. As arranged by the guide on the previous day, a different guide came with a sedan, and he would make stops on the way and deliver us to the hotel we booked in Luoyang.

We visited the Longmen Grottoes (Dragon Gate Stone Caves) south of Luoyang. It is a renowned world heritage site. The limestone sculptures of Buddha and disciples are carved individually alongside the mountain or as a group inside caves. Several large, elongated caves made the Grottoes unique. The gigantic statues in a cave could be a Buddha and a series of disciples, or lords in human or spiritual worlds, and soldiers on the battleground. Its grand layout is derived from storylines mostly found in Buddhist script. The ones from Chinese folklore could be out of a version of a local flavor of the rulers who assigned the resources to build the cave. We walked by the caves with large and small statues, and the sculptures sometimes connecting the caves. Parts of the history and folklore we had come across in visiting tombs and temples are illustrated in the works. Inscriptions in the stone caves left by the artisan are as old as 1500 years. Many of the sculptures have weathered over the years. The heads, especially noses, of many sculptures are badly damaged, resulting from the rites at different time periods in history. There are obviously missing pieces and empty slots where the works were removed. It is said that some of them were found in local construction, but others were on display in the museums in China and worldwide.

At night, we had the famous dinner called "water banquet." We were given a set of selections based on the number of guests. Every dish, cold or hot, was a type of soup. The dishes came one after another and were served in time, and each of them brought a distinct aroma and flavor to the surroundings. What mattered was probably the style that set the guests in a smooth and forever-flowing atmosphere. We enjoyed the soups, as well as the tiny buns and dumplings.

Our visit to Luoyang city turned out to be an overnight stay. Apparently, viewing the ancient capital of different dynasties requires visiting different sites, but we did not pass any on our way to the hotel. The best season to visit is in April during the celebration of peonies' cultivation. Despite the incompleteness, we visited the stone grotto and tried the water banquet, two of the few heritages.

Shaolin and Taoism Temple

Next day, we were on our way to Zhengzhou to catch a train back to Beijing. As agreed with the guide, we would visit the Songshan Shaolin Temple on the way. It was exciting for us since you were in karate in those days. On our way up to the temple, we passed a few Shaolin schools and saw groups of people of different ages practicing. The guide left us at the entrance of the Shaolin Monastery and drove away to meet his next customer. The Monastery was first built around the sixth century. It is one of the most authentic Shaolin temples. Its location, Songshan (Song Mount), is known as one of the five holy peaks in China.

As we were told, the Shaolin culture is composed of Chan Buddhism, martial arts, Buddhist art, and Chinese traditional medicine. From what I could understand, Chan Buddhism is a special branch of philosophy from Buddhist teachings, while the goal of Shaolin culture targets illiteracy and sickness observed anywhere and anytime in history. Such a temple had been an informal school to teach different trades to common youths who could not afford to go to regular school. When we visited, it was clean, quiet, and had not yet turned into a showplace. We passed a few monks sweeping the courtyard and walked into a temple where a famous monk left his footprint on the stone floor. Further into the monastery, we could see monks, old and young, in their different morning sessions. Indeed, it is a school coexisting with the daily functions in the temple for the local Buddhists. Out of the temple, we walked along the street, passing some other Shaolin schools and a large auditorium for local competitions and gatherings.

After our Shaolin tour, we visited the Zhongyue Temple, which was built several hundred years earlier than the Shaolin Monastery. The location was regarded as the center of heaven and earth because of the surrounding mountains, and therefore, the Emperor of Qin built the temple. Centuries afterwards, the temple expanded and became the largest architectural cluster for official ceremonies. The religious rituals worshipped here are Taoism, another major religion in China. In contrast to Buddhism, Taoism in Chinese history is rooted in the upper society and populated among intellectuals. Its teachings originated from those of Confucius and were integrated into the philosophy of ruling. It developed branches of ancient science in cosmology and medicine focused on longevity. A map at the main entrance shows that the area of the temple is huge, covering approximately 110,000 square meters with a north-to-south central axis of 650 meters. It is said that there are several hundred rooms, over one hundred of which function as a formal temple. We entered from the south end, visited the gate, the pavilion, and then several temples in different courtyards before we had to leave. In each courtyard, stone statues and monuments are surrounded by cypress trees. Each courtyard is characterized by a large hall facing south. In each hall, one or two enormous statues are at the center, with altars holding tributes. In front of the main altar, a few cushions are placed on the floor for people to kneel. What is set up along the walls in the shadow rather reflects local interpretations of the history and stories related to the main statue. Sporadically, I could see donation boxes side by side with the tributes or outside next to the huge incense burner. However, it was all quiet in the winter except for a few keepers dressed in Taoist gowns.

Country Bus and Train in Zhengzhou

We left the Temple, and it was time to head back by ourselves. As told by the guide, we waited for the bus going to Zhengzhou. It turned out that riding the long-distance bus was a unique experience. When the bus finally came, it was already quite full. We got on and went to the back of the bus to look for a place to sit. There were pullout seats in the aisle to let more people sit. Still, there were not enough seats. Instead of sitting on my lap, the conductor passed a stool for you. The bus was fully packed, and the road was not always paved. You were on the stool, and we could see dust rising because of the bumpy ride. While making stops on the way, the bus picked up more local people. By the time it reached the checkpoint to enter Zhengzhou, the bus was overloaded. It had to unload a few people before being allowed to enter the city. I dusted you from top to bottom after we got out of the bus.

We hurried to the train station and bought the ticket to Beijing. It was crowded in the lobby and waiting halls of the train station. Other than the packed people on and between the benches, who were waiting for different trains, there was no restaurant inside. The snacks or any food available at the food stand were simple. You went into the toilet but came out right away. The train ride was uneventful, and the facilities were relatively clean. The attendant came by and checked everybody's ticket. A different attendant, probably from the kitchen, pushed a metal cart with boxes of hot food. We bought two different dinner boxes. We had the only proper meal of the day, and it was delicious. Everybody was happy when we finally got back to the hotel in Beijing. It was an adventure. You slept well that night and had an extra big breakfast the next morning. The experience of sitting on a stool in the bus or having to hold up yourself until you reached a proper facility seemed all behind you.

Dinner in the Best

The highlight after we returned to Beijing was observing Christmas. We were in the crowd on the pedestrian streets on Christmas Eve. It was as beautiful as any place we had visited in other parts of the world. Strings of lights and decorations were on every tree, streetlight, lamppost, billboard, and storefront. Signs of the big sale were on store windows. People were shopping for good deals because the Chinese New Year was not far away. Ying's brother reserved dinner at the best old-style restaurant nearby. It was the wish of your grandmother. We went and took many pictures of the family.

In the restaurant, we had an individual room decorated with Chinese paintings and calligraphy. There was a merry-go-round in the middle of the large dining table. The dishes were served in style. Appetizers, cold and hot dishes, and fruits were brought to the table in several rounds. For drinks, besides the liquor we brought, we ordered green tea and watermelon juice (even in the winter!). There were sofa chairs and a couch along the walls of the spacious room for people to sit. From the south-facing windows, we could see the south entrance and the bridges of the Forbidden City. To its south, the famous Tiananmen Square is enclosed by the museums, conference hall, and one of the few remaining ancient city gates. Everything felt luxurious, and your grandmother was very satisfied that night.

Sadly, it was the last big gathering we had with your grandmother. She passed away after a few years. She was a housewife all her life and was remembered by families, neighbors, and relatives in the home village as a very kind woman. Unless she was at a restaurant, the food on the table for the family was always on her mind. She was an expert in southeastern Chinese dishes, appetizers, and sweets. In her eighties, she spent most of her day shopping and preparing food. Even with the helper hired to take care of them, she was still in the kitchen before the dinner and always the last to come to the table. Your grandfather missed her dearly as a companion for the authentic cooking and a few cups of warm rice wine the two shared almost every evening.

Tours in Southern China, Summer 2009

You were not yet seventeen years old, in transition to university life, when we went back to China in the summer. By that time, you could really enjoy the food offered at the Chinese restaurants. Your favorite was the breakfast buffet at the hotel, where you were used to a glass of warm milk and had fun selecting steamed buns with different fillings. You and your cousin Le Le even went out on your own. Your Chinese was good enough to pay for lunch at the Starbucks in the park, within walking distance of the hotel. The main event of our trip was Ying and you following his family going back to the home village for a brief stay.

Nanjing

Ying's family arranged a trip for us to visit several cities along the Yangtze River, and Ying and you would go to the home village afterwards. The first stop of our trip was Nanjing, which is the capital of the old republic and the center of several dynasties and kingdoms in Chinese history. My first encounter with Nanjing was after I finished elementary school. The city then served as the port on the Yangtze River to ferry the train across the river. A train had to be disassembled to fit onto the ferry and then reassembled. I felt a few bumps, and it took a couple of hours, as I remember. Many years later, a bridge, which was the second one across the river, was built with multiple levels to allow both rail and road traffic to pass through.

We were supposed to spend a day in Nanjing before joining the tours the next day to visit other places. We first went back to the port side for a view of the famous Yangtze River. By the time we visited, there were different bridges and even tunnels crossing the river. It was windy and overcast on the river. There were boats and barges on the water, and the section of the river was broad and calm. We could barely see the other end of the structures on the river. Historically, the river was a natural barrier because the locals were always superior in navigating it. In transition to a different ruling regime, the river served several times as the short-lived border between newer and older ones.

We visited the Presidential Palace, the residence and government building of the old republic. It was the site of the central Chinese government before 1949. It has been restored to be a historical heritage site, which is rather large and empty. The setting includes western-style buildings and authentic Chinese tyle gardens. We walked across the gardens and buildings and visited the exhibitions in the eastern area. Many pictures of the old government compound and government officials before and after the anti-Japanese War (WWII) are on display. However, we saw very few artifacts. What was not there reminded me of the scene often seen in movies — the big retreat when the government changed hands at the end of the civil war in 1949. The old regime spent many months moving the government and the riches to Taiwan; the new regime took control of the city after fierce battles on both water and land. All this happened even before I was born.

We had supper on the most crowded streets near Confucius Temple and Qinhuai River. With lanterns along the bridge and decorating all the shops, restaurants, and paddlers on the streets, we were in a moving crowd. Still, we had time to check the activities near the water below the bridge. We saw people on the covered boat with lanterns, and we could hear music from the slowly moving boats on the water. Hotels and restaurants are lined up on the riverbank on each side. It reminds me of the Riverwalk of San Antonio, a Texas town, where the culture is mainly Spanish.

It was raining the next day. We could not hike the trail near Zijin Mountain to visit Sun Yat-sen's Mausoleum, which is in memory of the first president of the Republic of China. He fought relentlessly for a few decades in China and abroad with a lot of overseas support. His party, the Nationalist (Kuomintang), won, and it ended the thousand-year-old monarchy system in China.

Suzhou

The second stop was Suzhou, which was the hometown of my family, although it was my first visit. Suzhou is known as the

"Venice of the East" because of the waterways inside the city. It is also famous for its rockery gardens. The local entertainment was Pingtan, a folk musical/oral performance that originated from Suzhou with a history of at least four hundred years.

A major stop of the tour was the famous Lions Grove Garden. It was crowded before we even reached the entrance. We were taken into the gated rockery garden that is sectioned into small courtyards. Each courtyard is an artful arrangement of rockery mounts, pavilions, and bridges over ponds. The rockery mounts are an imitation of a cluster of lions in action. The ponds are filled with lotus and other water plants with colorful flowers. Visitors enjoy viewing the flowers and many goldfish in the water while strolling on the covered walkways and resting in the pavilions. A small stage was set up inside a pavilion in the middle. There were benches and extra chairs so that the visitors could sit down and listen to Pingtan. Among the surrounding crowd, we got to sit near the musicians when it was our turn. It was probably just another quick show for you and Ying, but I was thrilled, as it was my first Pingtan in my hometown!

After the visit, we made another stop at the ancient pedestrian street with bookstores, tea shops, and a local museum. We had opportunities to visit several shops. It was not crowded, other than a few other guided tourist groups. In the museum, there was a long list of local officials on one display. I looked for my granduncle, who was the county magistrate at the end of the 19th century. I did not find any similar names. There were probably many counties then in current Suzhou.

In the light rain, we took a ride in the covered boat on the waterway. We passed a few bridges, local commercial areas, and even residences. There were just a few boats, and the water was dark green but clean. It was quiet, probably because of the rain, when the guide pointed out local docks and places where people came to wash clothes and fetch water. Compared to the opera-singing gondola in Venice, it was tranquil but somber, an analogy comparing the vivid oil painting to the Chinese ink painting, which is mostly in black ink and occasionally brightened by a few red or yellow spots for the viewer's imagination.

Shanghai

We were cramped into a van with another group of seven people on our way from Suzhou to Shanghai. Our first stop in Shanghai was the Yu Garden and the City God Temple. The streets were packed. On the way, the guide ordered lunch for two tables of six people at a nearby restaurant. The dishes were freshly cooked and plentiful. After lunch, we were given an hour on our own to visit the Garden and the Temple. Inside the garden, it was a stop-and-go situation in the flow of people, whether at an entrance of a section or on a narrow bridge. Following the flow, we went through its multiple sections, admiring the rockery or plastic statues in the ponds. We visited the main temple to see the calligraphy displays and to check on different snacks. It was just too crowded to find a relatively empty spot to make a stop and enjoy any snack.

At night, we were sent to a hotel outside the central area of Shanghai. We learned the city was preparing for the World Trade

Exhibition and there was a lot of construction. We, the foreigners, needed to stay away from those sites. A minivan picked us up early the next morning to join the others for the activities of the day. We had good food and walked along the old commercial streets, visiting a few shops and shopping centers. Across the Huangpu River, we could see the Bund, where the new financial center of China was symbolized by clusters of skyscrapers. We could also see the constructions along the banks of the Huangpu River, which was later known as the site of Expo 2010 Shanghai.

The next day, before we left Shanghai, we dragged our luggage and stopped at the Shanghai Museum. Because of our luggage and the lineup in front of the museum, I called the scholar on Chinese coins, and it was a pleasant surprise for him. He came out to let us in. After we stored our luggage, he led us to the exhibition room, showing my father's coin collection. This was the first time I had come back to visit the display room. Years ago, we, his children and wife, donated his entire collection to the museum. Two years after the donation, I attended the opening ceremony of his collection and the related museum publications. The display and the room brought back a lot of memories. The scholar showed us around and explained the content in the display. You were quiet and reading the English content. On leaving the room, we took a picture with him and thanked him. Certainly, I really appreciated the opportunity. On the way out, we briefly visited some other rooms, and stopped in front of a huge wall. In the inscriptions on the wall, we found my father's name on the list of the contributors.

Outside the museum, Ying and you headed for the bus station to take a long-distance bus to Ying's hometown in Zhejiang. I still

241

had a few hours, so I checked in my suitcase at the luggage room of the train station and wandered around. At the bakeries on the pedestrian street, I bought several kinds of pastries freshly out of the oven. They turned out to be a sensation for the relatives in Beijing.

Your Trip to Home Village

I was told that you were fine on your trip to Ying's home village. All of you stayed in the family's Old House. As the historical residence of the family, it was quite rundown when we visited in 1998 and was subsequently rebuilt in its original style. After further renovations in previous years, air conditioning and shower facilities were installed in the Old House. Therefore, it wasn't bad in the middle of the summer.

Visiting the home village became your grandfather's favorite tour once the condition of the Old House stabilized. He went there two or three times every year with the nanny and your uncle sometimes. During our visit to China, your grandfather was glad to have more companions along for his visit to the home village. One of his activities was to engage the professionals in local education to see where he could help.

With your cousin Le Le around, you had some fun with relatives of the same or younger age. Your magic tricks were a sensation at the gatherings when relatives came to visit your grandfather. It was your second visit to the village, and I hope that you still remember some scenes of the Chinese village and villagers.

I did not know at the time that there was a project in the hills to build the tomb for your grandparents. It is not far away from other ancestors. After your grandmother passed away, her picture and an urn of her ashes were always in your grandfather's bedroom. Ying told me that your grandfather was involved in planning every stage of the project, but he never went to the site. Years later, Ying and I went back to China for the journey to take your grandparents home for their proper burial. We and the villagers went up the hill and put their ashes side by side in the tomb and closed it. It was a ceremony that started with a few days of celebration in the Old House, followed by a parade through the village, and ended with a gathering at the tomb site. In the soil of their home village, the souls of the departed were finally at peace according to old Chinese beliefs.

Beijing, Summer 2011

The trip was again in summer, and you were almost nineteen years old. We went to Beijing to join your aunt, her grandchildren, Lili and Andy, from California. It was to fulfill the wish of your aunt to visit China for the last time since she was in her late eighties. She wanted to pay respect to my late parents and visit with my relatives. Lili and Andy would be the keepers of their grandmother besides having fun.

Trip with Lili and Andy

You just secured your next co-op job and came back with half of your hair tinted red. You told me you colored your hair yourself to avoid a potential offer that you did not want to accept. We met the Californian group when we picked up our luggage at the airport. Out of the gate, we were welcomed by Ying's brother. He arranged for the two cabs to pick everybody up. At the toll booth on the way to downtown Beijing, he even got out of the cab once to check if he had gotten everybody. Your aunt always remembered that he really took care of everybody. We were greeted at the hotel by my brothers. It was a quite welcome home for your aunt.

We stayed in a relatively upscale hotel in the central commercial district of Beijing. It was the first time you got your own room in the hotel. We did not have family trips outside Beijing like we did on the previous trips. Your task was to entertain your niece and nephew, who, especially Lili, were quite free-spirited, and to keep them safe. Lili completed degrees at Columbia University and had friends from both school and her ultimate frisbee practices. She would say that she found one of her friends visiting Beijing and then went out alone to meet her friend or attend a gathering. Eventually, we had to give her the only cell phone we borrowed from the relatives to track her. Andy was a homeboy, keeping company with his grandmother whenever needed. You accompanied Lili and Andy a few times to shop along the Wangfu pedestrian streets. The three of you explored the shops and food courts in the large shopping malls. With them, you were not shy, and helped a bit with Chinese. Lili could even bargain when buying some T-shirts

Wishes of Your Aunt

The ashes of my late parents, your grandparents on my side, are laid in Babaoshan Revolutionary Cemetery on the west side of Beijing. It is a place for government officials of certain ranks. My father, never a revolutionary, was a civil engineer all his life. He completed a master's degree in civil engineering from MIT in the States in the 1920s. He passed away in 1975, before the end of the Cultural Revolution. Upon his death, his contribution to the country was deemed important enough that he could join those who held proper ranks and levels in the cemetery. When my mother passed away after many years, we got permission to expand the space to place my mother's ashes in the same location. The location is a slot on the walls (of honor) inside a large but restricted garden. At least, it is a permanent place for my parents. Ying and I visit the cemetery every time we go back to China. This time, we brought your aunt and her grandchildren.

We went there in the morning before the heat settled in. Three of us went with Lili and Andy and took the subway and then walked to the cemetery. After entering the gate, we walked the long stretch of stone road that passes tombs and monuments among tall cypress forests. My brother came in his car to take your aunt so that they could drive past the gate and stop right outside of the restricted area. Your aunt bought a small plastic flower basket at the store near the parking lot. The guard at the entrance checked our documents before letting us into the gated garden hidden inside the walls.

Your aunt walked the distance of several long walls to reach the location of my late parents. It is a ritual of the family to refresh the flowers whenever somebody comes to visit. Andy climbed up the ladder and did the honor of removing the old flower basket and stringing in the new one. We then all bowed, and your aunt fulfilled her duty to bow for her late husband, one of my half-brothers. That was the ceremony; it couldn't be simpler since the quietness was the minimum respect to the other dead, whom we know nothing about. The areas between the walls and in the central courtyard, and the gardens, were well maintained. After the visit, we went to a restaurant where my brother had already arranged lunch. Your aunt was in high spirits, although she was a little tired because of the walk and the heat. She got her wishes.

Tourists in Beijing

The relatives in Beijing arranged several shows besides dinners. One of them was at the Grand National Theater. The architecture and the decoration inside and outside the theater were indeed amazing. However, the folk music played by Western instruments in a large hall had a mixed flavor in the grandiose setting and acoustics. Another show was in a newly renovated tea house. The entertainers on the small stage were comedians or narrative singers accompanied by instruments with a single, two, or three strings. The setting is in small groups with a table full of local snacks in front of each group. It was quite entertaining. We bought tickets from the hotel front desk and went to an acrobat show. It was quite impressive, technically, although not as colorful as Cirque du Soleil. The problem with attending the night show was getting a cab afterwards. We had to wait and wait to get a cab for your aunt before the rest could go home or to the hotel.

Ying took you, Lili, Andy, and Le Le on several sightseeing trips, such as the Great Wall and the Temple of Heaven. Hanchang, my brother, came in his car and spent a day with you, Lili, and Andy. He took you to the Olympic Village to see the Bird's Nest (the Olympic stadium) and the Water Cube (the aquatics center). Afterwards, he took you to the famous Tsinghua University. He gave you a tour of his laboratory of wastewater research in environmental engineering.

Lili turned out to be a girl with her own mind, which was not always ideal in a tourist group. Ying had a bit of a tough time gathering everybody in time for the stops amidst the crowd on the Great Wall. Ying brought back a broken camera after visiting the Temple of Heaven. You were bothered when Lili invited one of her friends to spend the night on the extra bed in your room. We called the front desk of the hotel to make it official. The cell phone, which Lili used, and I collected at the end, as I recall, was never returned to the owner after we left China.

Another time, while we went back to Ying's family for a gathering and Lili was out with friends, your aunt and Andy watched a movie in the hotel. They couldn't find any place open when they looked for dinner after 9 pm.

The Dinner for the Older

Ying and I arranged a banquet in a garden called Baijiadayuan to entertain the relatives of both families. We had fun at the place during our previous China trip. The setup is an imitation of the upper class of the Qing Dynasty. People who come to dine often stroll on the paths among the rockery gardens, goldfish ponds, and pavilions. From time to time, the visitors are greeted by girls dressed in traditional Qing costumes. The Qing-style greeting is a solute with right palm over left fist and slightly bending knees. Inside the banquet hall, there are shows of Peking opera and other entertainment while the dishes are being served.

It was a hit. The cost was approximately RMB 6400, about C$1500. It wasn't cheap, but it was really an honor for us because we had attendance from all the old relatives in town. We had thirty people arranged at three big round tables. Several of our guests, such as Ying's father, your aunt, and two of my cousins, were over eighty years old. There were four generations of ages ranging from eighty-five to eight. Lili, being almost professional, provided the best picture of the crowd afterwards.

It turned out to be a very memorable event. Several people in the picture left us or became homebound in the years that followed. It was the last time you were together with your grandfather, who passed away a few years later. He was a mathematician. The textbooks used for primary education in China were standardized, and the standardization of the math content was his job for at least two decades. He made important contributions to the math subject in the education plans and university entrance exams. He was quite up-to-date and often had foresight in his field. I still remember my discussions with him on topics of educational acceleration and the content of the textbooks.

Your aunt was overwhelmed by the friendliness of Ying's and

my relatives in Beijing and the service of our family of three. Other than all the happy memories of the trip, she got the impression that they, especially Lili, caused a bit of fuss in Beijing. Her last trip to Beijing is often brought up in our conversations on my bi-weekly calls. She is in her late nineties now.

Travel in North America

The trips in North America detailed here are the ones I remembered most. They are special because of unique places, a long journey, or visits with relatives or friends.

We drove long distances many times over the years and crossed the border, sometimes to the US side. We often planned to drive or fly somewhere for our summer, Christmas breaks, or a long weekend. Ying and I liked to explore, and in addition, we didn't mind driving, a hobby since our school days on this continent. For me, driving was a part of my job as a seismologist for many years.

Florida, USA, Winter 2001

You were nine years old. Our Honda Civic was a year old, and it was a quiet and smooth car. Ying and I planned to drive to Disney World. In this way, we could make stops on the way and have a car to drive around in Florida. I went to school to talk to your grade three teacher, asking her to let you go before the Christmas break started. Mme. King was excited about our plan. She said that you might learn more from activities like family tours than staying for the last few days of school.

On the way there, our stop on the first day was in Virginia to visit Ying's friend Lv. The second day was a long day on the road. The driving was not as fast as we expected because of the holiday traffic. In Georgia, we had a wonderful supper at one of the Bonanza Buffet places and checked into a hotel for the night. We started driving at 4 am the next morning and got up to speed. Once in Florida, the road had more lanes in each direction, and the speed limit was increased to 65 miles per hour. I recognized a few names of the popular resorts on the ocean side. At a truck stop serving Chinese dishes, we filled up on gas and had lunch. The people helping us were huge, speaking a draggy English, which reminded me of my school days in Texas two decades ago. The dishes were soy sauce-soaked fried rice and sweet-and-sour chicken. I would rather have traded for some authentic local food such as fried okra, cornbread, and biscuits with gravy.

Disney World

We checked into the hotel in Orlando in the late afternoon. It was the winter following the 9/11 incident in the States. There were probably more people from other countries than Americans in the parks. The weather was cooler than normal. We were all prepared since we drove from Canada. Some others who flew from Europe, Australia, or New Zealand were not expecting anything more than T-shirts and shorts. Despite the weather factor, visitors enjoyed shorter lines at each popular station and less crowded restaurants and shops in the parks. We spent a day or a half-day at each major park like Magic Kingdom, Epcot, Animal Kingdom and Disney's MGM studio.

I like the Magic Kingdom the most. Big Thunder Mountain Railroad was our first stop on the first day. You still had the attitude that you would only go if I went along. I experienced the up and down swings and some sharp turns. I survived with a pale face, and you were sympathetic enough to change your attitude afterwards. My participation at a point of interest was no longer mandatory. Accompanied by Ying, you had a lot of fun at the station of Buzz Lightyear and the field of bumper cars. You were barely tall enough at some stations. However, you did not want to try any babyish or girlish ones like those in the Storybook Circus. Still, there were enough kind-hearted and musical entertainments for all of us to enjoy peacefully. It was so beautiful. In the evening, we had fun exploring the Main Street and watching the Christmas Parade. We went to the light show on the lake one night. It was the first time we saw lights of such a grand scale dancing on the water. You insisted on staying until the end of the show, although it was a little chilly.

At the entrance of the Magic Kingdom, you used your allowance for the trip to buy a magic set. It was a smart trick requiring full-body coordination. It used very thin but good quality threads to connect the magician and any objects such as a card or paper folding. With some skill, the paper object would fly when the magician moved his body and arms. He would put his hands at almost a fixed, short distance from the flying object with his fingers following the toss and turn. To the common eyes in the dusk, he was remotely directing his dancing objects! I noticed the details and disagreed with your request. Ying thought that there was a certain airflow and good hand coordination. You promised it would be the only big toy (~USD40) you would buy for the trip, so you got it. The toy stayed with you for many years You got the hand coordination and showman skills to lead the audience. You used it for a few shows, although it took time to get the wiring ready for the trick. Ying also asked you to show our visitors a few times until he learned the truth.

We enjoyed the 3-D movies in every park, from *It's Tough to Be a Bug*, the Muppet Show, to *Honey, I Blew up the Kids*. Each of them had its distinct entertaining aspect. I liked the Muppet Show of the Magic Kingdom the best because it was authentic with typical surprises like virtual punches, kicks, and even stares. You liked the *Honey, I Blew up the Kids* of Epcot because you loved the entire series of the 2-D originals. In the movie series, the scientist and his family became big or small, dealing with the bad guys trying to steal his inventions. *It's Tough to Be a Bug* at the Animal Kingdom had some sort of crawling motion on the back of our seats and an imitation of mist; these caused some screams but were not scary.

It was a cold and windy day when we visited Epcot. There were not a lot of tourists around. In the World Showcase, we visited China, Japan, Germany, Mexico and some other pavilions. In the China pavilion, we watched a 360-degree movie about China. The first half of the movie was a series of snapshots spanning five thousand years of Chinese history. The second half focused on China's landscape and its famous tourist attractions. In the Germany pavilion, we saw the cuckoo clocks, many of which were bigger and fancier than the one we had at home. You stayed in front of a clock structure with little men, carts, and cuckoo for a long time. In a pavilion of one of the Middle East countries, we had delicious lentil soup, which became an addition to my cooking at home. The beans in the soup extended to not only lentil beans all the time, but the soup mix of the beans from Bulk Barn.

Kennedy Space Center and Disney Quest

On the extra day in Orlando, we drove to the Kennedy Space Center. There were displays of moon rocks and other things used by astronauts. There was a stage showing the US astronaut walking on the moon. We read the details about the history of space science. The persistence of mankind was very impressive, although it happened mostly among the so-called superpowers. While we only knew the famous few, the journey into space took so many resources, including many sacrifices, to advance.

A part of the tour was to visit an old launchpad. Sitting on a tour bus, we visited launch locations with space vehicles and visitor stands from decades ago. After we were dropped off at the visitor center, we walked on the compound and visited the Rocket Garden, more likely a space junkyard. It had retired rockets, space vehicles, and even some old fighter jets or bombers. It reminded me of Tatooine in the *Star Wars*. On the way towards the exit inside the center, we walked through the Hall of Fame of the astronauts. There were so many of them besides John Glenn, Neil Armstrong, Marc Garneau, and Julie Payette, the few Americans and Canadians we already knew.

In one afternoon, after we completed visiting a park as planned, we passed Disney Quest, a huge indoor arcade. I had done my studies before the trip and was amazed by the scale and technology of the entertainment. Ying was totally against going in because he always discouraged the activities along this line ("electronic games"). You and I went in. Besides lines of game machines, which we had seen in places like Midway (Ottawa), there were large theme games involving a group of people. There were early generations of the game set up for physical exercise. We selected a few and obviously needed to wait in line sometimes. To me, it was not only fun but also a reckoning of not spending time on inferior games. In the end, Ying took the car back to the hotel by himself, and we had to take a taxi to find our way back. It was probably the first time you saw your parents angry at each other. You were quiet.

We left Orlando after our grand Disney World tour and went to Fort Lauderdale to visit my brother and his family.

Homebound

We drove back to the outskirts of Orlando to catch the Auto Train after visiting Fort Lauderdale. It was a unique experience on the only Auto Train in the States. At the train station, we watched cars being loaded into the lower level of the train. We then boarded and got to our sleeper compartment. The space was limited but private. We had stools and a stand to pull out for board games. You and Ying played checkers. When everything inside the cabin was connected and flat, Ying and I laid down parallel while you were at the other end. We had a good night's sleep, although there was no space to toss and turn. In Lorton outside Washington DC the next morning, we got off the train and were back in winter. It started snowing.

By the time we got on the highway going towards Canada, the visibility was probably less than ten meters. In the storm, I tried my best to keep the car along the white strip of the road and away from the shoulder or the ditch on the side. Other than several vehicles parked on the roadside, I couldn't really notice any highway exit along the way. You were napping in the back at the beginning but woke up and sat straight, watching quietly all the way. Were you worried? It took probably at least two more hours further on the highway when the storm finally cleared. It was Syracuse, New York, and we were out of the hills and forests. After Watertown, we passed the customs at the border with a bright moon hanging in the sky. We got "Welcome back to Canada" and "Happy New Year" at the Canadian customs. The home stretch was well lit, mostly by the moonlight. We were all happy, and you went back to sleep since it had already passed midnight. Home, sweet home, I felt it was so well said.

Friends and Relatives

Virginia. On our way to Florida, we spent a night in Virginia to visit Ying's friend, Dr. Lv. He was a medical student in Buffalo when Ying was doing his doctoral degree in physics. When we visited, Lv and his wife were both working at the same medical laboratory. Lv's mother lived with them to take care of their children and help them with other chores. Ying and Lv had a lot to catch up on while you played with his boys. Lv later took the board exam for a physician and became a licensed family doctor, a dream he had from his university days in China.

<u>Fort Lauderdale, Florida</u>. Your uncle and his wife immigrated from Shanghai, China to the USA years ago. They were in their early seventies. They knew basic English when they were still in Shanghai. Once in the States, your uncle worked first as a data entry clerk at a credit card company and then as a guide at a department store, while your aunt worked in daycare. They worked for ten years before retiring to meet the requirements for social security benefits. Their children, your cousins, are my age, and we came to the States in the same year (1980) to study for different degrees. After ten to fifteen years of study and work, all of us settled down with our own families and careers.

Judy, their daughter, arranged a huge dinner in a restaurant to welcome us. It was your first time meeting your cousin and her children. You were "Uncle James" to Lili, who was in her teens, and Andy, a three-year-old boy. We had a lot of fun on the beach during the day. Lili was already a talented photographer. Andy had his own mind about everything. You had a friendly shell collecting competition with him, and the game ended with him collecting shells from your bucket into his. We remembered Andy's famous "pee pee in the sea" for many years.

The Maritimes, Canada, Summer 2003

You were almost eleven years old. Still with the same Honda Civic, we had our road trip to the Maritimes. Our plan to reach the first maritime province, New Brunswick, was to go southbound. It meant driving through Ontario and Quebec, crossing the border and driving east in Maine to enter the Canadian Maritimes. We started driving east in the late morning and stopped for lunch at a small restaurant in Quebec that served both local and Chinese dishes. We passed Sherbrooke, a major city in Quebec, and then drove through the forested area, following the signs towards the US-Canada border. South of the border, we were mostly on state or county roads, in the forest with denser and taller trees. Remember that I saw the signs of Vermont, but we were mainly in Maine. The wilderness in Maine was beautiful. In the years Ying and I stayed in the States, we somehow never visited Maine. By late at night, we were still in Maine, far from the Canadian border. We spent the night in a motel. I was glad that I had not reserved a hotel for our first night on the road.

New Brunswick

Early the next morning, we started driving towards St. Andrews, New Brunswick. We were soon out of the forest and along the water. After the sign of St. Andrews, we made our first stop in St. John. We visited the Reversing Falls Rapids, where the rapids of the Saint John River reversed the flow during high tides before entering the Bay of Fundy. The observation point was a large well and had the water flowing in multiple directions because of the underwater swirls. For lunch, we had plates of sandwiches, where the fillings, fish or cheese and lettuce, were all fresh — a change from the food we had the previous day. We then visited the local museum that displayed relatively young fossils of elephant tusks and shark jaws. The destination of the day was Moncton, which is close to several attractions we planned to isit. We stayed at a bed-and-breakfast home, which was our first me with a B&B. It was a very homey and clean setting with very nowledgeable hosts. To conclude our first day in the Canadian Maritimes, we had the famous lobster dinner in Dieppe in the vening. You had fish while Ying and I shared a lobster and some ort of seafood gumbo. The main point of interest was the huge obster statue outside the restaurant.

Our first stop the next day was Hopewell Rocks. We got there n time to go down to the sandy beach before the tides. The beach as not muddy, but with large leaves of seaweed everywhere. tanding next to the rocks with the watermark of the high tide ell above my head gave me fear. The work of nature has made he diameter of the columnar rock at and under the watermarks maller than that above. I looked around but did not find any roken rock pillars. It has been a fine work for thousands of years. mong the big and small columnar rocks, I was just in for a apshot in the middle of a long, slow but never stopping process. took plenty of pictures while you and Ying walked among the emnants of the tides. Soon enough, we heard the call to go up to he observation platform. We followed the instructions and were robably among the first group to return to the upper level. In ct, the call was repeated many times before we saw the water vel rising. We stayed until the lower-level observation points ere completely submerged. In the light fog from the upper-level latform, waves came until they reached cliffs, ponding on them ith bigger splashes every time. On the beach where we had been inutes before, the rock pillars, like clusters of guards along the ore, were unshaken and never retreated.

We stopped at a souvenir shop on the way to the Bay of Fundy. The outside of the store is a deck leading to a layout imitating the columnar rocks we had visited. For somebody coming from Hopewell Rocks, the layout was vivid, although there were not a lot of details on the wooden statues in the water. I took a few pictures from different angles. Thanks to the creator, who appreciated the wonder of nature and brought to the roadside its introduction to the tourists passing by.

We drove through Fundy National Park and bought a two-pound boiled lobster in a small town called Alma. We then drove to the Anderson Hollow Lighthouse. On its ground level, we bought more food for lunch from the country-fair-like tents and stands. We had lunch on its upper level, where there were fewer people. The boiled lobster wrapped in the newspaper was delicious and filling. Ying and I shared it and felt that we had all the lobster we needed for the trip.

Before returning to Moncton, we visited Magnetic Hill. The visitors were supposed to bring their car to the top of a gentle slope and then set the gear to neutral and let the car slide. Ideally, they would experience the pull of the "force" when the car slides backwards down to the bottom of the slope. It turned out to be a test of my ability to drive in reverse in a straight line, which I was never good at. When sliding downward, our car, with me managing the steering, was zigzagging all along. I wish it were a stretch with lanes! I parked the car in the parking lot to take a break. Ying and you went back to check the route to see if there were any magnets or forces. The answer was NO, other than gravity.

260

In the morning (of the third day of our trip), we said goodbye to the B&B owners after a quite formal breakfast. We made a stop at an Acadian village to learn the local history. It is a part of the history between the English- and French-speaking Canadians. On this piece of land, it was straightforward in local history that the British persecuted the French. The French afterwards stayed in the village, which was likely a similar cluster to the current reservations for Native Americans. Some of them went south to settle in the States, as far as New Orleans. We had some freshly made poutines in the gift shop. It reminded me of the mystery books of Anne Rice, each of which has descriptions of diverse backgrounds, along with a long and strange story. Someday, I will visit New Orleans and try Cajun food.

Prince Edward Island

We left New Brunswick and drove east to cross the Confederation Bridge, the world's longest bridge in the cold area. It was my first time driving across a bridge with a length of over ten kilometers. I could feel the minor swinging of the bridge, although it wasn't a windy day. I thought about ice engineering and other forces in nature related to slow erosion or corrosion. The tourist information center of Prince Edward Island (PEI) was right after the bridge. It had a nice playground and benches for the visitors to rest and have their first glance at the greenness of the island. The exhibition inside the center gave us the answers to building and maintaining the bridge.

It was green everywhere all the way to Charlottetown, the

capital of PEI. The hotel was close to the government seat. We went to the theater, and we were lucky that there were still a few tickets left for the night show, *Anne of Green Gables*. We went back to the theater after dinner, and it was a bit early for the show. The theater was a part of a connected building complex, including the provincial office, art gallery, and museum. It had a nice exhibition on local history and the author and the background of *Anna of Green Gable*. The girl in the story has been well-liked in Japan and other eastern Asian countries. It was really a very good musical with the same cast who had already traveled to several provinces of Canada and different places in the world for quite a few years. The narration was clear, and the characters were very vivid. There were songs and dances. You were never bored for the entire duration. This was the first musical we attended.

We visited the actual gable and the museum the next day. We walked along the path in the forest and along the lake, which inspired Montgomery when she worked on the classic novel. The story and the farmhouses hidden in the "rolling greens" seemed so well together. We drove along the red sand beaches and visited a few more lighthouses afterwards. You learned to skip stones. The water was calm and was close to the grass-covered area where we could collect some pebbles. The entire family looked for proper pebbles. A few of them were thin, flat, and elliptical. We then took turns skipping stones. You learned how to grip a piece of stone and move the arm soon. Using the pointing finger to give a final twist to enforce the spinning required some experimentation. A good one would hit the surface several times before diving into the water. We sat on the grass in the late afternoon sun. It was just so green and peaceful.

The next morning, we drove to Wood Island and boarded the ferry to the next province, Nova Scotia. At the dock, we were guided to one of the lanes to board the ferry with our car. The ferry was over an hour long, and therefore, the vessel was well equipped. We went up and down to check on our car, which was among many parked on the lower deck. It was clean. We had a simple lunch on the dining deck. It was an old-fashioned ship, so there were a lot of areas on the deck that were open to the water. The water was relatively calm on the way. I took a few pictures on the deck, one of which was a seagull flying towards my camera.

Nova Scotia

The ferry ended at a dock in Caribou, Nova Scotia. We didn't waste a minute after getting our car back. It took over two hours to reach Louisbourg on Cape Breton Island. We spent a good part of the afternoon at the famous Fortress of Louisbourg, including an old-style afternoon tea. The Fortress was built from a fishing village by the French approximately three hundred years ago. It was a stronghold to defend the French territory from the sea. It is a large compound with rows of old-style houses that were for both commercial and military purposes. The land, however, was really pieces taken by the French and British intertwined together. The British won more wars because the entire eastern coastal area of the States was a British colony with armies. During the wars, the French had to get help either from Quebec or overseas. It's hard to believe that the now miles of peaceful coastlines and lands were often a war zone in the past. The maritime provinces gave a good reason for the existence of bilingualism in Canada.

We settled in Baddeck before night fell. From Louisbourg to Baddeck, we passed a few cities and old mining areas, which were a kind of barren and not so green. In Baddeck, we stayed in the Telegraph House Hotel, where Alexander Bell often stayed. The building has wooden floors and many pictures and memorabilia of the hotel and its famous visitors. Mr. Bell came to Baddeck in the late 1880s and settled in the area as his second and later the primary home. Outside the hotel, Main Street had some gift shops and restaurants. Ying found a restaurant serving both Chinese and Canadian dishes. You and I walked up the street one night and had dinner at an Italian restaurant. It was a nice sunny day the next day. We had a substantial breakfast in the dining part of the hotel and, unavoidably, admired the details of displays along the way and in the restaurant. Then we left to spend our day driving around.

Baddeck is the place to stay for a drive on Cabot Drive, miles of highway in the mountains next to the shoreline. We thoroughly enjoyed the drive. As was said in the guide, we were driving Cabot Drive counterclockwise. Ying learned how to use different gears to handle long stretches of uphill and downhill. Once we came to the ocean side, we made stops at a few scenic observation points. At one stop, we could overlook a herd of whales swimming. With their black and white colors under the sun, the change of color was quite synchronized. They were probably orcas. It was lovely although they were likely meat eaters, I thought. At Pleasant Bay we stopped for lunch and joined probably the shortest whale-watching boat tour. We got to see a larger whale a few times. Those were not staying in a group. At one point, when the boat was near several whales, the guide stopped the engine in the middle of the water to let us listen to "whale talk." Other than the murmuring, the motion of the boat without the engine running made me almost seasick. You and Ying were fine, and it was quite amazing to listen to their singing firsthand. We came back to Baddeck after sunset. The last stretch of the Cabot Drive was downhill in the patches of forests and pastures. The day, which was spent at the east end of our maritime trip, was most satisfying.

We left Baddeck the next morning for Halifax. Before leaving the town, we visited the Alexander Graham Bell Museum, where the Canadian part of Bell's life was reflected. Being a resident of the United States, Canada, and the United Kingdom, Mr. Bell regarded himself as a "native son" without a prefix in all three countries. Across a lake, we could vaguely see the Bell residence, Beinn Bhreagh (Gaelic: Beautiful Mountain). It was his summer home first, but later turned into his favorite residence, where he had his large laboratory and even a boat shop. His inventions, which were mostly on display in the museum, went well beyond the telephone. They were devices for long-distance and marine communication in various aspects of life, including military use. He and his family claimed the Baddeck community "his own" and were well mixed with locals. I was glad that we had planned this visit to understand the brilliant inventor as a human being. Someday, I thought, we should go to Brantford, Ontario, to check on Mr. Bell, too, to learn how he learned the Mohawk language as part of his research on sound.

From the Bell Museum, we drove straight to Halifax, the capital city of Nova Scotia. There are quite a few museums in the city. We only went into the Maritime Museum of the Atlantic and then visited some old ships that were open to the public. We learned that a big trade in town was salvaging shipwrecks. It was said to have sourced from over 10,000 submerged ships related to warfare, natural disaster, and piracy. There were so many ship models and stories related to shipwrecks. We watched the 3-D movie on the Halifax explosion, which claimed to be the largest artificial explosion before the nuclear bomb. The incident started with a bump on the bow of a ship loaded with explosives. Another part of the exhibit we visited is on how Canadians responded to the sunken Titanic and its artifacts from the ship. In the end, it made me think that the huge liners and luxury cruises nowadays were really an evolution of all these actual human sacrifices. Out of the museum, we walked and went in and out of whatever military or commercial ships we could find an entrance.

In the late afternoon, we walked along the waterfront and visited Pier 21 and its Canadian Museum of Immigration. We watched a well-prepared show to illustrate how people from the other side of the Atlantic came to this country. This was the first historical pier I visited besides sailing past Ellis Island when visiting New York. The Pier is one of the five or six immigration entrances in Canada, and amazingly, it was in use as late as 1971. Nearly one million immigrants came through the pier. With the arrivals, there were likely many broken families and losses on the long journey. I felt sad. The vast structure contained several piers to match up with ocean liners of different sizes during that time. With connections to other office buildings, the compound was like a small town offering all the necessities to the newcomers. It is a part of our own history, I thought, although we "landed" via an office on the highway.

We were tired when we checked into the hotel in the evening. This time we got our first experience at a hostel. At least, we booked its only family type room for the night. The facilities were clean, sufficient, but simple. We went out and found a pho place nearby for dinner. In the morning, the hostel provided the minimum continental breakfast. Ying and I got coffee, and you got milk.

We used the morning to visit the Citadel (Fort George). Built at the top of a hill, the Citadel is in the shape of an octagonal star. The site resulted from multiple stages of expansion in history as a part of the strategy to defend Halifax Harbor. Its actual function has been a source for the Royal Navy. Interestingly, as the counterbalance to Louisbourg, it remained British and then Canadian. The potential enemies were French or Americans over the time of approximately 250 years. Never being a battleground, as shown in our guided tour, the site provided the central coordinates for the city's anti-aircraft defense in World War II. Inside or outside of the buildings, we enjoyed the openness of the hosts, who were eager to share whenever asked. We could visit different rooms of the fortress and were guided by a volunteer at the exhibition in a large room. Later, we were out on the compound to watch the cadet training. It is a nice educational site for a brief military history of different generations.

On the way west, we made a stop to have lunch in Peggy's Cove. The shoreline here is rocky! I took a picture of you jumping from one big rock to the next with waves hitting hard on the rocks. After the crash of the Swissair in September 1998, Canadians from these small villages arrived at the crash site with their private vessels first. They performed the initial rescues and evidence collection. Later, the local people accommodated visitors from all over the world who arrived at the crash site to mourn the 229 victims. Over the years, I came across reports, TV series, and some shows about the disaster and the pain and kindness afterwards. The fishing villages we passed through were quiet, with only a few people around, besides a few small docks, lobster cages, and boats in the waves and winds. Many years ago, everybody was out giving a helping hand and many families hosted unexpected guests. It reminded me of Kanata, a suburb of Ottawa. It was never crowded, except on Canada Day, which brought out people from every household. At the Walter Baker Recreation Park, local organizations always had a full set of programs throughout the day and fireworks at night.

After a stop at the Swissair Memorial Site, we left Peggy's Cove and drove southwest along the coast to the lower part of Nova Scotia. It was a very empty stretch of the highway. We spent the night in Digby, which is famous for cold-water scallops. The area is known for humpback whale watching. We did not book any tour but went out in the morning to check, anyway. It was too early, and the dock was entirely covered in fog. We walked along the shore and then on the stretches of boardwalk. We could vaguely see the waves hitting the platform. There was no horizon other than the waves under and around the boat ramp. It was spooky, and we did not stay long.

After Digby, it was a long day on the road towards Fredericton, New Brunswick. On the way, I was stopped by the highway patrol when the road was so empty, and I did not use the cruise control. My speeding was probably first picked up by the patrol helicopter. The patrol car with blinking lights appeared in my rearview mirror, followed by a few sirens. Oops, my speed was OVER 130 on a highway that already has a speed limit of 110 kilometers per hour. The police officer checked inside and saw Ying in the passenger seat and you taking a nap in the back. He advised me to watch my speed and reminded me that the speed limit in New Brunswick would go back to 100 kilometers per hour. He then left. That was very lucky. Ying said that I had a not-smiling, innocent face.

From Fredericton to Quebec City

We arrived in Fredericton in the rain. I had only planned for an overnight stay. I did not select any activity, although it is the capital city of New Brunswick. The city was modern, with streets filled with buildings labeled with well-known restaurant and hotel chains. It differed from the mixture of old and new in the small and medium-sized towns and cities we had passed in our previous days. We left the city as well as the maritime provinces the next morning and drove all day in the rain until we were near Quebec City in the early afternoon.

We had a package for a two-day and three-night stay in Quebec City. The package also came with free entrance to three points of interest. The Aquarium du Québec was amazing. We all loved it because we had a similar but small-scale experience before at the Biodome in Montreal. We also enjoyed our first IMAX experience, which was a movie about insects.

When we finally got back home, the odometer reading in the Honda Civic showed we drove approximately 3000 kilometers for the trip. The part of Canada we traveled to was like a kaleidoscope of different cultures and people: French, British and Canadian. History there is not repetitive nor in sequence, but a collection of colorful pictures. The impact of *Anne of Green Gables* resonated for a while. I bought the book and watched the different versions of the TV series. You had it for your English reading at school one time. Compared to Oliver Twist, the orphan in London, Anne Shirley did not encounter any real evil in her life; she grew up as an always truthful and enthusiastic girl among the villagers.

Rockies, Summer 2004

You were almost twelve years old. After the successful Maritimes trip, Ying and I planned another driving trip to visit the west. The purpose was to see the Canadian Rockies and visit relatives and friends. We flew to Calgary and picked up the rental car at the airport.

Edmonton

Our first stop was Edmonton. It was quite flat all the way from Calgary to Edmonton. We saw sporadic oil wells with dippers along the way. It reminded me of Texas in the States, where the roads are wider than those of its neighboring states and the dippers of the shallow-sand oil wells are everywhere. We checked into a B&B where we had the entire basement to use, and the basement had windows and a separate entrance. The owner provided plenty of information on Edmonton and how to start the trip to the Rockies. It was the end of June, and the days were very long. It was still daylight at 9 pm.

We spent a day visiting Edmonton. Alberta is famous for dinosaur digs. We visited the Royal Alberta Museum to admire the large and small fossils. The content here is a branch of Canada we had learned about when we visited the Museum of Civilization in Ottawa. It is about the great west here and has a lot more details on the mining and ranching in the Rockies and the great plain. We went to the Edmonton Mall to have lunch. The mall is said to be one of the three largest malls in the world. We spent the entire afternoon in the mall, doing a lot of window shopping, passing an indoor water park and ice rink. To our surprise, we visited a nice display of marine animals and enjoyed a round of indoor mini golf.

Canadian Rockies

We drove west and entered the Canadian Rockies early in the morning the next day. In Jasper, we took a gondola ride to the top of a mountain where we could have a bird's-eye view of the mountains. Unlike the Rockies in Colorado where I did my 6-week field course, the mountain peaks in Jasper are sharper. The folded rock strata are far above the forests and pastures. Driving toward Banff was kind of downhill. On the way, we passed small groups of deer a few times. We made a stop at the Columbia Glacier. Ying and you went to walk on the glacier. For me, I was more than happy to look at all the U-shaped valleys, a feature of glacial topology. The last force of nature in the Canadian Rockies is indeed the glacier.

We arrived in the town of Banff and had a quick lunch and window shopped at the stores on Main Street. We then went to Lake Louise and Moraine Lake. The site of Lake Louise is a lake and elegant hotels surrounded by snowcapped mountains. It was tranquil even with more than enough tourists around. Moraine Lake is mountains and lakes with shores of a range of living to dead trees augmenting the jagged rocks. The word "enchanting" seems fit, for example, a place where I felt I could see very far. No wonder it was on the back of the Canadian bill. We spent a bit of time there exploring the rocks. We then drove southwest to Panorama, where Club Intrawest had a resort. On the way, we had to stop to wait for a few North American buffalo to pass.

Soon, I had the rental car bumped. The accident changed the mood of our trip, at least for a few days. I was supposed to bring the car from a side road onto the highway. Unfortunately, the merging was not a ramp but a stop facing the traffic in both directions. It was too late when I realized my car should join the traffic on the "other" side of the road. I lost my orientation and was checking the traffic in the wrong direction. Fortunately, the driver in the on-coming traffic was alert. It was not a functional loss for either party. The other vehicle was a super pickup truck with solid metal frames. The impact only caused a scratch. My rental car suffered a visible dent on the driver's side fender. The owner of the other vehicle was a pastor from Texas. Neither he nor I wanted to wait to report the accident to the police. We left our contact information with him and promised to pay for his damages.

After meandering along the road that is quite close to the cliffs, we arrived at the resort in Panorama. For the next two days, we had to become accustomed to the stretch of narrow highway in and out of the resort. The resort was fine, and we had opportunities to do our laundry and play unlimited mini golf. For the dented car, Ying and I tried to check if a garage could replace the fender. However, the shops for body repair were almost non-existent. We went back to the Rockies to visit more lakes and look at more mountains. The most amazing observation was the color of the lakes, which could be blue, turquoise, or green. I checked online after our trip to understand the colors of the lake water and the related minerals.

We did not fix the car. It was my duty to report the accident to the insurance and the car rental.

Portland, Oregon

After three peaceful nights at the resort, we left Panorama in he morning and went south, entering the States. We drove over 000 kilometers that day. After a lot of mountains and forests in the morning and noon, we were "out of the woods." We were near the Columbia River. We passed a lot of farming areas. It was beautiful to see the mists and rainbows from the very long and moving irrigation systems in the afternoon sun. However, we had to spend the night about 100 kilometers from Portland for security reasons because of the Democratic convention that night. In the morning, we passed the Columbia Gorge, driving again on the mountainous road, and arrived in Portland. I believe we crossed the Sierra Nevada. The hotel I booked in Portland was the worst one we had for the trip. However, it was at least safe and had good air conditioning.

The purpose of visiting the city was for a reunion with a couple of old teachers and my cousin's family. The teachers had helped me learn English during my days at the Beijing Teachers Institute several decades back. My cousin's wife, who was a doctor by profession, was a visiting scholar at the university in Wisconsin, where I worked on my doctoral degree.

We visited the Oregon Museum of Science and Industry, which is one of the best science museums I have visited. We spent more than half a day there, even skipping the IMAX movie. At different labs in the Turbine Hall, I was really impressed by the environment designed with a mind for the school children, especially the youths. There are abundant hands-on stands and platforms; the legends and explanations were short and well-thought-out for the level of the readers. It was our first-time walking among holographic images. There were quite a few chemical experiments in the lab, besides the usual mists and frozen balloons. There were many things I haven't seen in place like Smithsonian museums in Washington DC, or the Ontario Science Centre in Toronto. Outside of the museum, we visited the retired submarine on display. In the late afternoon, we drove to the city's rose garden, and had a pleasant walk among acres of roses. After the Rockies and long drive in the States, it was probably a day more aligned with your interest in a beautiful city.

Vancouver

We left Portland for Vancouver the next day. On the way, we made a stop at Mount St. Helens. The mountain and its volcanic eruption were special to me. The volcano erupted in May 1980 when I set foot on this continent. It was in every news magazine. I spent two months at a language school in Dallas to prepare for the exams so that I could be qualified to enter a university in the fall. The volcanic eruption became the focus of my final essay at school. Subsequently, geology was my major for a bachelor's degree and geophysics was my research focus in the years that followed. On our visit, the Mount wasn't really smoking, but there were still a few fissures. From the observation deck, which was quite far from the mountains, I saw a few clusters of heavy fog on the Mount, likely the normal geothermal activities in the area.

Mount St. Helen is about 100 miles from the US-Canada border south of Vancouver. It took longer than expected to reach the Canadian side because of the lineup at the border. Our first stop in Vancouver was the University of British Columbia (UBC). It is a beautiful campus. I was there many years ago for a conference and was impressed by the museum on campus. Based on my memory, we went to the Museum of Anthropology, but it was closed. We passed a monument commemorating the people's demonstration in Tiananmen Square in 1989. We walked inside the student center and toured the cafeteria to give you an idea of university life. It was close to the end of the summer and, therefore, even the summer terms were over.

Our second stop was Chinatown, as marked on the map. It was neither lunchtime nor dinnertime, and therefore, it was not crowded at all. In the end, Ying and you went into a barber shop and had haircuts. We checked into the Sheraton at the center of the city, another Club Intrawest location. The space in the room was tight, but the location was ideal for parking the car and walking the blocks. After a brief rest, we went out to explore probably the most touristy street blocks downtown. We spent our evening window shopping and trying to figure out where to eat. The dinner, which included the famous Vancouver crab, was expensive and the 2-lb crab was cooked quite tasty and juicy. You enjoyed the dinner special that included a piece of grilled fish, salad, veggies and a dessert.

As planned, we took the ferry to Vancouver Island to visit Victoria, the provincial capital, the next day. Many years ago, after attending the conference at UBC, I took the cruise from Victoria to Seattle on my way back to the States. It was my first cruise in North America with my limited resources. This time, we had a vehicle to drive around on the island. It was quiet and peaceful on a summer morning. We drove past the area of the parliament buildings and made a quick stop at the maritime museum. Otherwise, walking along the harbor on a sunny day was very enjoyable. We took the ferry back to the mainland to catch the midday appointment with my friend in Richmond. Coming from Ottawa, where Chinatown is mainly one street, I was surprised by Richmond, a very Chinese town in the suburb of Vancouver. In the late afternoon, we drove past Stanley Park on our way back to the hotel. I felt Vancouver was a very modern city and quite oriental.

From Vancouver to Calgary

We left the city the next morning on our way back to Calgary. I did not book the hotel for the night so that we would have some flexibility on the unfamiliar road. In fact, we got lost at least twice after several detours to go around the areas blocked by wildfires. The CAA maps and the National Geographic Road atlas we brought along were not sufficient; there were hardly any road signs on the roads, which we referred to as "road for the locals." Occasionally, we were in the smog and could smell the smoke. I finally gave up on getting back to the highway that leads to Calgary on the map. Instead, we turned on any decent road going eastward to get out of the smoky forest area. It worked, and we were out of the Sierra Nevada and entered the Rockies. We spent the night on the west side of the Rockies, likely close to Panorama. It was a small town, and there were only a few streetlights. The sky was full of stars.

We had plenty of time the next morning to drive to Calgary. As planned, we visited my previous colleague at the University of Toronto. Other than driving past the streets for the annual stampede, as recommended by my friends, we did not make any stops. After lunch, we drove to the airport and left the car with the car rental. We were homebound shortly after. The long and complicated trip was over, and you were happy that we were on the airplane and going home.

For this trip, we drove over 5000 kilometers. It was the only trip we took to see western Canada. Compared to our trip to the Maritimes, the west, from a few glimpses in our busily packed travel schedule, is still wild. In addition, the visits we had with my friends and relatives were valuable memories because I would not see them again for a long time, or possibly never.

For the car accident, the pastor repaired his truck and mailed me the receipt. It was approximately US$100, and I promptly paid. When returning the rental car, I told the rental company that the car was parked and had been bumped. By that time, I had already communicated with my insurance agent about the incident while driving a rental car. I lied for two reasons: one was to avoid penalty, and the other was to protect the other party involved in the accident. It was the biggest lie I had ever told in my life. It was probably the first time you noticed I could lie. You were disappointed and angry at me for a few days. I hope you understand the consequences of these actions better now.

Friends and Relatives

<u>Portland</u>. We met with my cousin and my teachers in our shabby hotel room. However, it was air-conditioned and quiet for us to catch up in the afternoon heat. My cousin was a professo

back in China, and he was a lecturer at a college in Portland. His wife was a medical doctor by profession and a visiting scholar in Madison, Wisconsin, when I was a graduate student there. My teachers were English professors, and they helped me in English when I was in China, trying to figure out my new life after years in the countryside. In Portland, they worked on their new career in tourism, organizing several trips to China every year. The husband, an author of several books on linguistics, was active in the Chinese community. Interestingly, the children of both families were successful professionals who settled in California.

The crowd had dinner at a Chinese buffet place called "Wojia" (My Home in Chinese) in the techy section of Portland. In an enormous hall, the layout of the buffet included several aisles that led the customers to selections of appetizers, main courses, or desserts. The counters lined up on the side in each aisle were loaded with many small dishes of steamed, grilled, stir- or deep-fried food with various Chinese flavors. While you made many trips to pick up little things among the lines of food each time, we continued with our conversations about our lives and our children.

Vancouver. We met with the family of my classmate from junior high school. He and I were students in the same grade-eight class a few decades ago. After ten years of no school but re-education among peasants or herdsmen, many in the class reconnected. Somehow, he learned from others that I was in Canada, and sent me an open invitation to drop by if I was in the area. The family was doing well with my friend, who traveled between two countries to do his research and writing. The visit became lunch with his wife and their son, who was going to UBC and becoming a journalist. He shared a lot of information on college life and multiculturalism in Vancouver. When we departed, his wife gave me a couple of books written by my friend. His books focused on comparisons and contrasts of people's lives in different locations and different times. It took me another ten years to meet my friend and his family in Beijing. By that time, his son was a photographer and journalist and had a few publications of his own.

Calgary. On the day we were to catch a flight back to Ottawa, we had time to visit my previous colleague at the University of Toronto. After moving to Calgary, he switched his career from academic research to industries in petroleum exploration. His wife was an excellent cook, and they still remembered you when you were a toddler. Their two daughters, who had dressed you up as a girl when we visited their home in Toronto, already finished university. During the conversation, we learned that their older daughter had always wanted to become a doctor but got scared away by the cadavers in the lab. She then felt sick when she needed to look down at the black hole of a human throat all the time while trying to become a dentist. Eventually, she became a pharmacist. Ying and I talked a few times about her encounters. It takes a kind heart and determination to surpass quite a few fears on the way to becoming a medical doctor. The profession was never in my career planning, nor was Ying's. I was cautious in encouraging you, even when you were reading the family medical books.

Palm Desert and San Francisco, Summer 2007

You were almost fifteen years old. We took another driving trip in California to explore as well as visit relatives and friends.

Palm Desert to Los Angeles

We flew to Los Angeles and picked up our rental car. The stop for the night was a small town called Palm Desert, which is closer to Los Angeles than the better-known Palm Springs. It was 115°F in the early afternoon when we got out of the car in Palm Desert. We could see the heat coming out of the sand as we stepped on it. It was indeed a desert with sporadic cactus plants, whose fat leaves or stems stood firm under the glaring sunshine. We checked in at the resort and rested until sunset. We drove to Palm Springs to buy some juice and bread for the morning and then had a typical Mexican dinner before calling it a day. I still remember that the air conditioning in the suite was constantly triggered all night long.

Next morning, we drove towards San Diego. Our intention was to visit the famous aquarium. However, being less prepared, we ended up near the San Diego Zoo. It was not as hot as it had been in the Palm Desert the previous day. We got a map of the zoo and had an enjoyable walk visiting different sections. The panda residence was probably everybody's must-see for everyone visiting the zoo. Just getting up to walk, the creature would be rewarded with cheers and greetings from the crowd of visitors. In the section on wildlife in the desert, we stayed for the lecture on eagles.

It was well into the afternoon when we started driving towards

Los Angeles. To my surprise, we came to an aquarium on the way, which was the second unplanned event of the day. The aquarium had a huge lobby illustrating the evolution of the underwater world. It also had tunnels with display windows to show the world beneath the water. We ended up staying for the longest time with the large stingrays.

At the end of the long summer day, we finally arrived at Judy's home. Since it was our first visit after she moved to California, it took me several rounds of driving in the Calabasas hills to reach the right gate of the right compound.

Sequoia National Park

After two days exploring Los Angeles arranged by Judy, we left the city in the late morning and drove towards the mountain ranges in eastern California. The distance from Los Angeles to Sequoia National Park is over 200 miles on the map. Calabasas is already in the hills of the Coastal Range and out of the Los Angeles Basin. Specifically, we drove out of the coastal mountains and into the Sierra Nevada. The direction is almost due north, instead of east, as I had thought. We passed quite a few towns and villages and made a stop for lunch. The driving was smooth and almost endless until we started going up the Sierra Nevada. It was a day with light rain. The darkness settled in early because we were in the forests of very tall sequoia trees.

We arrived in Sequoia National Park before dark. I picked this park instead of Kings Canyon nearby because of the lodging. The Wuksachi Lodge turned out to be a wonderful place to stay fo the night. Built of stone and logs, the Lodge has a restaurant for food and a fireplace in the lobby to keep out the dampness. We had time and clear weather to walk to the Visitor Center before dinner. The air was very fresh and humid. It was dark when the night set in and unusually quiet in contrast to the previous nights in Los Angeles or the desert.

It was sunny when we checked out of the lodge the next day. We followed the park map and visited the monumental sequoia trees. The park is well managed for driving and hiking for all age groups. We visited the General Sherman Tree and the Giant Forest Museum. At each site, we took pictures and walked around to give the same amount of attention to other trees and plants nearby. In fact, the site of a monument is usually bare in terms of shrubs and moss. It made me think how far the "monument" roots spread — they must be hundreds of meters. At one site, we climbed up to the top of the large trunk of a fallen sequoia tree. The forest of very tall trees received sufficient sunlight as we could see. We then drove to Crystal Cave to satisfy my curiosity. We joined the 1-hour guided tour, the shortest one. Walking up and down the limestone caves was relatively demanding. Compared to the Rockies and the caves we had visited in the past, the local diversity from underground marble karst caves to miles of igneous-rock-based mountain ranges for the tall trees was unique.

The road from Sequoia to Yosemite included going out of and then going back in the Sierra Nevada. It is the only mapped road for tourists when I checked online. Including lunch in Fresno, it took over three hours to reach Yosemite.

Yosemite

We arrived in Yosemite in the early afternoon. Other than the famous peaks in the mountains, the park is a huge camping ground. We had reservations for a tent house, which has the furniture for a basic bedroom to accommodate three adults. The tent was set up on a deck with three steps leading to the ground. A metal garbage bin with a lock was next to the tent. This type of lodging was probably the best compared to the large and small tent rentals and the regular camping spots. The facilities were shared and not far away. The Yosemite Valley Visitor Center is at the one end of the campground, and it includes information, groceries, and a cafeteria for meals.

We spent two nights in Yosemite Valley. For the full day at the park, we first joined the guided bus tour. The tour takes visitors to the key scenic points inside the park. We also drove carefully along the park roads on the map to visit several well-known peaks. We could see people hiking seriously on the trails or a few climbers hanging on the cliff, such as the Half Dome. Otherwise, we enjoyed the fresh air in the forests during our brief break from the road.

Living in the tent house itself was an alternative lifestyle to explore. Ying and I were never keen on camping. With a roof of thick and waterproof cloth, the air inside the tent was fresh while we sat around in the comfortable beds. Ying and you walked together to the showers and washrooms. We had meals at the Visitor Center, which brought us back under the normal roof. The tent house we stayed in is possibly the most luxurious. The next level of dwelling is tall tents built by the park. People can stand straight inside. Normal campgrounds for campers are along streams and trails. It was hard to find one that was not occupied. Among the tents of various colors and sizes, we could see that a lot of families were here to enjoy the last bit of summer.

As we were told at the orientation, it was not quiet at night. Small groups of people nearby chatted into the early hours of the next day. Soon after it was finally quiet, I could hear animals coming near the tent and attempts to open the locked garbage bin outside. I thought about the potential impact of the night activities on the lodging of different sizes. I was glad that the animals around there were not known to attack humans. After a few hours, I was woken up by the start of the car engine, and the neighbor was leaving in the early daylight. On our way to have breakfast at the center, we saw clusters of smoke or steam rising near the tents on the campground we walked by the day before. It was the start of a new day in the wilderness.

The road from Yosemite to San Jose was very different compared to what we had in Southern California. I had been on this road in the past and knew it was treacherous. While descending in the Sierra Nevada, the road zigzagged and was signposted before every turn by a flipped U-turn sign with a speed limit of 15 miles per hour. We passed a town called Chinese Camp. It was at least my second time passing the road sign. Later, I found out it was a remnant of the Gold Rush, instead of the railroad construction I had presumed. Once out of the mountain ranges, we passed a few towns. The land we could see was almost barren except occasionally for a small garden next to a house. Our first stop in Northern California was San Jose, which at the time was already the center of high-tech.

San Francisco

After visiting two families in San Jose, we left the city in the morning and drove towards San Francisco. We visited Stanford University on the way. I took Ying and you there because it is an excellent school with many subjects ranked in the top 10 or 15 among the universities in the States. To me, its campus is always wide open, with beautiful landscapes and several historical yellow buildings. In terms of details, it is like any big university in North America, with buildings for lectures, labs, and libraries, as well as dorms with cafeteria. I shared my view on the benefits of its location, such as the thriving high-tech sector for work and the landscapes in California for recreation.

It was lunchtime when we arrived at Union Square in San Francisco. It is the terminal of cable cars that go up and down hills to reach many points of interest. The parks nearby are infamous for overcrowding of the city's homeless. My opinion of those people is that they were basically harmless and became homeless at one time in their life, hence losing the lifeline to connect with any help society has set up to assist. I have been to the city many times, mostly for conferences. One of my visits was just after the 1989 earthquake. The city has historical significance and is well-established for diverse social and ethnic groups.

We parked the car and took the cable car to the ocean side Fishman's Dwarf. In one of the small restaurants in the strip mall along the shore, I bought a crab for Ying and me and a fish sandwich for you. It was not crowded. We sat on the stools on the sidewalk under the sun. After lunch, we walked along the docks to look for an opportunity to sail on the water. Although most official tourist facilities were already out on the water, Ying and I found a man with his own boat and negotiated a price for an excursion. He would take us to the Golden Gate Bridge and Alcatraz Island. The tour would probably take an hour. He originally came from Europe, and his children grew up in the city. He was retired and just ran the boat on good days to talk to people from anywhere.

So, we were at sea. The sea was not smooth even with just a little wind. We were mostly sitting in the middle of the boat where there was no wind and under the sun. The man was quite familiar with what any tourist wanted to know. He navigated in the water almost under the bridge. Keeping the boat steady and close to the bridge obviously involved dealing with the complicated wave motions besides the wind. We took some pictures and watched the traffic on the bridge until he showed us how the boat would drift and swing if he stopped the engine just for a minute. He turned around and took us to check on Alcatraz, the famous prison built on an island. There were movies about big criminals who stayed at the prison, and stories about prison breaks. It was closed a long time ago. We circled around the island and the man explained who used it and when it was closed. No, nobody could swim ashore from the island.

After the excursion, we walked around in the area and had n ice cream. We then took the cable car back to the square.

Compared to Fisherman's Wharf, the square is surrounded by modern and commercial/financial complexes. Several street blocks are filled with upscale shops for people, especially tourists, to window-shop. We drove out of the city, and, this time, we were on the way to Foster City, where I would be reunited with my friends from Madison, Wisconsin.

Friends and Relatives

<u>Los Angeles</u>. We stayed at Judy's home. On the morning of our first day, we visited Getty Villa in Malibu. It was my first time to be in an upscale private collection and layout. Instead of the wide coverage of art usually found in a public museum, the content displayed in the villa is all classic from targeted locations in the world. It functions as an education center on art and culture of ancient times. We passed several groups of children engaged in activities. After visiting the villa, we went to the beach for lunch. It was a day with a few showers. We were in the crowd in front of a food stand that sold sandwiches or wraps filled with freshly grilled catches from the ocean.

At night, we met with your uncle and aunt — my brother and his wife. At dinner in a restaurant, we were a sizeable group, including Judy's parents-in-law. We had a lot to catch up on. These were the same relatives we had visited in Fort Lauderdale during our trip to Disney World in Florida. They moved to Los Angeles a few years ago. Her husband, who had won a Grammy award for innovation in lighting, was then the head of a lab inside Universal

Studio. Andy was already in grade school. You were the uncle to Andy and this time, you two had friendly visits together.

San Jose. We visited two families in San Jose. The friends we visited here were the big sister who had babysat you quite a few times when you were a toddler. Her husband moved to the States for a job suiting his academic goals. She and her two daughters followed and settled in San Jose. It was a joyful reunion because you knew these girls from Ottawa. In the evening, we stayed with the daughter of my cousin whom we had visited in Portland in 2004. We became acquainted in Madison, Wisconsin, where she was working on her degree in library science. When we visited her in San Jose, her husband worked for Intel. You were fine there because she had two boys about your age. We did not drive around in San Jose. However, I got to know the sky-high real estate prices for the area with good schools.

Foster City. We stayed with Emily Shih, whose family name is the same as my last name, and her husband, Gary. They were my friends from the time I was a graduate student at the University of Wisconsin–Madison. They were in biochemistry, and I was in geophysics. The couple came from Taiwan and went to the University of Wisconsin to work on their doctoral degrees. In the years we were in Madison, they worked hard in the lab and built their little family with two boys. Emily and I shared the same dorm room for a year before she moved into the family housing for graduate students to have her first baby. I was a good listener during her mood swings, and we became close friends. Gary always had tea ready whenever I visited. Ying became familiar with the family when he visited me in Madison. Emily and

Gary graduated and moved to the west coast to take positions in pharmaceuticals or university labs. Our visit was a long-promised one, and it was a happy reunion after over fifteen years.

You stayed in a large room, which was a garage but renovated by Gary to be the play space for his two boys. It is huge and with all kinds of game gear. You certainly enjoyed yourself that night after staying close to us on the road for so long. As for Ying and me, we had so much to catch up on with Emily and Gary. We were catching up on the whereabouts of all the others we knew back in Madison, and on how we raised our own families, especially our kids. We even checked the little river or canal at the back of their house. Gary made sure that you were having fun with the setup in the playroom, and I went to send you to bed long after your normal bedtime. Otherwise, we just talked and talked over beers into the night. The next morning, we drove out of the town together and said goodbye before we got on the highway bridge leading to San Francisco. It would be their turn to visit us in Canada next time.

Hawaii, Winter 2008

You were sixteen years old. I found the Pride of America cruise when I looked for a new place to explore during Christmas break. I thought that visiting several islands of Hawaii via a cruise would be much better than switching hotels. The dates of the cruise aligned with everybody's vacation. Flying to Hawaii turned out to be three hops, from Ottawa to Toronto, then to Los Angeles, and then to Honolulu. Arranging a trip with multiple connections in winter is risky. However, we were lucky, and there was no flight cancellation, and we got there the night before the embarkation as planned.

Honolulu

Unfortunately, I did not think about the closures during the holidays. We arrived in Honolulu on Christmas Day and the cruise ended during the New Year's holiday. We walked outside Pearl Harbor, but it was closed. It would have been nice if we could have been inside to feel the impact of the history that was known to everybody. Despite the closures, Christmas decorations lined the streets, and tourists were warmly welcomed everywhere. There was no rush-hour crowd, and therefore, we learned to take the local bus and read the map to go to different places. We had good food and plenty of fun.

On Christmas Day, we checked out of the hotel. We found our ship first and then walked to the nearby beach to watch people who went there to relax on the beach. We visited different local stores and food stands to try local sweets and fast food. Freshly roasted macadamia nuts were hard to miss.

When we disembarked on New Year's Eve, we took a taxi to the hotel. The taxi driver provided a lot of helpful information on how to tour the island of Oahu in one day. On the next day before our flight, we visited several points of interest in the city, besides going around Pearl Harbor one more time. I remembered two locations: downtown and the Chinese Cultural Center.

Walking in downtown Honolulu, I felt a sense of history from monarch times. We stopped in front of the King Kamehameha statue, the only statue of a king with a welcoming gesture as far as I could remember. It was he who unified the islands into the Kingdom of Hawaii in the early nineteenth century. To make his land prosperous, he welcomed foreigners and foreign investment. He commissioned Italians when designing the Ali 'Iolani Hale, a large cluster of buildings now behind the statue. They became the royal palace of the Hawaiian Monarchy, which existed until the end of the nineteenth century. After the monarchy, the buildings functioned as administrative offices. The square with the statue now holds both historical buildings and the current city hall, Honolulu Hale. The island grew first through trade between the outsiders and the natives and then through generations of immigrants and investors. Reading the description on various plates along the way, I don't remember coming across words like "invasion" or "colonization".

The Chinese Cultural Center is within walking distance of the government buildings. We saw the statue of Dr. Sun Yat-Sen outside the center. Dr. Sun was a medical doctor but very determined to overthrow the monarchy system that existed in China for nearly 2000 years. He became the forefather and the first president of the Republic of China. His uprisings inside China were heavily supported by overseas Chinese. This was the location where he and his followers came to raise funds and get ammunition. Ying and I took pictures in front of a monument with the inscription "Within the four seas, all men are brothers." Compared to the saying "We are the citizens of the world," the brotherhood elevated citizenship to a closer or more heroic level of bonding.

Cruise

This was the first real cruise for our family. We stayed in an inner cabin below deck. Besides considering our budget, I chose the below-deck unit because I got seasick on a smaller ship during our two-day Bahamas cruise. In the limited space, Ying and I used the twin bed on each side, and you used a pull-down bed.

The food on the cruise was excellent. This was the main reason that Ying and I continued our other cruise adventures with the Norwegian Cruise Line (NCL) afterwards. However, it turned out to be a part of this unique cruise. It was one of the few cruise ships flying the US flag. It was a fun-filled cruise around a relatively small area, the Hawaii islands, and on a relatively large ship. The many restaurants on board provide a variety of cuisines from Italian to Japanese, as well as from dishes from Texas to Hawaii. The food in the grand buffet from breakfast to dinner was very good, better than I had expected. In addition, there were temporary food stands almost every day at the poolside to celebrate dishes of special cuisines.

We spent New Year's Eve on the ship, and the dinner was formal with the ship's crew. However, we were among those who did not bring any formal dress. We just sat and enjoyed the waiting and the service. We left the party early because we were not big drinkers. Later, we went to the deck to watch the burning lava as the ship made its way back to Honolulu. It was the last exciting item of the cruise.

Volcanoes and Volcanic fields

I booked three volcano-related excursions to learn about the volcanoes on location or to satisfy my curiosity. On land, we visited an old volcanic field. It was not a hot day. We were among piles of dark brown and glass-hard porous stones, which are Hawaiian and cooled down from a type of lava flow called "aa". These were likely the distinctive, blocky flow advances, moving at a good speed, which can drag and burn everything in their path. Not in terms of any creeping lava, as it is often made available safely for tourists to observe. The cooled lava flow is raw and geologically fresh. My feet were on very rough and hard surfaces. Everybody walked carefully to avoid any falls or scratches.

On a different excursion, we visited the lava tunnels, which are again Hawaiian and called Pahoehoe. The tunnels were formed when fresh lava melted the underlying rocks. We walked in an almost horizontal one. We peeked into a nearly vertical tunnel and then went down the ladder to have a different view from the bottom. Temperature, pressure, and the original viscosity of the lava determined the type of volcanic field. The tube was said to form when the lava flow cooled down from its surface in the air or was in contact with other cold surfaces. The crust stayed while the filling moved on, while the mold was the existing earth. Like any natural disaster, such as an earthquake, mudslide, glacier, or avalanche, the aftermath sometimes looks like a natural wonder.

The most exciting excursion was the Big Blue helicopter ride. It was a sunny and calm day. We were driven to the site and assigned to a group with another family of three. Unlike any flying experience we had with commercial airplanes, the important part of a helicopter ride was load-balancing. Politely, the clerk asked for our weight, and we were assigned to proper slots to best balance the helicopter. The pilot came and instructed us to look only out or down on our own side. The pilot assured everybody he would fly in big or small circles so that the tourists sitting on both sides could have the same view. We flew over smoking and occasionally glowing lava pits and the boundaries of the active and inactive volcanic areas. Afterwards, the helicopter flew over beautiful cliffs and forests where land meets the water. It was my only helicopter ride so far.

Tropical Greens

When the ship docked for tours in Kauai, we joined a bus-and-boat-combined tour for the Fern Grotto. It was a great opportunity to learn about tropical plants. It was also a change of pace after several trips, checking out the bare and rugged volcanic landscape.

The tour guide loved his job and his islands. For the not-very-long bus ride from the cruise ship to the dock for a ride on the riverboat, he pointed out the farms and major types of trees on islands. We learned certain fruits grow at the top of a tree, while others are in clusters that are hard to detect. We also learned that sugar cane is a foreign crop, and the related industry and economy fluctuate under the influence of its counterpart on the mainland. One time, he pointed out an entrance to a large, forested area that was used to shoot one of the *Jurassic Park* movies.

We enjoyed a tranquil boat cruise on the Wailua River, which is said to be the only navigable river in all of Hawaii. The river is fed by Mt. Waialeale, one of the wettest spots in the world. Once we were on board the covered river boat, we were entertained by the songs and stories of old Hawaii. Occasionally, there were teams of kayakers. On the water, we met a similar boat, returning the tourists after their visits to the Fern Grotto. There was then a duet back and forth between the boats. It reminded me of the musicals about the love among ethnic boys and girls in China that I knew a long time ago.

After slowly navigating between the riverbanks with beautiful mangrove trees, the boat reached a dock deep inside the grotto. It is said to be a fern-covered lava cave. The more than sufficient moisture for the vegetation in the grotto comes from the run-offs on top of the cave. The short nature walk through a beautiful rainforest to the actual grotto was colorful. We were guided to observe the cave covered with ferns of different species from several viewing points. It is all dark green with different shades, shapes of the leaves, and symmetry of the leaves. Other than the tropical rainforest section of the Biodome in Montreal, this is our first time in a natural one. It is a small-scale but very dense tropical rainforest, indeed a natural wonder.

After our visit to the Grotto, we started identifying some tropical plants on the scale of bushes or trees as we took tours anywhere on land.

Culture: The Night with the Natives

One of our excursions was dinner and entertainment at Nawiliwili Harbor on Kauai. You refused to go because there was a magic show on the ship that night. You stayed.

We were bussed to the site, which is a combination of stage, dining hall, and market. The evening started with a fresh flower lei greeting, a process I had seen in many movies and TV shows. Before dinner, we had time to browse the wares at the craft fair of local artisans. We were then ushered to the assigned table, where there were already plates of fruits and local snacks. The main dishes were laid out on the tables lined up in the front. The food was plentiful and delicious. It was easy to tell the difference between the food on the ship and the local tables. The roast chicken and pork were in larger pieces and relatively hard to chew. My favorite dishes were the cold and warm salads and mixed rice with new flavors to me. It was nice to have large pieces of charcoal-grilled meat, fresh salad, and colorful rice in different flavors for a change.

People got a plateful of salad, the main dish, and dessert in front of them, and started enjoying the food and socializing with the others around the table. The show soon began, and its stage was in the center of the dining hall. The legend of Kalamakū was a thrilling theatrical performance with fireballs and knife dance. Its music, especially the rhythm of the drums, was loud and well echoed. Visually, the show was never short of gold, red, brown, and black colors, representing fire, feathers, animal skins, wood, and primitive metals. These were the basics on which aboriginal people lived and made weapons for fighting demons and evil in folklore. Before the end of the show, I went out and walked around the dining hall-theater to check the surrounding structures and feel the vibration of the music. It is a good setup with the atmosphere of early life on the islands to inspire imaginations.

Los Angeles, USA, Thanksgiving 2010

It was the second trip you took with me, and you were eighteen years old. The first one was in China when you were two years old. Although it was only the Canadian Thanksgiving weekend, the quick trip made me realize how much you had changed after your high school years. You had learned a lot more from your life with your peers at school than I thought.

Because of the three-hour difference between Ottawa and Los Angeles, I could go to the office in the morning. I drove to Ottawa airport before lunch and got on the flight to Toronto to meet you at the airport. By the time I went through US customs and reached the boarding area, you were already there, reading some printouts. You told me you took the GO bus and gave more than enough time for the traffic on Highway 401. You had enough time to walk inside the airport to check in and find the gate.

We did not have seats next to each other. I had a good nap during the flight across three time zones. We traveled light, and the flight was on time. We walked past the carousels and went out of the gate. Soon we met with Judy because she was driving and checking near the airport. It was mid-afternoon in Toronto but lunch time in Los Angeles. We were hungry since none of us had lunch before or during the flight. Judy took us to the oceanside. We walked along the water to admire the surfers. We had lunch at a simple restaurant named after the movie *Forrest Gump*. The fish and chips and crab cakes were delicious. After lunch, she drove us across the mountains and up the hills of Calabasas to her home. Her house and the beautiful compound were no longer new to us. Lili was attending the film school of UCLA then and Andy was in junior high. You stayed in Lili's room while I stayed downstairs in Henry's office.

Tours

We only stayed for two full days, but our schedule was full. On the first day, Judy and Andy took us to Universal Studios. The original and famous studio is a working place. We visited several workshops and movie setups. We were also in the office and lab where Henry worked before. What I remember the most from the visit was film making. A movie involves so many stages, some of which stack layers of colors, pictures, and even voice together, while others cut and filter. It is a very long and complicated process, from reels of what we occasionally encounter at a movie shooting on streets to the reels found at the movie theaters.

After the visit to Universal Studios, Judy took Andy to an appointment in the early afternoon and left us at the gate of La Brea Tar Pits, which is my favorite spot in Los Angeles. The park is in the central metropolitan area, where the urban development had to consider this group of seeping natural tar. It became a park with a museum and several tar pits, which have been used for past and ongoing research, as well as education. The open tar pits are just a few out of a hundred discovered so far. The excavation process can be learned from the exhibitions, and a few machineries are always at the live tar pits for the visitors to look at. It is a special case in paleontological study. A large part of the exhibition is on fossils found during excavations and their prehistoric stories from the subsequent studies. The biggest discovery is probably the nearly intact mammoth skeleton. Other findings include remains of a saber-toothed cat, dire wolves, bison, horses, and a giant ground sloth. In addition, the exhibit displays fossils of turtles, snails, clams, millipedes, fish, and gophers. They show the "pre-tar," likely a marine biological environment. What astonishes me, as a geologist, is the remarkable detail and variety of fossils found in the tar. As said in a line I read in the exhibition, "How the tar with abundant fossils of animals and plants was formed is ongoing research for paleontologists."

On the second day, we had our breakfast at the Corner Bakery in the Commons. It was my favorite coffee shop because I could mix my cup of coffee with several flavors. In addition, the portions of their freshly cooked Italian or Mexican breakfast selections were just right for me. After breakfast, Judy let me drive her old Honda Pilot to spend the day by ourselves. The first place we went was the California Science Center. We visited the retired space shuttle Endeavour. The journey of the shuttle from the airport to the museum was in the news for several days. It showed the platform for transporting the shuttle was not only huge but also very flexible while avoiding the trees, street signs, and billboards. It was definitely a good story and video clips about a space her coming home. Once inside the museum, we followed the guided tour to learn about the glorious contributions of the shuttle. It became a part of the educational functions at the museum. We also stayed for the discussion. I was surprised that you were next to the guide and asking questions.

We drove to the huge Camarillo Premium Outlets after visiting the Endeavour. It is a compound of several sectors with stores, mostly with brand names. We first had a simple lunch and then walked around to see if we liked anything. I was surprised again! You obviously knew a lot more about branded names than I did. You bought some plain T-shirts from Calvin Klein and then went in and out of Aldo, Guess, Levi's, Lululemon, Banana Republic, and even Versace. For me, I only knew Gap, Oshkosh, and American Eagle, for which I shopped for your clothes years ago. I noticed my favorite brands of shoes, such as Clark and Timberland, have their own stores. Never a fan of handbags and jewelry, I also stopped briefly to window shop at stores like Coach and Swarovski. In the end, I bought a small bag of honey pecans to share with Judy and Andy, and a small blanket for my brother to cover his legs when he was in the wheelchair. We got back to Judy's home safely in the late afternoon traffic. Los Angeles is very scattered, and you need to drive everywhere.

Relatives

Time flies while you and Andy were growing into young men or teenagers. I could feel the aging of my brother and his wife. My brother had a fall when playing ping-pong during a family cruise trip. The consequence of the long recovery from the fall was the overall deterioration of his health. In addition, he developed Parkinson's disease. He was in a wheelchair on outings. They invited us to a nearby restaurant for dinner on our first night. His wife pushed him to the restaurant and helped him move from the wheelchair to the seat. He still had a good appetite as always but was warned of his restriction because of his heart problem and diabetics. Looking at his purplish legs, I felt sad. When I was a child in Beijing, he was tall and walked in big strides. He always had a suitcase in his hand and a big smile on his face whenever he traveled to Beijing for business or leisure. That's why I bought the blanket at the outlet the next day. The dinner on our second night was at a buffet type restaurant with the entire family. I took the blanket with me and put the blanket on his legs when he arrived. He smiled and kept the blanket on for the entire evening. This was the last time I was with him because his Parkinson's disease advanced, and he passed away at home two years after. His wife, your aunt, moved to an apartment in a senior housing close to Judy.

Andy became a teenager, although he was still a mommy's boy, teasing her and creating trouble from time to time. He was a handyman. He could give himself a haircut and, in the car, he never stopped playing with the in-car GPS or Judy's camera. I think that we eventually lost most of the pictures Judy took However, he was with you, asking you to show him a trick every night. You entertained him well and acted like the uncle to play along.

Judy was the busy bee in three generations of the family. Sh was up before 6 to prepare breakfast for everybody, if needed, and then pack lunches for Andy and Henry, if needed. She then left the house to join the morning traffic of Los Angeles. For many years, on her way to and from her work, she called both her mom and her mother-in-law everyday so that she could check on them twice a day.

Lili, Andy's sister, was in the UCLA film school. She was quite active in sports. She started Andy on running long distances, and both took part in local marathons a few times. Her favorite sport, though, was the Ultimate Frisbee, and she was quite involved with her team. The tours and tournaments were part of the resources for her movie shooting.

Before the dawn of the third day, Judy dropped us off at Los Angeles airport. The return flight was smooth, and I got back to Ottawa in the afternoon. For the trip, you had a cool picture with their Tesla. You were in a purple T-shirt in front of the red sporty car.

Travel Other Places

We took vacations in a few places other than China and North America when you were growing up. The top concern for going to "other" places is that we don't know the language. The first or popular language outside China and North America may not be English (or Mandarin), but Spanish, Italian or Russian instead. To be safe and to maximize the benefit, I always planned the trip to be at least guided. Obviously, the trade-off is various restrictions and the cost. Ying and I continued our traveling after you left home for university. On your way to building your career and family, I hope that you have opportunities to travel and see other parts of the world.

Cuba, Winter 2000

You were eight years old. The trip to Varadero, Cuba, was the first Sunwing packaged vacation for our family. We went there for Christmas. We stayed at a 3.5-star hotel, which provided a clean room, swimming pools, a beach to walk to as well as nightly entertainment. As advised by some of my co-workers, I bought some school supplies beforehand so that the daily tip for the cleaning lady would be two or three dollars, along with a few school supplies.

Life of All Inclusive

It was a relaxing week with a lot of sunshine, without worrying about food, drink, and cleaning. The buffet at the main dining hall was excellent, with a lot of cooked dishes. We always had our breakfast there. The bar inside provided liquid from real liquor to nicely mixed non-alcoholic drinks. At the poolside, there were several drinks and fast-food stands. Around noon every day, the daily special was cooked at a temporary setup to provide freshly grilled meats or seafood. Under the nearby coconut trees, there were local men with a stick longer than the one we used to trim tree branches outside our house. It was fun to watch them fetch a coconut with the long stick and clean it with a machete. Then the fruit was offered with a straw. The fresh coconut juice tasted quite raw, but the pieces of coconut meat inside the shell tasted much better than the dry ones we bought from a grocery store.

We learned to check the flag on the beach every day. The green flag meant that the water was calm. You changed your mind and wanted to stay with us after going to the supervised activities for children on site for the first day. Our routine for the day was to get wet and sandy on the beach in the morning and come back to the hotel at lunchtime. On the beach, we watched others kayaking, water skiing and riding speed boats. We went into the water to feel the waves until our pants were almost completely soaked. At least twice, we saw a few pelicans flying low out of nowhere. Back at the compound, we went to different sites for lunch. Ying usually had salad and pasta at the buffet, while you and I enjoyed freshly cooked fast food such as chicken fingers, tacos, and nachos. Ying took a nap after lunch, and you and I wandered around the compound to watch other people playing water or sandpit volleyball. There was a pool table and other games set up in the game room, and it was not crowded in the afternoon. Our family of three learned to play pool.

Almost every day, you would run to the bar to ask for a San Francisco. Your favorite drink was colorful and probably made with Sprite and a bit of fruit syrup.

Havana

As Varadero is a peninsula, the excursions offered by Sunwing included a bus tour to visit Havana, the capital city of Cuba. It was a full-day trip. On the way, we passed the real world outside the resort area. It was bare and simple, reminding me of the slummy area on the hills outside Bogotá, Colombia. The tour guide was young and educated. He told us that the life there was around the poverty line defined in the world. However, the (socialist) system there kept the people well fed and, therefore, there is no real poverty in Cuba. He also proudly told us that there is no illiteracy in the country. So, it implied that the maid in the hotel could read Spanish, too. I was impressed.

We visited a cigar factory that made the world-famous Cuban cigars. The tour guide then led us to walk along the streets of shops and residences with balconies and occasional graffiti on the walls. We had lunch at a restaurant offering a buffet of freshly made local dishes that were delicious and quite different from those at the resort. After lunch, we visited a market that had aisle of merchandise ranging from dry foods and souvenir T-shirts to arts and crafts. I bought some souvenirs made from coconut shells or bark. We made a stop at the famous Jose Marti Square. The square was named after the national hero, who was the voice of the country, to fight for independence against the Spanish rulers. In the square, a little girl ran to me and asked to take a picture with me. I hesitated. Ying took a picture of me and the girl. Her mother soon appeared, asking for "dollars." This was our first encounter with the "local models" outside of China. I gave her a few dollars to send them away. Our last stop was an old church with a cemetery, which was distinctly Spanish, but quite run down.

We left the resort on Christmas Day. The dinner the night before was a celebration with the band. We learned Feliz Navidad, the Spanish greeting for Merry Christmas. Ying had two or three wines and you had your San Francisco, but we were not drunk. Everybody at the table was singing along whenever the band came by. On the way back to our hotel room, we bought a bottle of rum from the gift store. We were going home with sweet memories and Cuban gifts for our friends in Ottawa.

Europe, Summer 2006

You were thirteen years old. For our first family trip to Europe, Ying and I planned a grand bus tour with Trafalgar, which is a well-known tour company. The itinerary of the bus tour included the Vatican, some cities in Italy, a stop in Switzerland, Paris, and London. The purpose was to get a brief introduction to Europe, especially Italy, France, and Switzerland, where we don't speak the language.

Rome

To join the tour, we flew to Rome from Ottawa via Montreal. It was probably our first flight after the 9/11 incident in the States. All the airlines had updated the restrictions on carry-on luggage. You were singled out at the security check of Ottawa airport because of the soft drinks in your backpack. The cans were confiscated. Although it was embarrassing, Ying and I appreciated your thoughtfulness. You had your bag well packed and were probably going to share with the family when needed. The flight was uneventful. The service of the Air France flight from Montreal to Rome included rounds of drinks and two meals and was superior from beginning to end.

We wished that you still had soft drinks once we landed in Rome. It was much warmer than Ottawa. Somehow, we had to wait for over an hour for the Trafalgar pickup. It became hot and sticky when we finally reached the hotel. The heat and humidity soon affected me, and I started getting rashes. It was unfortunate that the rash lasted throughout the entire trip. The rest of the group (about thirty people) looked at my red and lumpy neck and ears every day. An American lady pulled out a tube of cortisone cream, which amazingly addressed my need to reduce the itching

The activities of the trip started shortly after we checked in. After the orientation and the welcome cocktails, there was a walking tour along the Spanish Steps and piazzas led by a local guide. I got to see the skill of the bus drivers on the bumpy ancient Roman streets. In the late afternoon, every tourist attraction was filled with people. The buses, when picking up their passengers, parked less than two feet apart and moved in and out of a parking spot with side mirrors completely folded. Because of the jet lag, we were not hungry and just walked and walked, following the guide. It was exciting to be close to the buildings and monuments that we had read about in history and fantasy books and seen in the movies. Like the others, we threw a coin into the Trevi Fountain and took quite a few pictures to capture the amazing sculptures. We also looked for a soccer jersey for your cousin in Beijing because he was very into the world series that year. From a distance and in the middle of the crowd, we admired Piazza Navona, and the guide busily introduced us to the names and history of the surroundings. Walking along the Spanish Steps was not as crowded as it was near the piazza. It was beautiful at sunset, and then the sculptures were lit up by lights everywhere. It was completely dark when we got back on the bus. The guide never stopped talking, and our tour ended with the view of Rome at night. It was hard to keep my eyes open because I was exhausted.

Our bus tour in Rome continued in the afternoon of the second day. The guide was experienced in pointing out the famous architecture that was likely known to his visitors. The bus once drove by a large ancient complex with an open theater (Baths of Caracalla), where the famous three tenors held their first concert. We made a stop at the Colosseum. We were only guided to walk through a few sections. In our short free time afterwards, we continued strolling inside. Our conversation covered the Colosseum-related movies, such as Gladiator, James Bond movies, and others by Bruce Lee or Chuck Norris. It was exciting. Historically, real or in stories, it was a battleground in which good and evil settled physically.

The Vatican

It was the visit to the Vatican City on the morning of our second day in Rome. We were in the Holy City before the heat arrived. We did not wait long before entering the compound as a tourist group. Once inside, we were guided through St Peter's Basilica and were told several stories about the precious pieces on display. We rushed through the Sistine Chapel as the guide checked us in and then went to the exit to collect his group. We were told to move along with the crowd inside. Indeed, it was fully packed with several streams moving in different directions where some groups attempted to stop and explain. Reluctantly, we had to move along, but we were moving as slowly as possible past Michelangelo's frescoes. At least, the famous Sistine Ceiling was vividly presented from the top and everybody could see with no obstacle. Already, I told myself that I would come back to study the details, although it would likely still be crowded. Once out of the Sistine Chapel, we had time to walk around St. Peter's Square. By that time, the sun was high and glaring. We got sandwiches from a store on the street. Was it great? Impressive? Yes, you agreed. But none of us could really describe much. Obviously that we were inside and saw these great works with our own eye was more important than any details for the precious time we spent inside.

We had an Italian dinner before leaving Rome for Venice. You really enjoyed it! The five-course meal was served elegantly in a sequence of an appetizer, a salad, a plate of spaghetti noodles, the main course, and the dessert. Unexpectedly, the noodles were harder than what I prepared at home and the sauce was simple but fresh. The salad had oil and vinegar dressing and it is from the home of the olive oil. You finished the whole plate of noodles, and probably thought that the pasta was the main dish until the main course came. You then tried your best to finish the roast chicken and the veggies, and then the dessert. Ying and I were trying hard to finish our dishes, too. It was the best meal of our entire trip.

Venice

We arrived in Venice in the late afternoon. The bus dropped us close to the canals. The tour guide passed people who had reservations for gondola rides to the local guide. We were assigned to a gondola, and it left the crowd at the dock quickly. The man, the gondolier, guided the gondola along with several others in the canal, some sections of which were wide enough to entertain even speedboats. Once it was away from the crowded open area, the gondola slowed down. We passed several bridges along the canal, which could probably hold the traffic of three or four gondolas. The sectioned areas connected by bridges are large and small squares of either historical or commercial buildings. The gondolier, with the long oar in hand, started singing, very classical and almost professional. There were other singing gondolas nearby or far away. The beautiful music echoed from time to time when the gondola navigated in the canal. I believe that the singing part made many tourists feel very romantic.

We spent one night and a good part of the next day in Venice. Our activities in the morning started by visiting a glass factory. Inside the shop, a man dipped his tool, a pipe with a round top, into the molten glass. His expertise lies in knowing the plasticity of the liquid at the exact moment, so that he can blow with his mouth while shaping the tube with the tool in his hands. The precision of the work is admirable. First, the initial bubble was pulled and sectioned into connected elongated tubes of different diameters. The subsequent process made a bent or more complicated curl or twist. A final product could come from one or several bubbles. The display in the shop showed glassware with hollow and solid parts and different colors. The transition of colors and connection between the hollow and solid are amazingly congruent. It reminded me of the little and cute glass animals I had from China. They were probably made from small solid drops of molten glass. I would have bought a small piece from the shop if we were not at the beginning of our trip.

After visiting the glass factory, we had half a day of free activities. It is such a beautiful city. To start from the far end, we crossed the canal to visit the art institute museum. More than half of the paintings there were rather contemporary. At lunchtime, we walked towards St Mark's Square (Piazza San Marco). On the way, we visited a few shops and passed souvenir stands. We guessed over the Italian descriptions on the functions of a building or gated structures that surround a fountain or a few monuments. From one square to the next, the most noticeable were the decorated fences and walls. The decorations could be colorful plants and flowers, metal charms or even masks. Meeting our first human statue in the middle of a street was a pleasant surprise. Among the ancient architecture, we saw a few more human statues. They were fully painted in silver or gold and held still with a meaningful gesture for the occasion. Eventually, we reached St. Mark's square. For lunch, we had cold sandwiches and ice cream. There was a long line outside the basilica, and therefore, we just had a relaxing break, watching people feeding or playing with herds of pigeons. We then walked around the square to check on postcards at some stores or stood in the crowd to watch live performances.

For dinner, we sat down at a table in front of a pizza place in the square. The cheese and pepperoni pizza there was rather thin, not as thick and rich as its counterpart in North America, but the dough and sauce smelled very fresh. We still had the appetite for dessert afterward and good pastry and ice cream were nearby and very tempting. We were back on the bus after dinner on the way to Switzerland.

Visit in Switzerland

It was two or three hours on the mountain road in the dark before we arrived in Lucerne, Switzerland. The good thing about this trip was that our luggage was always dropped off and picked up at the door. Your bed, half or full-sized, was always ready in the room. Everybody went to bed as soon as possible after the long day. However, for the first time in our trip, the room was not air-conditioned. The evening breeze was not enough to clear the heat during the day. It was hot. You fell asleep shortly while I was in bed, wide awake, listening. It was quiet without air conditioning, and the streets were all dark, very different from Venice or Rome.

It was pleasant and fresh when we woke up in the early morning. As we were told, we had to walk next door for breakfast. The breakfast was rather basic, with fresh coffee and bread. Soon, we were on the bus in the bright daylight. The bus did not dwell in the town long before getting onto the mountain highway. We were taken to the tram station on one of the peaks. We had a ride to admire the Alps. Thinking of the movie *Sound of Music*, I appreciated the jaggedness of the mountains and the towns and villages we quickly left behind. We did not go back to Lucerne but went out of the Alps on our way to Paris. On the way, we made a stop for the washroom. The guide talked about paying for the toilet since a few in our group, who were first timers in Europe, had noticed and were shocked. The guide was a veteran on the road and therefore, she knew the few free ones where you don't have to pay "to pee."

Paris

It was my third time in Paris, although the previous visits were on business or just passing by. We arrived in the early afternoon. It was hot as we were in the middle of a heat wave. It was also the peak season for tourists. Our first stop was the Louvre, th museum brilliantly designed by Mr. Ian Pei. My distant relatives of his generation talked about Mr. Pei from time to time since he was a native of Jiangsu province in southern China. I read articles about the diversity and grandeur of his designs. A person must have a very rich background knowledge and imagination to have done so.

Once inside the museum, we walked several sections of stairways, where we passed works, such as the *Venus de Milo*, the famous statue without arms. After a long hall of paintings and sculptures, we reached the *Mona Lisa*. It was probably one of the musts on the list of every tour guide. It was very crowded in front of a relatively small and dim oil painting in a case with quite wide borders. The masterpiece was smaller than I expected, despite its significant presence in literature. However, the piece is original, as we were told. Later, as we were introduced to other paintings and sketches on display, quite a few more of Da Vinci's works were not large either.

The visit of a tourist group was clocked, I believe. After seeing the *Mona Lisa*, the guide hurriedly led us to a few other pieces of display. Among the artworks I recall are the *Winged Victory of Samothrace*, *Virgin of the Rocks*, and *The Coronation of Napoleon*. Then we went out of the famous museum. Obviously, there was a lot of French content we did not get to see. I really need to come back and visit, I told myself.

The remaining evening was reserved for free activities before the bus came to take us to the hotels. In the Napoleon Courtyard, we strolled around the unique transparent pyramid symbolizing the museum. Then, we walked along the streets near the river, looking at the Eiffel Tower from a short distance. We came back to the meeting point to wait for our bus. It was a beautiful evening, and the streetlights and the lights of the Tower suddenly came on. As I had thought during my previous visits, the Tower, the fountain below, and the streets around the area all together were glorious at night. The pyramid, which I always wondered why it was accepted by Paris, was adding a nice glamor among all the lights.

The first thing to do the next day was to visit the Palace of Versailles. We caught a glimpse of the city along the river, passing Notre Dame. The short ride between the city and the palace was dotted with castles and church-like structures. I thought it would take months to visit all the historical places and years to get to know a different culture. Suddenly, the glorious palace and the garden were in front of us. We didn't wait long in line outside. Once inside, there were enough tourists gathered for endless photo opportunities in the rooms and on the steps leading to the garden.

Versailles was the residence of the royals and Napoleon. It functioned as the capital a few times in history. It had been restored into the original layout of a palace and museum over the years. We spent most of our time in the palace, the museum (of French History) and the garden. Like visiting the Palace Museum in Beijing, I liked its originality the most. Each chamber has its own uniqueness with stories of past residents. In contrast, the chapels, especially the Royal Chapel, were of a grand scale for various public presentations in history. The paintings on the wall and ceiling in the chapels require careful observation or reading to understand.

Large oil paintings are in the museum to characterize the stages in European history wherever France was an important part. Artifacts and sculptures for each stage are on display to provide more details. The Hall of Mirrors leads to the garden. Outside the building, many tourists stood next to the statues at the top of the steps, overlooking the garden and the fountains. It was a bright sunny day, and we saw rainbows amidst water from fountains and sprinklers. We took pictures of ourselves and the garden in the mist. We walked down the steps to the garden and probably became a part of many pictures taken by others. The Palace is a vast place functioning alternately or parallelly as residence and office of the ruling class. It was obvious we knew very little about the complicated history of Europe.

Once back in Paris, we had a brief tour of the city. The guide pointed out a few famous buildings and important locations, one of which was the corner of a memorial for Princess Diana. She was in the car with Lafayette, chased by paparazzi, and died in the accident. The guide also provided information on taking public transit to our hotel. We were dropped off for a few hours of free activities in the afternoon. We walked along the Champs-Élysées to have a light lunch, reached the Arc de Triomphe, and then returned to the Eiffel Tower. There was a line for tickets to go to the top of the tower. After a quick discussion, both Ying and you were not keen on waiting for the ride to the top. I was a little disappointed in the diminishing spirit of the family. We walked to Notre Dame Cathedral, but it was closed. From the souvenir stands along the river, we bought two small oil paintings of Paris before going back to the hotel. For dinner, Ying picked the Chinese buffet that is just a few minutes' walk from the hotel. That was the last thing we did in Paris.

London

We were on the bus the next morning to travel on land and then on a ferry to cross the English Channel. A few years later, I realized we crossed the narrowest part of the Channel, which was quite famous during the Second World War. We watched from afar the famous white cliffs of Dover Beach, and the guide elaborated a bit on the related literature. On the ride from Dover to London, we did not make any stops. However, the guide focused on the history and evolution of the local landscape. This was the last part of our trip, and she discussed things like gratitude, feedback, and what to see in London. Once in London, we said goodbye to the tour guide and the Trafalgar trip of four countries across Europe was over.

We had options to explore ourselves or to take a double-decker bus to tour London. Ying chose two or three points of interest to explore on his own while I took you on the double-decker bus. To me, this was where the double-decker bus originated. and probably the open-top double-decker bus for the tourists started as well. Many buses are still completely red, without a lot of extras to promote business. It was fun and classy to move along the narrow but relatively crowded streets. We passed some old red telephone booths. The guide on board read out street names and talked briefly about related points of interest from time to time. I tried hard to refresh my mind. My knowledge about London started when I was still a child in China. You were tired after following a large group on a tourist bus for more than a week. Being able to sit in the open and see the sky and the top of the architecture was an agreeable change, and you happily came along.

The places I found most memorable were Big Ben, Westminster, Buckingham Palace, Tower Bridge, and Piccadilly Square. We hopped off at Buckingham Palace and waited patiently in the crowd for the changing of the guard. The world-known event began on the other side of the gilded metal bars. Somehow, you got a spot in front without a visitor blocking your view. I had to hold my camera high enough to get a few pictures without other people's heads. Otherwise, everybody had a full view of the procession. Did I feel like a royal subject as a Canadian? Not really. More likely, I had observed a traditional ceremony in a monarchy system; it is again original compared to those practiced in front of the parliament buildings in Ottawa.

We then got off at the stop for Piccadilly Square. I am familiar with the streets and shops here. In 1989, I, a citizen of China then, was blocked from returning to the States after I finished my collaborative research with a group of scientists in Edinburgh. The reason was the Tiananmen incident in Beijing, and anybody with a Chinese passport needed to be re-assessed by the US government. On the morning of my last day in the UK, I walked and explored every street junction in the square to kill time before my appointment at the US Embassy. As soon as I got the letter of permission from the Embassy, I took the subway to Heathrow airport to catch my flight. It was fun to be with you this time. We walked by many stores and bars/restaurants of medium and small sizes. I told you about my experience with the delicious food in the bars and the "authentic" Shakespeare I bought in a bookstore with old and new books. We practiced crossing the street, following the instructions in the sign "Look right and then left" in the middle of the road. The time was tight for the hop-on-off tour of London. We had to ensure that we had time to return to meet Ying.

Mexico City, Winter 2011

Mexico City

You were nineteen years old. The trip was offered by Air Canada, and it covered the return flights and a week-long hotel stay in Mexico City. For the excursions listed online, I booked the Pyramid outside Mexico City and a riverboat cruise.

The hotel was right in the center of the city, and it was safe to stroll on the streets in the evenings. In the morning, we got up and walked a block down to the coffee shop to have a sizeable piece of pastry and coffee or milk. We usually had lunch at the places we visited during the day. At night, there were plenty of restaurants around. Pretty soon, we found a Chinese buffet place. We talked with the people there about China and about our past. The friendly owner of the restaurant offered to make some special dishes for us instead of his buffet items.

We arrived in the city right before Christmas. and there were beautiful Christmas decorations. After a quiet Christmas, we spent one day in Zocalo, the city square. We got the map and were prepared for the crowd. However, we were still overwhelmed by the variety of the gatherings. The vast square is an artistic venue of local popular culture. These are loving people! Having been on this continent for over three decades, I was still amazed by the peaceful co-existence of different cultures and different fun. Strings of lights formed "Feliz Navidad y Prospero Ano Nuevo" on the walls of government buildings across the square from the City Cathedral. The tour guide in the Cathedral told us that the square was in a James Bond movie and the name Zocalo is in several music pieces worldwide. The square is a gathering place for parades, concerts, and other cultural events. Outside the Cathedral, we stopped at a few gatherings from art and craft sales, small concerts of local wooden musical instruments to magic shows.

We visited the city zoo, and we enjoyed it. We only met a few people. Even the panda bears were there peacefully. After visiting the zoo, we had a typical bean-based Mexican lunch at one of the food stands near the park. The plate of food was fresh and delicious.

On the afternoon of our last day, we explored a big shopping mall to check out the 2012 decorations. It was New Year's Eve. On the way back, we passed people setting up the gathering place for the New Year countdowns. The armored city police were also there, ready for any potential riot.

Excursions

Our visit to the pyramid turned out to be better than expected. The location is in Teotihuacan, an area in the valley of Mexico. The site is a mile long and includes pyramids and other ceremonial structures with puzzling orientations. As explained by the guide, the study of the Teotihuacan and later Aztec civilizations is ongoing and worldwide. The Sun and the Moon pyramids, the two most visible structures on the site, were originally built about 1500 years ago. The original structures became ruins over the years, and the current ones were restorations in the early twentieth century. Residents of Teotihuacan from various origins excavated ancient records and labored. It had been an effort of several generations to find ancient records and reconstruct the monuments at the site.

Our bus stopped near the Moon pyramid, which is best restored for tourists to climb. It took some effort for the three of us to reach the top. The view at the top was excellent, looking at the Sun pyramid not far away and the aligned platforms in the entire square. I could imagine how populous it was in ancient times if their ceremonial site could be so grand. Once we came down, Ying took you to conquer the Sun pyramid. It was steep with loose pieces. I walked around to read every sign and plate for more information. I noticed the division in history called "Pre-Columbian civilization." The discovery of the new continent a few centuries ago brought Spanish civilization but destroyed a lot of aboriginal cultures along the way.

It was a good afternoon to be out of town and learn a bit of history. It was my first time visiting a pyramid. A year later, Ying and I visited Chichen Itza, the Mayan site near Cancun, with curiosity about the end of the Maya calendar. The ruins of the pyramids are original.

The river boat cruise was in a privately owned boat on a canal of not-so-clean water. Mexico City has a layout similar to the

Great Toronto Area, with many cities. The city Xochimilco is in southeastern Mexico City, and it is known for its canals and lakes. The cruise used the very colorful local gondola called a trajinera. While we were meandering along, some other boats were selling locally made food for lunch. We only watched because I strongly rejected the idea of having lunch on the boat. The uniqueness of the cruise is probably the tree-made islands, canals, and the colorful boat. One comment I found online said, "Arriving at the Xochimilco canals is like seeing an explosion of Skittle colors—a rainbow piñata of boats." Indeed, it was wonderful entertainment.

Peru, Winter 2012

You were twenty years old. Planning for this trip was rather complicated. It was the holiday season, and I wanted to book a trip to explore South America, where we had never set foot before. I found Globus, which arranges trips for small groups. I had an insightful conversation with a lady online. The itinerary would fit in with your Christmas break, while Ying and I had plenty of vacation days to spend. I checked with the travel clinic on diseases and the required vaccinations. The response was nothing serious enough to require a specific vaccine. We were given some readings on basic sanity and safety when traveling in that part of the world.

Prior to Lima

I noticed one place, Cusco, on our trip was not very far from the area of our World Vision child, Jimmy. I communicated with the organization and the response was a pleasant surprise. A visit from the sponsor was very welcome, although the visit usually included volunteer work, and the duration was often longer than a day. However, a day trip could be arranged, provided I went through the security check and produced proper documents for the visitors.

It would be an adventure, but why not? I called the Kanata Police Station and booked an appointment for a security check. Ying and I went there one night to provide the fingerprints. We got the security clearance within a few days. I communicated with World Vision again, and this time, the local workers were contacted. They were excited, and the date of the meeting was set on the day when we spent two nights in Cusco after our visit to Machu Picchu. On your side, you just went through the physical checkup required by your co-op with Shell in Sarnia. It was your co-op term after Christmas Break. You were concerned about your contact with the locals during our trip because your job would be affected if anything in your health changed after our trip. I reassured you with the information from the travel clinic. You were still worried, as I could tell.

There was another twist before our take-off. Two days before our departure, I got a call from Expedia, saying that our flight from Ottawa to Toronto was canceled because of the weather. Instead of offering me a different flight, Expedia would give me a full refund. I panicked because we were left with the remaining two connecting flights from Toronto to Bogota and then to Lima. I called places like Newark and Chicago and found no flights indeed. Ying and I discussed, and our decision was to drive t

Toronto and ask my nephew to keep our car for ten days. It worked out all right. My nephew and his wife are always very helpful. We had a little party at his home with his parents-in-law the night before, and he dropped us off at the airport the next morning. The rest of the trip was relatively uneventful. For the transit at the Bogota airport, we had to pick up our luggage and open every piece to let the security check thoroughly. In Lima, we met with the friendly Globus staff at the airport and were chauffeured to the hotel.

Lima

A trip with the Globus is semi-private. The tourists travel to their destination, and the local Globus agent arranges the hotel and sightseeing. The local agent handles the airport pickup and drop-off. In this way, a local agent can serve multiple groups, while the tourists can join different organizations for sightseeing. Flexibility exists for both sides with a streamline of redistributions. I chose the semi-private style because our family of three is all adults and in good physical condition. The agent gave us sets of tickets for the activities we booked for the next day. He then talked about safety and places to eat and shop nearby. He made sure that we were confident during our stay and fully understood how to take part in the activities. Before he left for his day, he also told us he or a different Globus agent would come back to see us on our last day in Lima.

We had the city tour the next day. The prime tourist spot was the Plaza Mayor de Lima, where we had guided tours and then free time to explore. The bus dropped us off at the corner near Lima Metropolitan Cathedral. We walked as a group and the guide pointed out the beautiful architecture surrounding the square. The names of several buildings contain "palace" and others "club" or "headquarters." Quite a few of them are still functioning as government or organization offices. We had time to make a full circle of the square after our visit to the cathedral. It was a nice sunny day, and we could read some descriptions of the buildings and check the details of the sculptures outside or on the building walls. The buildings in the square were constructed during the Spanish colonial time. Some of them survived earthquakes, and others were rebuilt in the twentieth century. Therefore, what we were facing are colonial and republican architecture. The lawns and flower beds we found near some buildings were green and beautiful. Obviously, it is summer in the southern hemisphere.

The most important building in the square is the Lima Metropolitan Cathedral, where we visited as a group, following our guided tour in the square. The cathedral was said to be Spanish and in Renaissance style. Once inside and after an introduction, the guide let us move freely, but quietly, because there were ongoing daily programs. Everything inside, including the naves and many chapels, was grand and rich in details. To me, the uniqueness is the persistence in the style of its architecture buil in different phases over three hundred years. The background wa that the cathedral started from a rare acquisition of the Spanis conquerors to formally own the plot of the land that was an Inc shrine.

The one-day sightseeing tour was a colorful bus ride in Lima, a city with a mix of Spanish, Republican, and contemporary flavors. We passed several churches, clusters of buildings from a certain historical period, and several government buildings. However, we did not have time to visit another cathedral or a museum. The bus also passed several large and colorful entertainment grounds, which are a must for a large city. Parks and shopping centers are along the coast. In the late afternoon, we hopped off at the stop before our hotel. It is the Park of Love, facing the Pacific Ocean. For pedestrians, the park has paths covered with mosaic tiles. At the center, surrounded by colorful paths and waves of walls, is a tall platform holding up the brown sculpture *The Kiss*. It is tall, broad, and raw, symbolizing the love between the two people who won the competition for the longest kiss.

We enjoyed dining next to the ocean. The delicious but simple chicken soup had large pieces of corn and carrots. We agreed that the large and tasty ones are likely the result of sufficient sunshine year-round. The salad and later the fish fillet were very fresh. After dinner, we walked along the beach, and the Christmas decorations were still on. The Christmas trees were conical, either plastic or cardboard, like those we had seen in Hawaii and Beijing. It was bright and pretty at night.

Cusco

We flew to Cusco after spending two nights in Lima. Cusco is at an altitude close to 4000 meters above sea level. Handling the high altitude was the first lesson tourists were told. We were offered tea made from poppy leaves when we checked into the hotel. Supposedly, the tea will invigorate everybody's blood circulation to meet the demand of the high altitude.

We had our first tour of Cusco in the afternoon. The tour guide, a native of thick and short build and dark brown skin, told us to walk slowly and try to take deep breaths. A short bus ride took us to the Cathedral of Santa Domingo, the main Spanish architecture in Cusco. Outside the cathedral, the guide explained that the cultural content included Killke, Inca, and Spanish; the first two are indigenous, and the third brought and spread Christianity in the Andes. Cusco was the center of this cultural involvement and built on layers of cultures. The Inca Empire was built on Killke structures. The Spanish replaced indigenous temples with Catholic churches and Inca palaces with mansions. We had opportunities to be inside the cathedral and later in a different church (Church of the Society of Jesus) near the plaza. The guide led us to the front of a large canvas on the wall in a hallway. He introduced us to the Cusco School of Painting that injects local content into the Bible stories. Indeed, we saw holy creatures like monkeys and llamas in the painting. Later, we found a dish of roast guinea pigs in an imitation of da Vinci's *The Last Supper*. The localization reminded me of the Canadian geese we saw at the end of the ballet *Nutcracker* when it was performed in Ottawa. Our next stop was Cusco Square of the Warrior, a large plaza in the center of the city. The market had hundreds of tents and stands fully open. We had a quick break to admire the arts and crafts created at high altitude. Most of them are earthenware and wool-woven clothes and blanket with patterns, and they were mostly in brown, maroon, and black. However, the memorabilia, cups, and dolls, which were sold as souvenirs, have patterns of bright red and blue for the sun and skies. We then walked up and down through some streets while the guide pointed out structures before or after the Spanish conquest.

The real Killke and Inca indigenous culture is away in the mountain. We were taken to the famous ruins of Sacsayhuaman. We could barely repeat its name after the guide, and we were told that the journey of these rocks to where they are around today is still a mystery. Indeed, the wall complex made of meters high rock blocks was alone on the pasture, far from any visible valley or basin indicative of previous queries. There were locals in traditional dress. We took pictures of a local and his llama. We went to an even higher altitude afterward. Along the mountain trail, we could see the herds of llama grazing on a higher slope. The soil was thin, and the guide said that it was close to 5000 meters above sea level. He then led us to the caves and underground passages. Historically, the area was used by the locals to leave their dead and often well-preserved mummies. He discussed how the mummies were made. I thought that there must be hundreds of ways to preserve the physical bodies of the dead, historically and worldwide.

The sightseeing of our full day in Cusco was focused on Inca culture and local life. We were away from Cusco on the bus all day. The first stop was the Pisac Inca town. The ancient town was built halfway up the slope of a mountain ridge. It has well-maintained stairways to the ruins of a building complex overlooking the village. We were at the foothills of the mountains, with the ancient city on one side and the village on the floodplain on the other. Farther down the road, instead of terraces for farming, the caves for burial filled one side of the mountain. As we were told that the Inca believed in reincarnation and that each cave of burial was an environment for the mummy and its supplies necessary for its new life. Ying and I walked down and visited some households and a small farm in the village. You were up high checking out different sectors of the ancient city. The photo op there was the locals with alpacas, which are smaller with finer wool as compared to llamas. I still have a picture of our family of three, the locals, and the animals. You were in your "Chem Eng" T-shirt at Waterloo University.

On the way, we made a stop at a local bakery. The first thing we saw in its courtyard was a kitchen with a large built-in oven and an elongated table with freshly baked bread of different sizes and shapes. Looking around, I noticed piles of firewood, nicely stacked cages for live guinea pigs. I also saw a fire pit where the grilling was being done. At the entrance of the courtyard, a list showed different price tags of the products, including grilled guinea pig. It was not a good feeling when the expensive pet at home became a dinner delicacy in front of me.

We made two unplanned stops on our way back to Cusco The first stop was in a town, where we met a local parade. We go off the bus and waited for the crowd to pass. It was December 25 Christmas day. It was a local celebration, and the participants wer face-painted and in colorful costumes. In the same town, ther was a different gathering in a schoolyard. As explained by th guide, the crowd was organized by a foreign charity organization. Participants were given school and household sanitary supplies for holiday celebrations. The second stop was after a rainy stretch on our way back to Cusco. The guide asked the driver to make a stop on the roadside for rainbows. It was the right time and the right spot, and we were close to double rainbows. What a photo opportunity! I was overwhelmed by the beauty of the highlands and the culture, which I had known almost nothing about before I was there.

It was the first time our family spent nights at a high-altitude place. You and I slept fine. Ying felt short of breath a few times throughout the night. Regardless, he was alright in the morning and had a good appetite for breakfast. Luckily, we had very experienced tour guides and slow-paced tours. The content of the tours, which covered the history and cultures, was right at the level of the tourists with curiosity.

We got on the PeruRail Vistadome after two nights in Cusco. The destination was Machu Picchu, one of the world's wonders. With the panoramic view of the train, it was a beautiful ride in the Andes. The train had one engine at each end and passed the hills with a zigzagging route. Instead of turning around, the two engines just switched roles to pull and push the train up or down the hill as needed. We could see the next train below us meandering, maybe dangerously sometimes, while we, on the same route, were feeling fine. The journey was a transition from the high plain to the mountainous area near the Amazon River.

Machu Picchu

We could hear the roaring water once we got off the train. We soon learned that it is one of the headwaters of the Amazon: the Urubamba River. The hotels are in the valley with the Inca Trail on one side and the Machu Picchu on the other. It is a crowded tourist area because it is famous.

It was a mixture of rain and sunshine the next morning. We joined the lineup early to get a ride to the top of the mountain. It was amazing to see that all the transportation was mid-size Mercedes vans. The road to the top of the mountain was a single lane with bubbles. The rule to yield applies to the first-arriving vehicle; It stops on a bubble to wait for the oncoming vehicle to pass. The drivers were very skillful, driving fast whenever they could. I took many pictures of the road and the torrent below, but only a few of them were good because of the many turns, uneven slopes, and the crazy speed. It was still raining when we got there, and everybody got a blue or yellow poncho. On passing the entrance, many of us handed out our passports to get a Machu Picchu stamp. A short distance after the gate, the entire picture of the "Lost City of the Incas," the ancient royal estate or citadel, is in front of us. We could see the Inca trail on a slope across the valley. The visitors of the trail at that time were limited to 1,000 per day

We walked on the terrace and then entered the well-sectioned ruins. The guide emphasized the uniqueness of the site — the structures related to the astronomical clock or calendar. I also learned some general rules of the Inca culture from his lectures. The site of the ruins was regarded as a legend by the locals based on the unique earthenware found at a much lower altitude. There were no written or graphic records at the site. The site, deeply covered in the jungle, was reached at the turn of the 20th century after multiple attempts by foreign explorers. Based on many studies of the Inca cultures, people originally lived along the river and later moved upwards to terraced land on slopes. They then built better structures on the ridges of the mountain as permanent sites for governing organizations. The changes in their life were related to the climate, floods, and other environmental factors such as diseases and animals. At Machu Picchu, the ruins we looked at were only composed of small and large sections of stone walls. All the roofs and accessories of a room or building, made from different natural material like trees, vines, and leaves, were long gone. Interpreting the world wonder is ongoing archaeological research.

Afterwards, we used our free time to climb up to the main astronomical features of the site: the temples of the Sun and Three Windows and the magic rock (Intihuatana). The walk, sometimes on all fours, was slippery in the mist of light rain and hot in a poncho. But it was all worth it after we understood a bit more of the architecture and geometry of the structures. The measurements to follow the sun were amazingly accurate. The rain was on and off; we did not have many opportunities to check the shadow of the sun or wait in front of a window. However, I could imagine that the local people and ceremonies were passionate when the lights shone through hundreds of years ago.

After visiting Machu Picchu, we had a few hours to have

lunch and tour the local streets. I bought two very colorful mosaic glass vases as souvenirs.

Visit by Jimmy's Family

Visiting our World Vision child turned out to be an ever-changing arrangement. At first, the plan was to travel to Jimmy's home on the day we were in Cusco. While we were in Machu Picchu, we received a message from the local World Vision staff that Jimmy's family lived quite far from Cusco. It would be impossible for us to make a round trip and come back to catch the flight to Lima. The arrangement was to bring the family to Cusco to meet us at the hotel. We would entertain the family in Cusco. The Globus guide volunteered to coordinate all the parties and told me on the phone not to worry. Many years ago, he grew up in a village that was in the program of an organization like World Vision. Therefore, he was very willing to help and make the meeting happen. I was moved.

We met the guide the night we were back in Cusco, and he told us about the arrangements for the next day. What we would do was wait at the hotel, and he would track the progress of the matter. The World Vision staff would drive to the remote village after midnight to bring the family in. What a great effort!

The group finally arrived before noon the next day. There were three World Vision staff; one was from Lima, and the other two were local. Jimmy's family included his mother and younger sister. Our tour guide was the only one capable of communicating with all parties. We used the lobby of the hotel, which was graciously provided by the hotel staff. Everybody there thought it was such a wonderful thing. For me, it was my first time experiencing "such a wonderful thing" in my life. We hugged and shook hands. I brought Jimmy a new school bag and some school supplies, a picture book of Canada, and some small things I bought from Canadian souvenir stores back in Ottawa. Jimmy's mother gave me a woven handbag, which she made herself from scratch. It was truly authentic! It brought back my memory of me, in my previous life, making threads from camel wool and using them to sew a leather coat or the cushion of my felt boots. Her work was probably very similar. We chatted and took a lot of pictures.

After the gathering at the hotel, we took them to the food court in a nearby shopping center. We ordered a plate of lunch for everybody as instructed by the World Vision staff. It was nice to try the local dish, which was quite filling. After lunch, as instructed by the staff again, we went grocery shopping. Unable to visit their village, I was totally willing and felt obliged to do the most for the occasion. You asked me to be excused from shopping. Remembering your concern about contacting the locals, I let you go. The group then went to the local grocery store, which we would never notice if it was not for the occasion. They, the World Vision staff, were familiar with what the villagers needed most. We checked out two full loads of the shopping cart. It was already mid-afternoon, and they hurriedly loaded the car with people and groceries. As we waved goodbye, the car started its long journey to send Jimmy back to his village.

It turned out to be a complete visit with everybody's effort. A long time ago, a professor told me that my wish may come true if I keep trying. I was proud to be one of the few World Vision parents who tried to meet their sponsored child. Jimmy's village graduated from the World Vision sponsorship after two years. I don't know what trade he took. As arranged by the World Vision, I moved on to a child in Venezuela. Back at home, I washed the hand-woven bag from Jimmy's mother after the trip, and it is one of the few souvenirs I still have after moving from Ottawa to Toronto.

Lima: Homebound

The Globus guide in Cusco was quite excited about his extra contribution to our meeting with Jimmy's family. He talked a lot about the locals and the improvement in education and sanitation that the world charities had made in the area. He left his name and phone number with me when he dropped us off at the airport.

The flight from Cusco to Lima in a small airplane was smooth. We met the Globus agent in Lima and checked into the hotel. At the same ocean-side restaurant, we had a large dinner to say goodbye to Peru. We ordered the same chicken soup with chunks of corn and carrots. During the dinner, we talked about the roaring torrent, sunny valleys and terrace, and the ancient citadel along the mountain ridges. It is a unique civilization with wisdom and bravery. In the hotel, we had a room with three parallel beds. For the first time, you had a bed that was the same size as the other two for Ying and me. However, there were only a few hours of sleep to enjoy before the agent came to pick us up around midnight. He had to pick up tourists at the airport before our departure. We had an early flight to Bogota and then to Toronto.

We arrived in Toronto in the early afternoon. There was plenty of time for us to drive back to our sweet home in Kanata. You were quite relieved once we were home. A few days later, you happily left home with your almost-new Toyota Matrix, the vehicle for your co-op job. You collected your belongings in Waterloo and then went on to your co-op with Shell. The snow was light that year and the car's tires were in good condition.

Epilogue

In early 2017, Ying and I bought a condo in Toronto. It would be the place we retire to, and at least we would be in the same city as you. Ying was already retired, but I was still working full time. After some debating, immediate change and moving were deemed to be impossible. We rented the condo to an Italian couple, who wanted to try condo life as their first step of downsizing and moving out of their house. Before the summer of 2018, I completed my negotiation with the company on working from home part-time. My immediate bosses understood my switch as a transition to retirement in a different city. Starting from June 2018, I worked three days per week. My plan was that Ying and I could spend a year to first clean the house and pack the contents, and then sell the house and move to Toronto.

Our house, which we had for over twenty years, was full of stuff! The size of our Toronto condo is equal to the area of the living-dining and bedrooms of our house. Therefore, the downsizing should be equal to the area of the basement and garage. As you remember, the basement was sectioned into a laundry, entertainment room, Ying's workshop, and the cold room. Even the hallway had two storage closets to make use of the space under the stairway. Things piled up in each section could be from generations of renovation or years of celebration/birthday parties. The entertainment room was furnished for recreational and office-use purposes. The recreation area included a treadmill and ping-pong table, while the office space had a desk, chair, and bookshelves. In the large room, especially the recreation area, you left behind what you did not need or want from each co-op term. All the stuff in the basement should go. The garage of a house usually functions as the storage for outdoor and seasonal items. Luckily, we had kept the garage empty enough to park two cars in the winter. However, things like garden furniture and tools are not a part of life in a condo. Therefore, all the stuff in the garage should go as well.

Besides space consideration, the major function of moving is getting rid of the stuff stored for years without being used. My expectation was to start a new life with enough space to move around inside the condo. There were bags and suitcases of clothes and linens packed when we upgraded the carpet to hardwood floors years ago. They were never unpacked and obviously were not useful anymore. Over the years, I packed and donated sometimes when I was informed about a donation on the way. Ying is not a hoarder, but he usually keeps things he thinks are worth keeping for reuse, use in a different function, or for memory. I do not touch his own collections. However, I occasionally found clusters of old pots or your clothes, which I had packed to give away, inside the house, in the garage, and under the deck in the garden. To start the project, I had a list of locations and a list of items. Closets on the second floor were on the location list; the items included old and unopened sets of bed sheets, countertop medicines, souvenirs and the little bags from the dentist's office.

Among my belongings, files for each bank, insurance, utility companies, and tax offices were kept for years. I also kept folders of records from your years of education and extracurricula activities. I was not a good note taker for my school years, but I kept a few good textbooks and copies of my own publications. There were even a few data tapes and many bundles of slides from my days in Wisconsin.

Your belongings defaulted to me. Boxes of outdated toys, either from kids' meals or bought as kids' favorite in different years, were in the basement. Your schoolwork, certificates, and diploma from kindergarten to high school were in your bedroom, and your game gears and games were in the game room. The piles of leftovers from your co-op terms were a mixture of household items and clothing. You told us to throw them away if they were not useful to our lives. I categorized them by potential destinations like the library, game store, and the condo. I don't recall that we ever directly asked you to help, and therefore, you never came to help.

It took several months of hard work to convert the contents of a fully livable house into ready-to-go furniture and many boxes! We bought many packing boxes from Dymon in Kanata. We posted on Kijiji, a popular online classifieds service, many times and took many trips to the nearby Value Village, a thrift store chain. Several times, we put small furniture and mattresses at the end of our driveway in the night before the city pickup day or regular garbage collection day.

We were probably active at the Kijiji Ottawa website for half year, with joy and anxiety. The ping-pong table, treadmill, and bicycles were posted and sold. So was the BBQ. I then got a call from a church that was doing spring sale. They would come to pick up whatever (in good shape) we wanted to downsize.

However, they will not enter the house. Ying and I spent two half days moving desks, bookcases, coffee tables, an entertainment unit, dressers, nightstands, lamps and fans. That was probably the time when my knees were overworked, although Ying always held the heavier or lower ends. He had a strong back and the proper BMI (Body-Muscle-Index). I only had strong arms and the will to persist. We were surprised that the items from the second floor and basement filled the entire hallway and living room. We then moved everything plus the two-section sofa, sofa chair, and rocking chair outside to the garage. With the cars in the driveway, we filled the garage. We had to move our cars away when the church people came. They filled their two pickup trucks and a car. They came back with the same pickup truck the next day and got a full load one more time. While they got their goods for the church event, Ying and I felt relieved — almost all the extra furniture in the house was finally gone.

With the same Kijiji, we got scammed. I posted the piano for sale and got an email from a niece intending to buy the piano for her uncle. Her uncle then contacted me by cell phone messages to coordinate the shipment. Soon I got a letter with a money order from him for the piano and its shipping cost. He asked me to deposit the money order and pay for his shipment in a bank account so the piano would not miss the carrier pickup. Ying went to the banks and completed the two errands promptly. But the carrier never came, and I was informed by the bank after a few days that the money order was a fraud. Re-examining the address from which the check was sent showed that it was a Toront apartment. I was spooked! With all the messages, emails, an records of transactions, I wrote a report detailing the sequence of communication and exchanges. I took the report and the stack of my evidence to the police station. I got a lesson from the man on duty that my case was just one of the many. Police never provided me with any update. That was the first lesson I learned along this line, since I had always been on guard with my credit cards, bank account, and junk calls.

By the end of April 2019, the content of the house was almost 100 percent ready for moving. We decided whom to hire as the real estate agent after a few rounds of viewing and feedback. There were quite a few minor fixes to make the house more salable. Ying found a painter, who could come in his spare time after work or on weekends to do minor fixes and touch-ups. He loved music, so we gave him the piano besides his pay. He happily asked the professional mover to ship it to his home. Meanwhile, the agent brought a professional photographer to take pictures of the house for publication. Unfortunately, we missed the peak of the market before summer. The house had quite a few visitors and several open houses, but it was not sold until the end of August. By the end of May, we had to set the move to Toronto in early June because Ying's relatives were coming.

The condo then was in good shape for new residents. The couple renting our condo bought their own condo and wanted to move out in February. Ying and I traveled to Toronto and released the tenants. We set up a minimum for our temporary stay in the condo. We spent a few days hunting for vinyl flooring. Before going back to Ottawa, we planned the project of a new vinyl floor after discussions with the condo management and a flooring company. The new floor was installed in mid-May, and Ying was in the condo to monitor. After the new floor was in, he tried his best to clean away the dust with a vacuum and a dry or wet mop. At the end of the renovation, I took my work stuff and did a test run between Ottawa and our Toronto condo with Greyhound and public transportation. To stay connected on my working day, I spent the morning at McDonald's and the rest of the day at the city library in the same strip mall across the street from our condo.

We moved on June 2nd. The schedule was for the mover to load his truck in the afternoon of June 2nd and bring everything to the condo in Toronto on the morning of June 3rd. By that time, we also rented a series of sturdy Eco-moving plastic containers from Dymon. They were handy and filled to the weight Ying and I could handle. A couple of our friends came to see if we needed any help. They taped the room or content labels onto the boxes. The moving truck came with a group of three people. They were late, and the loading was not smooth. A major piece was our king-size bed, which included the bed, its wall section, and storage units. It took at least an hour to move and load all the pieces onto the truck, although we had already unscrewed and separated them as needed. After that, the group was tired, and a bit frustrated because it was obvious the truck could not fit everything in. We were not happy because the mover did not bring the largest truck of his company as he had promised. The second trip from Ottawa to Toronto would be required and at our cost. The truck with the driver and one of his helpers left well after dark.

Ying and I needed to take our cars to Toronto. Our neighbo

who had checked on the loading in front of our house several times, invited us in for a simple meal. It was hard to refuse and badly needed. Other than attending the movers in the afternoon, we had fully packed the two cars with small and fragile items. Both of us were tired from the long day. We went in and stuffed ourselves with dumplings and a bowl of soup. We then said goodbyes and on our way to Toronto. Ying drove the RAV4 and I my B250. It was a dark night without the moon. It was my first time using the cruise control of the B250, and it was user friendly. In the light traffic of the night, I got off Highway 401 at Warden within four hours. It was past midnight, and I sat with a cup of hot chocolate in the same McDonald's for a quick break. Rejuvenated, I drove the car, passed the gate, and went down to the underground parking. I parked my B250 in our second parking lot for the first time and brought up the minimum. The condo had already switched to air conditioning for the summer. Ying showed up at the condo after less than an hour. He had to stop and take a nap on the way. As usual, he did not need me to worry for too long.

We reserved the usage of the specific elevator for the next day, and the mover brought in his truck in the late morning. It took many trips from the truck to the staging area, to the elevator, and then up to our condo at the end of the hallway. The unloading was not as complicated as loading because the elevator was tall and spacious, and the mover had the right gear to move every item around. Getting all the pieces of our king-size bed was not troublesome either, although the trip and the handling damaged the board and broke one leg of the wall unit. The movers left around four in the afternoon. Ying and I needed to catch up on some sleep. We went across the street to the Sam Woo BBQ and had our usual steamed fish and vermicelli soup. We finally moved to our new residence.

The days that followed were focused on getting the rooms ready for guests from China. We bought a sturdy bedroom set for bedroom #2 and set it up two days before the arrival of our guests. We unpacked the stuff to cover our king-size bed, the new queen-size bed, the sofa bed in the solarium, and the single bed in bedroom #3. Bedroom #3 is Ying's office. The large solarium is my office with my office desk unit at one end and the sofa bed and a large coffee table at the other end. For the rest of June, the condo entertained four guests from time to time when we were all at home. I learned that the car rental price was higher for drivers older than 70 years old, when I had to rent a van for group travels. All of us went to Waterloo to attend the commencement of Ying's niece after a trip to Kingston. We flew to the States for a tour of four cities. Back in Toronto, Ying and I took his sister and niece to Ottawa and then Montreal. Our guests liked the tours and were impressed by the convenience and the Chinese atmosphere of our condo.

In July and August, while I worked part-time at home in Toronto, Ying made a few trips back to Ottawa to house-sit. He analyzed the real estate market, and communicated with ou agent, and finally sold the house at the end of August. The las piece of furniture he sold on Kijiji was the metal bunk bed, whic was well-used when you had friends to spend the night yea ago. As the handyman of the house, he replaced a mirror in washroom and tightened the doors of the closets in the basement. Ying found a mover with a super cargo van. I went back for the last time to pack and clean with Ying. We left the keys with the lawyer and moved out of the house at the end of September, about three weeks before the closing day. The cargo van was full, and so was our RAV4. Our move from Ottawa to Toronto was finally complete after the van unloaded and left our condo.

Your belongings were mostly sent away on trips to Value Village. We asked your cousin in Waterloo to send a few textbooks back to the university bookstore. There was a game shop on March Road, Kanata, that still collects games of outdated gear. I gave them all the game cartridges and CDs from Game Boy, PSP, and PS2. I made a few trips to Beaverbrook Library to disperse your books and my books. However, I kept the sets of *Harry Potter* and *Lord of the Rings*. I also brought over all your music books, thinking I may use them after I retire. For the memories of your years at school, I packed all your certificates, diplomas, and plates. I also brought all the belts with stripes you had for your karate training. They are all in boxes in our storage space of the condo.

Time flies. We are now spoiled by convenience. Everything is within walking distance, and the recreation is in the basement. If not for the pandemic, we could have flown off Pearson Airport to a few more places in the world without airport layovers. In the same building, we have made some friends who followed their children to Canada. They are well-to-do in the sense of being neither dependent on nor in debt to their children. Occasionally, we meet for a meal or a walk, and we talk about our adult children.

We rarely drive, although we still have two cars. The Presto card for public transit takes us to downtown via either Route 53 with Subway #1 or Route 68 with Subway #2. We go downtown to pay a quick visit occasionally. Our communication with you remains very sparse, although we are in the same metropolitan area. Remember the trick of skipping stones we figured out when we were in the Maritimes? A perfectly round, flat, and thin pebble is the best. An odd-shaped one flies away, no matter how hard it spins, quickly submerges, or only achieves one or two bubbles after it hits the water. That's our communication these days. Life is not perfect, but we have to try.

Printed in the United States
by Baker & Taylor Publisher Services